Daily News

KEY ATLAS

TO A

RECONSTRUCTED WORLD

The NEW FRONTIERS

An Invaluable Guide without which
no existing Atlas is complete

Price, Full-bound Cloth, 5/6
POST FREE
Size - - 12½ by 10 inches

56 pages of Maps Lithographed in Colours, Introduction by
J. Wilson Harris, Indices to Places of Recent Importance
and Names Changed as the result of the War.

**Prepared at the Edina Works, Edinburgh
by W. & A. K. JOHNSTON, LIMITED**

*Descriptive pamphlet, list of contents, and sample map
free on application.*

THE
MODERN CYCLIST

A

HANDBOOK

FOR

CYCLISTS AND OTHER ROADFARERS.

—

PRICE **1/-**

· OLD HOUSE ·

CONTENTS.

                                                            PAGES
PART ONE ... ...   5—37

Choosing a Bicycle—Heavy Riders and
Light Ones—Frame Height and Crank
Length — Position — Traffic Riding — The
Woman's Bicycle—Variable Gears—Traps
for the Unwary—Learning to Ride—Toe-
clips—Care of Bearings, Saddle, Chain—
Tyres — Lamps — Luggage — Women on
Tour—Wet Weather Riding—Touring from
a Centre—A Hundred in a Day—Laws and
Customs of the Road—Cycling for the
Unsound—" Spare Spokes."

PART TWO ... ...   37—85

" Potted Tours " in Great Britain, Ireland,
and France.

PART THREE ... ...   85—135

Resthouse Directory, with over 3,000
Addresses. Forewords. List for Great
Britain. List for Ireland. List for France.

INDEX ... ... 136—137

FOREWORD.

Known throughout the British Empire by his pen-name "Kuklos," Mr. Fitzwater Wray, author of this handbook, has been a Journalist of the Road since 1892. His cycling experience dates from the days of the high bicycle and the introduction of the solid-tyred " safety "; and his motoring from 1898, when he drove a tricycle from Bradford to Harrogate. His first motorcycling was in 1901, and his first car in 1907.

The Evening News has described him (November 15, 1911) as " an acknowledged authority on road transit."

In *Sport and Play* for September 23, 1922, the following appeared from the pen of the editor, Mr. J. Urry, *doyen* of wheeling journalists :—

" Throughout the wheel world, ' Kuklos ' is regarded as an authority, and thoroughly deserves the reputation, and, though I am inclined to think that he knows the value of his own work, he is a genial and charitable soul, and has a soft side to him that is very admirable and attractive. Like every strong personality, he has his hobbies, and sometimes he rides the high horse on them; but he knows his book, is wonderfully and shrewdly entertaining, and is a real and enthusiastic cyclist and motorist, without a bit of prejudice for either tribe so long as they are gentlemen of the highway. He has a pretty wit, sometimes on the sarcastic side, and, though he prefers the rapier to the battle-axe, can use both with skill and dexterity. A fine friend, but an almost implacable foe; and one of the foremost figures in the great world of wheels."

" Kuklos " has been associated with *The Daily News* exclusively since 1905. An article from his pen on cycling matters appears therein every Saturday and another on motoring topics on Tuesdays. He also conducts private postal correspondence on such matters of the wheel as are not dealt with in this book, the only rule being that a stamped addressed envelope for reply must be enclosed.

THE MODERN CYCLIST

CHOOSING A BICYCLE.

Most cyclists are riding machines which are unsuited to their physique or temperament. This is the reason why so many people (ignorant and unfortunate) condemn cycling as " hard work," the simple fact being that the bicycle is a mechanical device for reducing labour. If people gave a fraction of the attention to the selection of a bicycle that they do to the choice of their clothes or the implements of their other pastimes there would be less disappointment and less silly talk about " hard work." The build of the bicycle should be according to the build of the bicyclist.

Men of average weight and height are not confronted by any great problem in choosing a bicycle. There are about eighteen firms with well-known names whose " standard roadsters " will not be far wrong. They may make their choice, for instance, and be confident they will at least get good value for their money, between (in alphabetical order) Alldays and Onions, Ariel, Bradbury, B.S.A., Centaur, Enfield, Gamage, Humber, Humphries and Dawes, James, New Hudson, Raleigh, Rover, Royal Ruby, Rudge-Whitworth, Singer, Sparkbrook, Sunbeam, Swift, and Triumph.

If the bicycle is required only as a common hack for strictly utilitarian use within a short radius, and is likely to get little attention in the way of cleaning and oiling, top price should be given for a first-class machine, with all-black finish, a single gear, a well-made metal gearcase, and the best tyres. Only high quality can stand up to habitual neglect.

If such men of average physique want their machines for something better, i.e., for week-end runs, touring, and intelligent riding whenever possible, they should choose a " standard roadster " (according to their purse) equipped with 3-speed hub. Such machines have 7-in. cranks, and 71 or 74 gear either as single speed or as the normal of a 3-speed hub. In the hillier districts 71 is the better in either case.

GEARCASES.—Whether or not to have a gearcase, each must decide for himself. There is considerable added weight in a full gearcase of metal, perhaps up to 3 lbs. There is increased wind resistance. If you are prepared to give the modern chain the attention it deserves, if you have the time and inclination to treat it as described later (page 18), then the gearcase may not be worth the extra weight and windage. If you have neither the time nor the inclination to treat that beautifully minute and exact mechanism humanely, then it is criminal not to have a gearcase. If a bicycle is used all through the year for business purposes and there is no time to look after it, the gearcase would be worth while if it weighed 10 lbs. After all, it is really the cheap and bad chain which requires coddling in oil baths more than the first-class chain.

But the chain-case must be a good one. Laced-up things of bad leather and celluloid are worse than worthless. Many of the " detachable " variety are good protectors, and if the chains inside them are once a year removed and treated as directed they are being excellently treated. But I would not trust the " detachable " kind to hold oil. It might be all right until the machine was reversed for tyre repairs, and then——? The best oil-bath gearcase is the Sunbeam.

HEAVYWEIGHTS.—These standard roadsters may be fully relied on to carry riders up to 14 stone, *plus* luggage, anywhere, though it would pay men of this weight to specify a bigger and better saddle and heavier tyres than are usually found on standard roadsters. The top-weight man, 15 stone and over, should have his bicycle built to suit him.

LIGHTWEIGHTS.—The lightweight man of 10 stone and less usually buys the wrong machine, forgetting that the standard roadsters are designed by their makers to carry riders up to 14 stone with a wide margin of safety. He is misled by the expressions " lightweight," " road-racer," " speedman," applied by the makers to models which are not standard roadsters; he fears his neck will be in danger unless he buys the latter, but he is quite wrong. There is hardly any difference in weight and strength in the *frames* of both models. The difference is in the equipment, the lighter model having smaller wheels, lighter tyres and saddle. The " light roadster " or " sporting roadster," or " clubman's " or " speedman's model " sometimes has the top tube sloping towards the head. As a matter of simple fact, the *same frame* is used as on the same firm's " road-racer." Put an upturned handlebar into the latter instead of its dropped one and you have practically the same machine. The makers know quite well that their " road-racer " must sometimes be used by a muscular man of 12 stone weight, and they provide an ample margin of strength.

These machines are also fitted with 1⅜-in. tyres, which are not roadsters and are often called " road-racing," and the novice is afraid of them. Let him reflect that the same tyre which is hardly a " roadster " for a 12-stone man *is* a roadster for 9-stone and 10-stone. If the light man insists on having the same " roadster " tyres as the heavy man he is simply driving round a lot of useless weight.

One word of warning is necessary. Too many of these lighter roadsters are foolishly fitted with the same higher gears as the " road-racer " models. They should be geared the same as the standard roadsters, see *ante*.

ROAD-RACERS.—I do not regard the real road-racer or speedman as being quite adequately catered for by the big firms named, and the fact is that most of such cyclists have their mounts built for them out of B.S.A. or Chater Lea fittings by intelligent mechanics whom they personally know; and it is the best way.

FRAME HEIGHT.—The prospective cyclist should decide for himself what size of frame to order, and not accept the advice of the agent. Take the inside measurement of your leg from fork or crutch in a straight line to the ground while wearing cycling shoes. If it is 30 ins., for instance, then a 23-in. frame is the highest that you *could* ride with comfort and efficiency, crank-length being 7 ins. It is, however, wiser to decide on a frame-height 2 ins. less than this, because you may want a very low position for traffic riding and because the shorter frame is easier to sell when you have done with it. The formula, then, to give you your frame-height with 7-in. cranks is: Leg-length as measured above, *minus* 9 ins. If you are so heavy as to require an extra large and deep saddle the subtracted figure should be 10 ins.

POSITION.—The leg should never be fully extended in cycling. If the knee is still slightly bent at the lowest point of the pedal circuit your position is right in that respect. While standing on the camber of an ordinary road, with the bicycle between you and the gutter, you should be able to put your leg over the machine on to the far pedal and push off comfortably from it.

The vertical poker-back position is mechanically unsound and means waste of energy. The egg-shaped back of the scorcher is unnecessary except for pure racing. The straight spine should be inclined slightly forward from the hips. The arms should be perfectly straight. Your power is put out with the arms as well as the legs, and you cannot pull in hill-climbing with bent arms.

If a plumb-line dropped from the nose of the saddle hangs 2 ins. to 3 ins. behind the centre of the crank-bracket the position of the saddle in relation to the cranks is about right, but it is largely a personal matter. Most cyclists will find a horizontal saddle best for all-round use. If a slightly-dropped handlebar is used, the peak of the saddle should be slightly lowered, but this is also a matter of taste. The saddle must not lean to one side or the other, and its peak must not point to left or right of the steering-head. The rider should sit on the broad part of the saddle, and his weight should be divided between saddle, pedals, and grips.

CRANK-LENGTH.—For nearly 21 years now, practically all my riding has been done with 9-in. and 8-in. cranks, and the campaign that I have conducted (almost single-handed) since 1899 in favour of " crank-length in proportion to leg-length " has seen the standard crank-length raised from 6½ ins. to 7 ins. Before the war some thousands of my readers also equipped themselves with cranks proportionate to their leg-length. Most of these reported their experiences at length, and all but one expressed extreme satisfaction. The only claim I make in respect of longer cranks is that slow pedalling is more enjoyable than fast pedalling. Everyone with 33 ins. of leg-length as measured above can ride 8-in. cranks, and everyone with 34 ins. and more can ride 9-in. The normal gear should be increased by 10 ins. for every inch that the crank is longer than 7 ins. My present " battleship " has 8-in. cranks with the Pedersen 3-speed hub geared to 54, 81, and 120. The corresponding gears with B.S.A. or Sturmey-Archer 3-speed hub would be 61, 80, 106, or 64, 84, 110.

But such machines have to be built accordingly—with rather longer wheel-base and rather higher crank-bracket. (It is worth noting here that no rider with very long legs can be comfortable on a machine with the usual wheel-base length.) But trade and factory conditions since the war have reduced the number of models offered, and makers are very reluctant to build " special machines." Messrs. John Marston offer to build Sunbeam bicycles with 8-in. cranks for an extra charge of one guinea. Otherwise, the tall rider who wants long cranks is another case for the intelligent local builder, who can get any length up to 9 ins. from Elson and Co., New Summer Street, Birmingham. I have a few addresses of such local builders.

TRAFFIC RIDING.—Cyclists in large towns who expect to do most of their riding in dense traffic should not only select the model with 26-in. wheels (with 1½-in. roadster tyres if the cyclist is of normal weight), but should fix the saddle a little farther back and a little lower down than is usual, so that it is not necessary to dismount before the feet can be put on the ground.

THE WOMAN'S BICYCLE.—The ease and enjoyment of cycling as experienced by men is almost unknown to women, because of the impossibility of adapting the skirt to the bicycle. This impossibility has led to the very unsatisfactory compromise called the " lady's model," which is really only half a bicycle. When the top tube is taken out of a bicycle to accommodate a skirt the frame is so weakened that heavier material is then used in an unsuccessful attempt to equalise the strength. Skirts have also made necessary the added weight and complication of devices to keep them out of the chain and spokes. So the " lady's model " weighs more than the masculine bicycle, although the man is, as a rule, both heavier and stronger than the woman. The lack of rigidity in the " scoop " frame further wastes the woman's energy. Most women, therefore, do not regard cycling as a delightful and healthful pastime, but as a necessary evil for time-saving, and decidedly " hard work." The women who have adopted the real bicycle and who dress accordingly are the only ones who know what cycling means. But their numbers are increasing.

It is difficult, therefore, to take the skirted cyclist and the scoop frame seriously. The big leading cycle-makers refuse to do so. At least, the only machine they offer to all women is one which would safely carry a 12-stone rider. They may possibly have heard of women who weigh rather less than this, but they decline to cater for them. When asked why, they always reply that women will have big machines because they " look better." So it is not entirely the fault of the makers that most women buy " bicycles " that weigh nearer 40 lbs. than 30 lbs.

In my experience (25 years of heavy correspondence with cyclists of both sexes) the average weight of the woman who cycles is about 9-stone, and huge are the numbers of those who only weigh eight. The " lady's standard roadster " of the big makers, then, I do not advise to any woman who weighs less than 10 stone. Most skirts as now worn do not reach the chain, and so the gearcase is unnecessary. If the woman of 10 stone and upwards specifies a single gear with this " standard roadster," and has the gearcase taken off and thrown away, she will have made the best of a bad bargain.

For the average woman there is painfully little choice among the " ready-mades." Her chief hope appears to rest at present with local builders as soon as the latter wake up to the rich possibilities of the situation. The chief items in the specification of the best possible scoop-frame bicycle for women of 7, 8, and 9 stone weight and 5 ft. to 5 ft. 6 ins. in height I should set down as follows :—

19, 20, or 21 in. frame, see page 7; 26-in. wheels, Roman rims, 1⅜ " road-racing " tyres, see page 6; B10L saddle; 6½-in. cranks, single gear about 63; Hans Renold chain, gut or " pike-line " dressguard, no gearcase, flat handlebar, two rim-brakes. But if you are so ashamed of your legs that you must entirely cover them, you must also spoil the machine with a gear-case. If the machine is to be used for touring as well as " calls and shopping," the specification should also include the Eadie 2-speed hub, geared to 68 and 53. Taller women among these lightweights, and apart from the higher frames necessary, should specify 7-in. cranks and about 70 gear, or 71 and 56 with the Eadie 2-speed hub.

" RATIONAL " DRESS.—Women who use bicycles merely as time-savers, in shopping, afternoon " calls," riding to tennis-courts, and so forth, will stick to the skirt and one of the compromise bicycles just indicated. They are not real cyclists and never will be. The others are those whose cycling opportunities are restricted by their domestic or commercial duties (or both) to certain definite times—week-ends, "half-day closing," Bank Holidays, the long summer evenings, and annual holidays. This kind cycles for enjoyment and health, not as a regretted necessity. Her bicycle is much more than a vehicle for a skirt, a tennis racquet, and a bag of cakes. She is free to choose

her bicycle as a chum, and free to dress for cycling as a pastime and not for "afternoon tea" as a penance.

So she chooses a real bicycle of the so-called masculine variety, and dresses accordingly. In so choosing, she saves money at the outset, for the "lady's model" actually costs more to buy than the equivalent "gent.'s," although heavier and weaker! Her most economical course will be to buy one of the "light roadster" class—see under "Lightweights," page 6. But

8-stone riders of either sex should have specially light machines
built for them.

The *decently*-dressed woman on a bicycle (my italics are
deliberate and significant) no longer attracts any unpleasant
attention. In fact, she attracts *less* unpleasant attention from
men *because* she is decently dressed. A practical and comfortable costume, of three-quarter length coat, breeches, and closely-
fitting hat or cap, is already in considerable use and favour.
The one illustrated was designed by Miss Dorothy Bishop, of
" The Daily News." Paper patterns of coat, No. 320, or
breeches, No. 321, can be sent for 9d. each or 1s. 3d. the two
together. Address Pattern Department, " The Daily News,"
Bouverie Street, London, E.C. 4.

VARIABLE GEARS.—I do not regard the touring bicycle
as complete without a 3-speed hub, so far as men of average
weight are concerned, though the speedman will have none of
them ; and the mere hack bicycle—despised, neglected, ill-used,
borrowed and lent—does not need one. When the lighter
roadster machine is in question (see page 6) an Eadie
2-speed gear may be specified by way of saving a little weight.
The gears of a 3-speed hub are low, normal, and high ; of
the Eadie hub they are normal and low. The low gear is a
necessity ; the high gear a luxury.

The B.S.A. and Sturmey-Archer 3-speed hubs are now the
only ones available to the general public, and both are excellent.
The latter is also available in combination with a coaster (or
back-pressure) brake.

The only 2-speed gear now available to the general public
is the Eadie 2-speed coaster hub, made by the B.S.A. Company.

There are two proprietary 2-speed gears, the James and the
Sunbeam, in both cases on the crank axle. The James is a
" reducing " gear, *i.e.*, normal and low; example, 74 and 56,
68 and 51. The Sunbeam is an " increasing " gear, *i.e.*, normal
and high ; example, 66 and 88, 69 and 92. In the James, the
higher gear runs solid ; in the Sunbeam the lower gear runs
solid.

When you hear a cyclist say that he has a 3-speed gear, but
never uses it, or that he has tried one and found it no good,
write him down an ass. He never learned how to use it ;
hence his disappointment. He has tried to work up speed on
the high gear when the conditions were unfavourable, · and
found he could go faster on the normal. Still more commonly
he has never learned that his low gear is for *power* uphill, *not*
speed. The rider's physical energy is applied to the work in
small doses, and the pace necessarily falls off. The strong
rider who drives his single gear to the top goes up faster, but
his output of energy is much greater. Always pedal slowly on
the low speed of a variable gear.

TANDEMS.—There would be a great deal more use for the

tandem bicycle if it were better realised that it can be a light
and convenient machine and need not be an understudy of a
tank. The man who wants to cycle with the lady of his heart
and is deterred by her nervous fears or inferior physique should
take her on a tandem. The woman who wants to take the
man of her heart cycling, but is deterred, etc., etc. The tandem
should be made to order and to suit the two riders concerned.
Wheels need not be more than 26 ins. and tyres need not be
bigger than 1½ ins. Palmer Specials or Dunlop Magnums,
except in the case of heavy riders. I have known several
instances of the successful use of the Sturmey-Archer 3-speed
hub on tandems. Such a machine, locally built, should cost
from £25 to £30. In hilly districts, a second rim-brake on
the back wheel, operated by rear rider, is advisable, and
is preferable to a coaster brake. A really light and
fast tandem for a " mixed " team is possible if the lady will
dress as on page 10.

TRICYCLES.—The 3-wheeler is under an undeserved and
unnecessary cloud because of the surviving monsters of 20 and
30 years ago. It would be as logical to condemn the safety
because people once rode boneshakers. You can have tricycles
made to-day with the same difference. The intelligent local
builder will turn out a 3-wheeler very little heavier than the
bicycle—lighter than some bicycles! Sunbeams offer a tricycle
which, even with oilbath gearcase, 2-speed gear, and roadster
tyres, weighs but 44 lbs. The James Cycle Company also make
a modern tricycle with bracket 2-speed gear.

TRAPS FOR THE UNWARY.

There is a small but active section of the bicycle-making
trade which devotes its whole energies to the making of
worthless machines which they proceed to get rid of through
the small advertisements of private sales in the columns of
newspapers, daily and weekly, London and provincial.

As a matter of fact, these people really " make " nothing.
Their so-called bicycles are assembled from parts which in the
main are the " scrap " of better firms. The wheels may go
round for a time, and in a way, but nothing save wasted
energy, disappointment, and additional expense can be expected.

The advertisements offering these " second-hand " machines
always emanate from private addresses, generally suburban,
and never from cycle agents or factories. Not often are the
advertisers local residents; they are of the " here to-day and
gone to-morrow " type. The following typical advertisements
are word for word as they have appeared :

" Cycles (Lady's and Gent.'s). Two high-grade machines,
1911 models, recently cost £10 10s. each; receipt shown; ridden

twice.; sacrifice £3.10s. each; must sell; urgent; officer, ordered abroad (Alexandria)."

" Cycles (Lady's and Gent.'s). Two high-class machines, practically new; cost £8 15s. and 9 gns. this year; accept £3 10s. each; professionals, engaged for Tropics."

Those machines were made for the purpose of those advertisements, and their wholesale value at that time was about 33s. each. One of these people advertises regularly from a private address in the Hyde Park district (printed on his note-paper), and I have seen some of the letters he sends out explaining that he has " bought Daimler car."

One of these machines was technically examined by the " Birmingham Daily Post," which published the following report :

" The bearings were old. On one side of the machine there was a 7-in. crank, on the other a 6 in. One of the pedals was screwed in; the other fitted so badly that it could not be screwed in. On the tyres were new covers (for obvious reasons) bearing no maker's name. The inner tube of the back wheel boasted 21 patches, and those on the front tube were too numerous to count. The handlebar was made for one system of adjustment, but it did not fit, so a rivet had been put through it, and the handle was fixed without any adjustment. The hubs were old, while the balls were visible from the back and front. The chain wheel and the free wheel were odd ; one was for a three-sixteenths chain, and the other for a one-eighth chain. The brakes were unsafe, and the tubes were soft and could be broken across the knee."

Sometimes the advertiser is a regular resident who has succumbed to temptation. He has been approached by one of these firms in the following way—I quote facsimile from an actual pre-war circular :

" To specially advertise our £12 12s. models we require a reliable person in your town to store two of these up-to-date machines so that we can advertise them very cheap for cash in your local paper. All you would have to do is just show them to callers and sell them and then send the cash on to us by postal order. We will allow you 5s. on every machine sold. We shall then send others in their place, and so on throughout the season. In this way you will sell about 100 machines. On receipt of your reply we will send you two cycles at once. We will pay all carriage and every other expense, and all advertising. We will insert the advertisement ourselves, and shall always advise you. We send you copy of advertisement, which will be altered from time to time. Please state name of your best paper for advertising, and say price for six daily insertions. Are you a householder and how long have you been at your present address? "

The suggested advertisement, to be " altered from time to time," ran as follows : " Gent.'s cycle, fitted with 3-speed gear, this year's model, perfectly new; £4 14s. Worth £12 12s. (Your address here.)"

Yes, a B.S.A. or Sturmey-Archer 3-speed hub is sometimes included in the machine, and it is the only good part of it. But it is a bait for boobies, because even a first-class 3-speed hub is of no use in a rotten bicycle. Often the advertisement is so worded that the name "B.S.A." appears to be associated with the whole bicycle. Whenever you see such an advertisement, cut it out and send it to the B.S.A. Company at Small Heath.

Another dodge is to describe these machines as "B.S.A. pattern," which means nothing at all. A rotten egg is of the same "pattern" as a new-laid egg. If a bicycle is really built of B.S.A. fittings, one of the two following marks—(1) the well-known three-piled rifles or (2) the letters B.S.A. will be found stamped as follows:—

Steering-head : On the front of the handlebar clip under the lamp-bracket, on the crown, and on the lock-nut.

Crank-bracket : On the face of each crank near the axle, and on the cups, chain-wheel, and axle.

Seat-pillar lug : On one side only, in line with the seat-post.

Back fork-ends : On the outside of each fork-end and on the adjuster cams.

Back-fork bridge : Between the tubes.

Back-stay bridge : On the top.

Hubs : In two places on the barrel of each hub, near the flanges and on the spindles.

In addition to these bicycles locally built from B.S.A. fittings, there are the machines built throughout in the B.S.A. factories and sold complete. These have all the marks just enumerated and in addition a special transfer on head and mudguard consisting of the name and the three stacked rifles within a garter shield.

Remember also, and spread it abroad, that the ancient and honourable firm of J. B. Brooks and Co., Great Charles Street, Birmingham, makers of saddles and other leather goods for cyclists and motorists, *do* NOT *make complete bicycles.*

———————

LEARNING TO RIDE.

The usual way—getting someone to hold you on with one hand and preventing you from steering with the other—is a laborious misuse of time and energy. There are two separate and distinct things to be acquired, and (like most other things) they are best learned one at a time, not both together. These are :

(1) The art of balance,
(2) The art of pedalling.

Take them in that order and ignore the second until you

have acquired the first. Put the saddle at the lowest possible point. If your feet cannot then rest on the ground while seated, hire or borrow a shorter bicycle. Get on a slightly falling road where the machine will just run by itself for one or two hundred yards. Let your feet touch the ground alternately, and don't use the pedals at all. A little preliminary practice with a scooter or a roller-skate would be useful. Keep your eyes on the road ahead, and don't look at the front wheel. If the tight-rope walker looked down at his rope he would fall off.

When you can thus free-wheel a hundred yards or so without falling off, raise the saddle. Push off from a kerb, bank, or ledge, and descend the slope again a few times with the feet resting on the pedals but not turning them. This is the end of Part One. Before proceeding to Part Two, learn the mount and dismount. The most easily-acquired way of mounting is to stand on the left side of the machine on the right-hand slope of the road, so that the machine is slightly below you, and the right pedal just in front of its highest position. Throw the right leg over the saddle, place the foot on the pedal, and push off. The difference in the case of women is that the right foot is put through the frame on to the right pedal, from which the rider lifts herself into the saddle and starts at the same moment.

Learn to dismount while the bicycle is descending the slight incline, slowly. Put all your weight on the left pedal and ride on it. Men should then bring the right leg round, women the right foot through the frame, all very slowly, and hop off. A still easier dismount is to stop the machine with the brakes, and put either foot to the ground. This is only difficult when the saddle is too high.

Part Two, learning to turn the pedals round and drive the machine, should be first on the level, and then on a slight up-gradient; it is easy when Part One is acquired.

When quite at home on the machine, learn the indispensable art of correct pedalling. The broadest part of the foot must rest on the centre of the pedal. When the descending crank has just passed the horizontal position, point the toes downwards, so that you can claw or pull the pedal past its lowest point. At the same time and on the other side, just before the ascending crank reaches its highest point, drop your heel sharply so that the toes point upwards, and then you can push the pedal past its highest point. This ankle-action enables you to exert your power all round the pedal circuit, instead of only on the down-thrust. Practise the movements very slowly on a level road, and if you have a variable gear, on the highest.

TOE-CLIPS.—These are not recommended to the beginner. Their chief use is in very fast pedalling to keep the foot in position. They should never be used as a substitute for ankle-action, of which there is some danger. I do not agree, however, with those who say they are of no advantage at all in driving, for when the rising crank is horizontal there is a fractional moment when the pedal is lifted by the toe-clip. The simple hook is the best shape in toe-clips; those shaped like stirrup or loop are unnecessary and risky. But if your ankle-joints are moving all the way round the pedal circuit, as they should do, you will have little need of toe-clips. When used, they should always be adjusted so that the foot is correctly placed on the pedal, see *ante*. The most practical and sensible clips I have found are the " Lito " aluminium, 2s. 3d. or 3s. 9d. (rat-traps or rubbers), by Frank Ashby and Co., Stirchley, Birmingham.

CHILD-PASSENGERS.—When a small child is occupying a carrier of any kind on a bicycle, there is less risk of a spill than when the fond parent cycles alone, because in the former case the f.p. takes no risks. If, then, you are a cycling f.p., but afraid to risk the children, calculate how many spills you had in your last thousand miles, add 100 per cent. extra caution, and you can then say (to five places of decimals) what risk of a spill the child will run if you get a kid-carrier for your bicycle.

There are carriers for the front of the bicycle and for the back, and for the top tube behind the handlebar; not merely parcel carriers, but comfortable seats of careful design.

Carriers over the front wheel should only be used on sound machines of recognised reputation. On bad bicycles, the fork-crown is a danger-point. Very young children should not be carried in front, unless you rig up a celluloid wind-screen, because air-pressure at cycling speeds is injurious to tiny lungs.

Back carriers are usually home-made. The child and the cyclist may sit back to back, and though the ordinary masculine mount and dismount become difficult, the child is in shelter from wind, rain and dust.

Ask your local cycle agent to show you illustrations of the basket work child-carriers by Brown Bros., Ltd., at 17s. to 22s. Send also for cycle catalogue to A. W. Gamage, Ltd., Holborn, London, E.C. 1.

The " Universal Cycle Saddle " is a carrier or seat for children up to six years. It fits to top tube of the bicycle (either man's or woman's) behind the handelbar, so that the child is between the cyclist's arms. There are foot-rests and back-rest. I know it is good. This is sold for 8s. by Saxessories, George Street Works, Coventry.

The sidecar (Gamage), weighing about 20 lbs., is also quite practicable for 3-speed riders in average country, though Papa should first take a bag of potatoes for a practice-spin.

The parents can also couple their bicycles together, side by side, and carrie Willie in a hammock seat between them. These couplings can be obtained from the Unito Coupling Company, Vange, Essex, and from A. W. Gamage, Ltd.

CARE AND UPKEEP.

Bicycles should be stored in cool, dry places; cool for the sake of the tyres; dry for the sake of the plating.

If you have a bicycle with plated parts, cover them up with vaseline as soon as possible. Apply it carefully with a brush, turning the machine upside down after working round it. Dirt will adhere to the grease, and " appearance " will suffer; but it will look at least as well as a rusty machine. Water can then do the plating no harm. The coat can stay on as long as you like, and paraffin will always reveal the plating as new. Of the handlebar, grease only those corners that you never touch.

BEARINGS.—Oil freely when new—the machine may have been sent out dry from factory and shop. Price's Axle Oil B is recommended. There are seven bearings to oil—front and back wheel hubs, crank bracket, pedals, and the upper and lower bearings in the steering-head. If you can find no oilers for these last, write to the makers. Give a few drops of oil every 500 miles. After doing so, see that oil is not running down the spokes to enter the rims and rot the tyres. Carefully adjust all bearings at least once a year—oftener if any perceptible " shake "or lateral movement develops.

SADDLE.—This is the most neglected part of the bicycle. It pays well to give saddles some attention. When new, a saddle is firm and level, and you sit on the flat rear portion as on a chair. Nine out of ten saddles are then neglected till they sink and stretch into a crescent-shaped line, and the rider is sitting on a rail. At the peak of your saddle there is a nut on a tensioning screw. As soon as a saddle shows signs of becoming hollow, tighten up that nut a few turns.

Colza oil, castor oil, or dubbin should be used on the under side of saddles; otherwise the leather may perish and crack just as boots and shoes do. Polish, such as is used for brown boots, should be used now and then on the upper side of saddles, but not those which also contain stain. If they are wet, they should first be allowed to dry naturally. Exposure to moisture for long periods, whether rain or perspiration, is what makes these dressings necessary. If possible, do not ride on a wet saddle. A waterproof cover can be bought for half-a-crown from Gamage.

When a saddle squeaks, turn it upside down and run a very little oil all round the cantle-plate and nose-piece, between the steel and the leather.

I can sincerely recommend the " spring seat saddle " made by Herbert Terry and Sons, Redditch (25s. for either sex), to any rider who has not found sufficient comfort in the usual patterns of saddle.

CHAINS.—The modern roller chain does not require oil on

the outside. A mixture of oil and road-grit is not a lubricant so much as an excellent grinding medium which would wear anything out, tool-steel not excepted. If the little rollers can revolve freely *on their axles*, the lubrication of the outside of the chain hardly matters at all, for the rolling contact of the chain with the fixed cogs is just about equally effective when dry. Oil put on the outside of the chain does not get between those little axles and their rollers.

A new chain should be removed from the machine, coiled up so that it will lie flat on the bottom of a shallow pan, and covered with fairly thick lubricating oil, or (much better) a semi-solid lubricant like Rangraphine (Price's Company, Ltd.), or Nixey's Graphite Gear Grease, or Vasol (County Chemical Company, Ltd.), or Brito Graphite Lubricant (Brown Bros., Ltd.). Any of these should be warmed till thin. Boiling is quite wrong, as the temper of the steel may be affected. The Coventry Chain Company state that at a temperature of 200 degrees F. the grease will penetrate the joints of even the smallest chains. Keep the grease liquid and warm for a few minutes, shaking the chain now and then, and then allow the lubricant to set stiff again with the chain still immersed. If you are using just heavy oil, hang the chain up over the pan to drain after its oil-bath. Then, in either case, wipe off as much of the lubricant as possible from the outside of the chain. What is left is where it is wanted—out of sight. This treatment applies to the Hans Renold new " improved " chain also.

If your present chain has only been oiled on the outside, and you now repent, remove it, and steep it in a bath of warm paraffin, shaking vigorously, and lay on a flat board or plate to drain. It may want brushing while in the bath. When dry, proceed to the oil-bath as above.

To keep chains ordinarily clean when in use after this treatment, remove rough dirt with a brush, dust with a dry cloth, and give a final rub with a paraffin rag. They will often show traces of external rust, after even a slight shower, but early use of the paraffin rag removes it at once.

If a chain is kept correctly adjusted for tension, there will be hardly any visible sag when at rest. This is important, but if a chain is kept at the correct tension it will rapidly become too tight during a ride in heavy wet, and must be slackened *pro tem*.

If run very slack, it may cause an accident by coming off or (worse still) catching on the rising crank. In those close-built machines which have very little clearance between chain and crank, it is vital to keep the chain correctly adjusted.

When a cracking noise begins in your chain it is a sign of wear and tear or (less likely) of insufficient lubrication. As a test of the former, press the two halves of the chain towards each other by grasping in one hand, and with the other try to pull the chain away from the chain-wheel at the point farthest away from the back of the machine. If it can be pulled away ever so little from the cogs, it is badly worn.

If you put a new chain on to old chain-wheels of which the teeth have been worn into hook-shape, loud noises will follow. Have the hooks filed off first.

Gearcases : See pages 5-6.

If you lose your chain-bolt on the road you can get home with a wire nail in its place, and I have known a hairpin also used with success.

TYRES.—Oil or grease of any kind if allowed to remain on tyres will do them serious injury. Great heat is also injurious to rubber.

Apart from the tubular tyres used by racing men, tyre covers are of two kinds : those held in the rim by a beaded edge and those by a wired edge. The wired-on cover is slightly lighter, slightly cheaper, and slightly faster on good surfaces. The beaded-edge cover is slightly easier to handle in case of repairs and slightly more comfortable on indifferent surfaces.

Most novices get into trouble in handling their tyres through failing to realise that the covers are held in position not only by the pressure of inflation, but also by the flanges on the valve-stems, the edges of the cover being gripped at that point between the rim and the flange.

Before proceeding to detach the cover of a deflated tyre, make sure that the valve itself is not at fault ; the rubber sleeve may have split or perished. Inflate, and put saliva on mouth of valve, watching for bubbles. If at home, immerse the valve in egg-cup or wine-glass of water, turning the valve to the top of the wheel for the purpose.

Search for the cause of puncture before removing cover. Most times you will find nails, old iron, or bits of flint or glass still embedded. Mark the spot before you pull the tube out. If it is a beaded-edge cover and the puncture is not near the valve, the cover need only be detached for a few inches and the valve need not be disturbed.

If no puncturing instrument is found in the cover, remove it, and feel all round inside. If you then discover it, examine the corresponding portion of the tube and mark the puncture with pencil. (A little copying-ink pencil should be in every repair outfit.) Then withdraw the intruder, preferably from the outside.

If nothing is found on either side, remove the whole tube, inflate it till stiff, and pass it through water, stretching a few inches at a time. Mark the puncture at once when found.

If there are no bubbles, it means that the leakage only takes place under greater pressure than you dare put into the naked tube. Examine old patches with your finger-nail and stretch them to see if their edges are lifting; and, if they are, pull them slowly off. Examine the joint in the tube in the same way. If the leak is still undiscovered, tighten up the little lock-nut that holds the tube to the flange of the valve.

To detach the edge of a wired-on cover, push it down into the rim all the way round until it forms a loop which can be slipped over the edge. It cannot be pushed to the bottom where the valve is in the way, so that the operation should always be begun at the opposite side of the wheel to the valve. The same course should be followed in replacing a detached wired-on cover, or you will find that levers are required at the end to force the last bit of cover on. It may be admitted that levers are usually necessary to get a wired cover off. The most popular are the One Minute Tyre Levers, 6d. per set of three. In replacing, when the last bit of the cover has been lifted on, the valve should be pushed well out from behind the rim to let the wired edge get under the flange as you pull the valve back. With both kinds of cover, the tube should be slightly inflated before the cover is replaced; but this is easy to overdo, and often the tube must be deflated a little before the last stretch of cover will slip over. The novice, after repairing a tube, will often put it back with kinks and twists in it, and many of them will be corrected by this slight preliminary inflation; but every twist must be straightened before the cover is put back.

The beaded edge cover is now usually made with the bead on one edge so extended that it forms a flap, which lies in the bottom of the rim and covers the spoke-heads. This side is not intended to be disturbed unless the whole cover has to be removed from the rim. The opposite edge overlaps it and is the one to remove. This is clearly indicated in lettering on the wall of the cover. When pumping up a beaded-edge tyre that you have detached, stop once or twice and make certain that the bead is properly bedded into the rim all round.

The punctured spot should be cleaned with sandpaper, or with the sulphur sticks in some repair outfits, or with saliva and the head of a brimstone match. Sandpaper is best because it slightly roughens the surface. The place must be quite clean or the patch will not stick. Apply a little solution to both puncture and patch, and let it be nearly dry before you press them together. There must be no wrinkle in the patch. Wipe a little French chalk over the repair, or fine road-dust, or put a bit of thin paper on. In the absence of a repair outfit, a small puncture may be mended *pro tem.* with a postage stamp.

Always assume that the nail (or whatever it is) has punctured *the other side of the tube as well*, and examine carefully.

A patch should never overlap another. If the old patch cannot be pulled off, rub its edge down with sandpaper where the new one is to go.

Always carry a " tyre gaiter " or outside repair band in case of a burst or a bad gash. In fixing, it must be tucked under the edges of the cover. The best I have tried is the Hermetic. Tyres should be pumped till you can only make a slight impression on them with the thumb; they will then slip less than soft tyres, wear longer, and be less liable to puncture.

A deep cut right through an outer cover can only be repaired properly by vulcanisation; but if minor cuts are promptly and carefully treated, the life of the cover can be greatly extended. "Tyre fillings" for such cuts are suspiciously regarded or roundly condemned by most cyclists, but their bad reputation is due to the fact that they are not usually given a fair chance. The cut and the canvas underneath it must be quite dry. It must be *thoroughly* cleaned—petrol and an old toothbrush are useful. It should twice be treated with rubber solution, the first coat well rubbed in and allowed to dry, and the filling worked in with a blunt penknife when the second coat is tacky. All this should be done when the tyre is on the wheel and inflated as far as is safe. Let the repair stand as long as you can conveniently, at least overnight. The "Chemico" tyre stopping is the best I have found.

If you set off on a very hot day with tyres blown hard they may be much too hard by noon for comfort or safety.

Go over your covers now and then and pick out embedded bits of road-metal.

When you have been forced to ride or wheel over fresh tar dressed with small metal, it is wise to scrape your covers.

You can save some punctures by stretching a piece of wire across the forks just clear of the tyre. It will either eject anything that has got its "first bite" or give you audible warning.

Water does a tyre no harm as long as it cannot get to the fabric base. A cut which reaches to the fabric admits grit and water and an early burst follows. Tyres ridden through a watersplash will take no harm from the water if the canvas is nowhere exposed and if they are blown up enough to prevent water getting in by the rims.

Particularly in hot weather, the rubber sleeve of a tyre valve is liable to become gummy and to stick, so that your pump cannot force air past it. With the valve in a horizontal position, hold a lighted match under it for a few seconds, then pump again.

If the resistance in your pump disappears, screw out the plunger-rod and put a few drops of oil on the washer.

Tyres should not stand empty. When the bicycle is out of use for long, hang up or turn upside down.

LAMPS.

The oil lamp is still prime favourite with cyclists; acetylene is a good second; electricity is beginning to compete; paraffin and candle lamps are "also rans."

The cyclist who wants the best light procurable from oil will get the Lucas No. 300 or 300 B (plated or all-black respectively), use Price's cycle lamp oil, and Chemico wicks. He will keep the latter absolutely dry and change them every three weeks, whether in constant use or not. To get the best results, the inside of the lamp should be frequently cleaned and the reflectors polished. Wicks suitable for paraffin lamps are not suitable for cycle-lamp oils. The wick should be of the same size as the burner, and should reach the bottom of the oil-well. Some riders soak their wicks in vinegar before use, and then dry thoroughly. Others put a bit of camphor, the size of a pea, into the oil, claiming that a whiter light is given. See that air-holes do not choke up. Cut top of wick off now and then with scissors. Boil the burner twice a year with soda in the water. If you run out of lamp-oil in the country and cannot get any, use any oil except paraffin. Never oil the rubbers in the lamp hinges.

Acetylene gas-lamps give a much more brilliant and penetrating light, but are much more trouble. The greatest possible amount of light among all cycle-lamps is obtained by the Lucas No. 310 projector set, with silvered mirror reflector and separate generator; 22s. 6d., without rear lamp.

The secret of success with acetylene lamps is absolute cleanliness. The needle valve which controls the supply of water to the carbide should frequently be taken out, washed with hot water, and slightly oiled. If the lamp is used often, the carbide chamber should be cleaned out at least once a week with hot water and a stiff brush. The burner is liable to choke, as the holes through which the gas passes are extremely fine; a piece of wire of the right gauge should be carried for clearing these passages.

Turn off the water a minute or two before the end of a ride. The flame should be blown out before it has dwindled much. A small flame causes soot to form in the gas-passage.

If the lamp is being used for a number of *short* rides only, a useful sieve can be made by punching a lot of holes in the base of an old tin. Empty the partly-spent carbide into this, and shake until only unused lumps are left behind.

As carbide expands when wetted, its chamber should never be filled above the limit-line marked on it. The water-chamber should be quite filled. For rides of more than about three hours carry spare carbide in an air-tight tin.

If your flame flares up turn off the water and open the front—before the glass flies. Too much water is the cause.

When lamp-springs break on the road, they can be replaced *pro tem.* with a couple of Bowden take-off springs fitted to the plates which connect the bracket and the body of the lamp. They must be fixed diagonally, one on either side, forming an x. Oil, gas, paraffin, and candle lamps should ride in a perfectly horizontal position.

ELECTRIC LAMPS.—In these you have the choice of two kinds—the dry battery type and the self-generating or dynamo type. (The acid accumulator seems to have weighed itself out of the question.)

The extreme cleanliness and convenience of the dry battery type have brought it into considerable popularity. Generally speaking, the light is better than oil-lamps give but less good than acetylene, and, of course, it is a diminishing quantity. The self-contained lamp, resembling a pocket flash-lamp in appearance, is the simplest form of this type, costing from 6s. 6d. to 10s. 6d. More satisfaction is got from the dry battery carried in a leather case on top tube or behind saddle. For front light only these sets cost from 18s. to 20s. The sets for both front and rear lights cost 30s. to 32s.

The principal makers of these sets· are :

Siemens Brothers and Co., Woolwich, London, S.E. 18.
Efandem Co., Fallings Park, Wolverhampton.
Ever-Ready Co., Hercules Place, Holloway, London, N. 7.
Ward and Goldstone, Pendleton, Manchester.

Spare batteries for these sets cost 2s. to 3s. 6d. I have had a total of nine hours of light, in intermittent spells, from one of Messrs. Siemens' sets, several of those spells being an hour long, before the battery became too weak.

When using dry battery lamps one or two spare bulbs should always be carried.

The chief advantage of the self-generating type, in which the current for one or two lamps is generated by a small dynamo driven by a pulley-wheel in contact with the front rim, is its very small weight. The price of these sets varies from 27s. to 52s. No light is given until the bicycle begins to move, and the power of the light varies according to the speed of the machine. There is a constant buzz from the dynamo. The amount of the rider's power absorbed is negligible. This type is more complicated than the dry battery type, and there is usually pulley-slip in wet weather. An experienced user wrote to me : " By using smaller lamps than makers supply, I can get a light like acetylene, but this requires a third lamp to be switched on going downhill, or the lamps are burned out." Some cyclists use the dynamo to charge an accumulator, and thus obtain a constant light.

Messrs. Ward and Goldstone are the principal makers of this type. There is also the Talmo, by Brown Bros., Ltd., obtainable from most cycle agents. The Philag set, German made, has been recommended to me. Apply H. W. Koehler, 10, Wood Street Square, London, E.C. 2.

FOG.—A white light is not satisfactory in fog. Gas lamps in particular require the lens or glass to be covered with some thin yellowish material—muslin dipped in coffee, for example. A circular cap may be made of such stuff with an elastic edge to slip over the front of the lamp.

RENOVATION AND ENAMELLING.

Remove everything you can from the patient—chain, wheels, tyres, brakes, handlebar, saddle and pillar, mudguards, and even pedals.

Wash all bearings out with paraffin, allow to drain well, and wipe off dry. Treat chain as directed, page 18.

If the old enamel is found to be in fair condition and not cracked, well wash over with turpentine, benzine, or petrol, but not near a naked light! Get some hot water, adding about an ounce of soda to the gallon, a piece of cloth and some fine powdered pumice, and scour the old enamel all over with these. Rinse with hot water and allow to dry. Then touch up any bare places with enamel, allow to dry, and apply a coat of enamel all over. If put on too thickly it will run; two fairly thin coats will dry harder and look better than one thick one.

If two coats are given, allow the first time to get hard, then slightly rub down with the pumice; wash off clean and apply the second coat.

Allow at least two or three days before assembling the cycle. Before it is taken out, wash over with clean cold water and dry off.

If the old enamel is in a bad condition, scrape it all off. (Previous careful heating with a blow lamp is the best way, using a large soft flame.) Scour down smooth with emery cloth, remove all traces of dust, and proceed to enamel as above. If a first-class job is required, flat the second coat with fine rottenstone on a wet cloth and wash off well and dry. Then apply a third and fairly full coat. A very fine and hard finish can be got by a final coat, after two days interval, of transparent enamel. When this last is hard, wash off with clean cold water, using a soft sponge and chamois leather.

The above instructions are taken mainly from those issued by the makers of the Robbialac range of enamels, Jensen and Nicholson, Ltd., Robbialac Works, Stratford, London, E. 15, whose goods are excellent.

I am also trying a new enamel with a bitumen base called "Bitufilm," which can be had in nominal half-pint tins, 2s., post free, from Structures Waterproofing, Ltd., 3, Broad Street Buildings, London, E.C. 2. It promises very well.

Enamelling should be done in a clean, warm room—it is of vital importance to avoid dust. New brushes should be soaked in water overnight before use. After use they should be washed with turps and then with soap and water.

After enamelling, even the amateur can decorate his machine with lines in gold and colours by utilising the transfer process of the British Decalcomania Company, Rugby, who are ready to send particulars. The only difficulty is with the panel transfers for curved surfaces like mudguards and front forks. One of my readers advises cutting these into sections.

LUGGAGE.

What you take with you in the way of luggage on a cycling tour is largely a matter of your age and the distance you are going. The young man will set off for a week with nothing but a waterproof cape—I have done it very often. For a shirt is good for a week, even worn day and night. If your knees and stockings are wet when you cease riding for the day you push newspapers down inside your breeches, one in front of each leg, and it is sound practice in both physics and physiology. You don't worry about wet stockings, because the area of evaporation and radiation is not large enough to chill the whole body. If it stops raining after tea or supper, a sharp walk will dry all your clothes and destroy the last chance of chill. This tourist does not carry a shaving kit because there are barbers *en route*. He may carry a spare soft collar and " hanky " in his breast-pocket; and if he has any disreputable old hankies he may take two or three and leave them behind as he goes. After these elementals, you take just what you " cannot do without."

Owing to the fact that so many bicycles are equipped with back-wheel carriers, a popular way of dealing with luggage is to wrap it all in a sheet of American cloth (putting little hard things in the middle of the bigger and softer ones) and strap it to a carrier. More serviceable is the double-texture Paramatta which can be bought in towns at the shops where waterproofs are made. Used like this, however, no wrapping material lasts long—too many carriers have sharp edges and projections.

The Japanese basket is an improvement on that way. When it is to hold nothing that will harm with crushing, it should be of the telescopic variety, which adapts itself to much luggage or little. But the woman who carries her Sunday bib and tucker for evenings in hotels should have the more rigid kind of basket, with an ordinary lid. " Each of us," writes a correspondent, " carries on his back carrier a small Japanese basket, each half of which we line with American cloth. After the lower part is packed, a loose piece of American cloth is also laid over it, overlapping all round, before the lid is put on. The baskets can be bought in any size required, and they are lighter and more accommodating than fibre or cardboard valises."

Apart from these methods there are several proprietary luggage-holders designed specially for the cyclist, some of which may be described in detail. There is no " order of merit " in the following list, and the articles illustrated are not drawn in comparative proportion. " A " illustrates the " cyclist's week-end bag " made by Gough and Co., Ltd., Park Road, Hockley, Birmingham. I find it useful and practical. The two straps behind go through the tool-bag holes in the saddle, while a third strap in the back (which is stiffened) goes round the back forks. It is made in two sizes, 10 ins. by 9 ins. by 3½ ins. at 8s., and 12 ins. by 9 ins. by 4 ins. at 10s., *plus* 9d. postage. My own, which is the larger size, weighs 1 lb. 4 ozs.

" B " is the " Any-size hold-all," designed by Mr. T. H. Holding, and obtainable from 7, Maddox Street, London, W. 1. It is an unstiffened bag to roll up, made on one side of brown canvas and on the other of linen. Brass rings are sewn to the outer side, and long thin lanyards, which pass through the rings on the rolled-up bag and are used to fasten up the bundle or to secure it to the handlebar, or both at once. The upper figure B shows the bag rolled up out of use, when it goes easily into a pocket. My own is about 26 ins. by 15 ins. when flat

and empty, and weighs about 11 ozs. The present price is 10s. 6d.

" D " is the patented pannier-bag made by T. W. Crampton, Castle Bromwich, Birmingham. It rides on a special light carrier which can be used for ordinary purposes when the bag's three straps are unfastened. One of the covering flaps has an inside pocket for maps, etc. Bag and carrier are supplied together, 17s. 6d. It is a very sound high-class production.

" E " is the " Handy touring-bag " sold by A. W. Gamage, Ltd., Holborn, E.C. 1, with an end pocket for maps and a handle for carrying when detached. Two straps enable it to be carried on handlebar, top tube, or behind saddle. The size is 14 ins. by 8 ins. by 5 ins. In tan mail cloth the price is 11s. 6d. ; in motorhood cloth, 8s.

" F " is a telescopic touring valise sold by Brown Bros., Ltd., and known to them as No. 5374a. This should be ordered from local cycle agents and not direct. It is made of brown canvas and rides on a carrier. Its size is 12 ins. by 7½ ins. by 6½ ins. and the price is about 10s.

" H " is a pair of front pannier bags in brown waterproof canvas, which hang on the top bar and are secured by one strap round the head. It is of Dutch design and is sold by Camp and Sports Co-operators, Ltd., 4, New Union Street, E.C. 2, for 10s. the pair. The weight is 11 ozs. One of the pouches holds my big cape, loosely folded. They do not touch my knees even with 8-in. cranks; they are not suitable for an X-frame. There is interference with top tube change-speed control in those cases where the lever bracket is brazed on and well forward, but adjustment is fairly easy when it is on a movable clip.

Mention may also be made of the large twin pannier-bags in waterproof canvas which hang low on either side of the back wheel, the piece which connects them lying flat on the top of an ordinary rear carrier and leaving it quite free for all ordinary use. These are of most use to the cycling camper, for tent, pegs, guys, ground sheet and ground blanket will all go into them and then leave some room. They are obtainable from the same addresses as the Any-size hold-all and the little Dutch pannier bags referred to previously.

WOMEN ON TOUR.—The following note is contributed by " Klossie " : " When on tour I carry a change of underwear, spare stockings, a pair of light evening shoes, a simple one-piece dress of some uncrushable material for hotel wear in evenings, and a princess petticoat made of washing silk to wear under it; a silk nightdress (warm and takes up little room) brush and comb, etc. All this goes easily into a small Japanese basket—not the telescopic sort—which then slips into an American cloth cover or bag which I made to fit the basket exactly. This straps on to a back carrier.

" For riding when not in ' rational dress ' I wear a fairly short and well-cut tweed skirt and knitted jumper to tone with it, and I also carry a knitted coat that matches the skirt to wear if cold. Hanging from my handlebar in front is an ordinary school satchel, and this carries either waterproof or the woolly coat—they are not often needed together. I never buy a ' lady's waterproof '—the masculine garment is much more satisfactory. Mine is an Aeromac, see page 28, but for ' rational dress ' a big cape is best.'

WET WEATHER RIDING.

After many years of experiment, I have given up the water-proof jacket in favour of the more popular cape or poncho.

The advantages of the coat over the cape are three, but not very important : pockets, freedom of the arms, and appearance. The advantages of the cape (when properly made) over the coat are three or four : better ventilation and, therefore, less moisture underneath by condensation ; much better protection for the legs, and ditto for the hands.

But the ordinary cape of commerce is a delusion and a snare, being too short and too skimpy in the skirt. You have to drag it tightly against your back and sides before you can get a bit of slack in front to put over the handlebar, and this means that your steering is affected, that your thighs get wet, and that you are soon sitting in a pool. Very many users of such capes simply give up the attempt and ride with a balloon on their backs—they are getting less than half the protection from the cape that they should do.

The cycling cape for all people of average build should be 118 ins. to 120 ins. in skirt circumference and about 40 ins. long. Ponchos in black oilskin, weighing but 1 lb. 5 ozs., are made to these measurements by J. Barbour and Sons, Ltd., South Shields ; 39 ins. long, 15s. 6d. ; 36 ins., 14s. 6d. It fastens with strap and buckle at the neck-opening, which has a tongue or gusset to keep wet out, and the collar is velvet-lined. It extends well over the handlebar and is long enough to sit on, which is occasionally useful in a gale. Driven rain is necessary for the knees to get wet. These " Beacon " ponchos and the many oilskin garments made by Barbours can be re-dressed again and again as long as any fabric remains. They are stormproof.

So also are the Aeromac ponchos, made by Rogers Bros., 5, Princes Street, W. 1, which are rubber-proofed single texture garments of very fine material. The speciality is the system of proofing. Never before has rubber proofing been known to withstand heat and to remain proof for more than a few months of the misuse which the cyclist's cape usually receives. But I know by experience that the Aeromac garments are still stormproof after seven years of use, and they are indifferent to tropical climates. The Aeromac poncho is 4 ozs. lighter even than the Beacon, and packs into less space. It costs 2 guineas, and is a cape for the connoisseur. They have a more popular line at a guinea, of proportionate value, called the Hydromac, weight 1 lb., 140 ins. skirt circumference, 36 ins. length. Made to order in about ten days.

Waterproof leggings and overalls are much too hot to ride in, and few cyclists use them. There are those who can hardly avoid it—clergymen, and many of those who ride to business—and their concern should be to get them as light and loose as possible. Barbours stock light black shaped leggings in oilskin for cycling, 11s. 6d. Brown Bros. (through agents only) also have a variety to offer, and their Cyclospats are quite unusual. They are open at the back of the leg, where the cyclist rarely gets wet, and are, therefore, much less hot. They cover the knee and foot well; there is a leather toe-piece into which the shoe fits, and three straps to fasten behind the leg; about 9s. a pair.

Women have always been devotees of the full-length water-proof, but they no longer need it. Now that their skirts are reasonably short, they would almost certainly find such a cape as that described a better protection than the full-length mackintosh, which can always be relied on to admit water all down the front fastening in heavy rain. When the full-length waterproof is worn it should be at least 2 ins. longer than the skirt, an effect which is often secured by fastening the skirt up *pro tem.*

The cyclist's lamp, when carried in the usual (and best) position, is sometimes awkwardly placed when a cape of ample size is in use. This is a case for a spare lamp-bracket on the right-hand fork-blade, high up—a position which may yet become universal for another reason.

Whether your cape is oilskin or rubbered, it is entitled to far better treatment than it receives at the hands of most cyclists, who strap their capes tightly to frame or carrier, reckless of destructive friction and sharp edges. Most cyclists also forget that heat and direct sunshine are, next to oil and grease, the worst enemies of rubber. Heat has a bad effect on oilskins. If the cape must be strapped to the machine, it should first be wrapped in a piece of some light and tough material. But the best way to carry any kind of waterproof on a bicycle is in a bag or satchel from handlebar or saddle, loosely rolled. When wet they should be allowed to dry naturally before being put away; and when not carried on the machine they should be hung up in cool and dry places.

Most people have too much fear of getting wet. Even drenched clothes will do you no harm *if only you take steps to keep warm.* The water is not harmful in itself, but if your own temperature is lowered below the safety point your power of resistance to evil is also lowered. That safety point varies according to your condition; healthy people can stand cold better than unhealthy ones. The lowering of your temperature is caused either by the continuous contact of cold rain or by the subsequent evaporation of the moisture in the clothes. If caught without a cape and thoroughly wetted, the rider should make for home and ride at the pace necessary to keep warm. Rather than coast down a hill in that condition, he should either drive hard down it or get off and walk briskly. If you have been foolish enough to go on tour without a cape and have got soaked, either ride hard till your clothes have dried on you, taking a hot drink now and again, or go to bed (with a hot drink) while your clothes are being dried. It is foolish to make for the railway, because of the loafing about involved and the probability of cold draughts while you are inactive; but if you could get without waiting into a compartment warm enough to maintain your normal temperature, the wet clothes would do no harm at all. It is common in the country, and especially in Scotland, to see people working in the open all day in heavy rain in their ordinary clothes.

With a real cape on, the cyclist need not worry about rain at all. Even if his shoes, stockings, and the knees of his breeches are sodden, it is unlikely that the small area concerned will cool the whole body down below the safety point. But if you are forced to ride in a cape for a long spell, it is best to reduce your average pace. All real waterproofs are warm things to ride in, with two distinct results : there is a greater tendency to perspiration, and as the body gets warmer there is considerable condensation, under the cape, of water-vapour. Many an excellent and innocent cape has been accused of admitting rain because it has been found wet underneath for this reason. A big loose cape is much cooler to ride in than a skimpy one drawn closely about the body. Thin stockings dry much more quickly than heavy " roll-tops."

Sensible cyclists ride when it is not raining with nothing on their heads; there are very few days in our climate when direct sun-rays are hot enough to be injurious to even the hairless cyclist. (I have a bald-headed cycling relative whose scalp is like mahogany.) Many are also content to ride bare-headed in rain, and I do not blame them, though it involves fastening the cape rather tightly about the neck. But many of us who have to wear glasses like to keep the rain off them. I never had a great opinion of the cap, even in the long-ago days when it was sensibly made. But the modern cap is an atrocity. I do not want a Yorkshire tea-cake projecting over each ear and another in front of the peak. So I have bought no cap for many years, and have divided my vote between those soft tweed hats (now lighter than caps) which can be worn any shape or no shape, and Barbours' " Haydon " oilskin hat, which goes into my touring kit in view of possible all-day rain. It weighs 4 ozs. only; 6s. 6d.

Sooner or later it will happen that you finish a day's ride on tour with sodden shoes, which are still wet in the morning. There is not the slightest need to be afraid of them. Don't put them on again until just before leaving, but if the feet continue to feel cold, walk sharply up the first hill.

TOURING FROM A CENTRE.

This is a plan which would be much more often followed if its advantages were realised. Even a fairly large company with mixed tastes can bring off a successful cycling holiday if a central headquarters be chosen, and daily radial rides made. If the H.Q. is carefully chosen—it should be personally known to one or more of the company—success is almost certain.

A more luxurious equipment becomes possible than in point-to-point touring, because it can be sent on in advance. If a town is chosen as H.Q. there will be something to count on in the way of evening entertainment, whereas the " moving-on " system may find you resourceless in the matter. I have the Easter Holiday most in mind, and Whitsun to a less extent, when weather may be uncertain and evenings dark.

You leave all your luggage behind every day, except your cape. The rest-house people will pack your midday meal for you, to be eaten *al fresco*, with the assistance of a thermos flask or Sirram tea-set; and you return to a certain roof, and dinner or supper in the evening.

In South-East England, Canterbury, Tunbridge Wells, and Horsham are good " centres "; in the West, Exeter and Taunton, the latter being much the easier. Hereford, Warwick, Bedford, Norwich, and Cambridge are all good. Farther North, Shrewsbury, Harrogate, and York are good, but Harrogate can be a bitterly cold place early in the year. North of the Border, Castle Douglas (in Galloway), Aberfeldy or Dunkeld, and Inverness would be good centres. Bournemouth is an excellent seaside H.Q. (though hardly a " centre "), because of the proximity of the New Forest and an abundance of good and easy roads.

North Wales, the Lake District, the Yorkshire Dales, and Cornwall are, in my opinion, better seen by the " moving-on " system.

A HUNDRED IN A DAY.

Though 50 or 60 miles in one day may have been your maximum hitherto, there comes a time when it would be of immense convenience to you to double that distance, if only as a matter of dodging a railway journey.

Any cyclist, man or woman, who is good enough in physique and health to ride 50 or 60 miles on a Saturday or Sunday holiday, can double it in the course of a long summer day without undue fatigue and without special preparation, supposing that he is decently mounted and does not encounter a strong head wind all the way.

The two chief factors in success are an early start and a slow start. Do not cut too big a slice out of the preceding night's rest; but if you are in bed by 10.30 you should be ready (for once) to get up at five and be off at six. A cold bath, or cold sponge and rough towel, are then worth more than the time they take. Eat a good breakfast, but not more than usual.

If there are any steep hills to climb in the first part of the day, walk them, variable gear or no. Remember that if you average eight miles an hour, including stops, for 12 hours, you will have covered a hundred soon after six p.m., and there

B

are still three or four hours of daylight left. Aim at riding so easily that your last 50 will be faster than the first.

Do not go much more than 20 miles or two hours without food, but do not be always eating. Carry raisins or chocolate or even biscuits in your pockets, or in a little bag where you can reach them without dismounting. Chew these things very thoroughly and keep them in the mouth till they disappear. Apples and oranges are better than any drinks. Drink as little as possible, and never take alcoholic liquors on a long ride. Mineral waters are utterly useless by themselves, but if lemon-juice is squeezed into them, they become refreshing and satisfying drinks. Only people who perspire heavily need drink a lot. Lemon-juice in tea, without milk, is a really good thirst-quencher and pick-me-up. Do not be afraid of a good dinner, but don't exert yourself for an hour after it. Tea should never be drunk strong, unless it is China tea, and never with a meat meal. China tea is far more wholesome than the other kinds.

Do not wear anything that is tight, especially at neck, wrists or knees. The best way to rest is to lie full length.

If you can neither eat nor sleep at the end of a ride, you have dangerously over-taxed your energy. It is a case for bed until you *can* sleep, and it is one of the few occasions when a glass of hot toddy is medicinal and beneficial.

LAWS AND CUSTOMS OF THE ROAD.

Keep to the left when meeting traffic and when you receive audible warning of overtaking traffic. This is Law, not merely Custom. When you are riding between tram-lines and receive warning from an overtaking motor, you are legally bound to make way and should do so also as a matter of common courtesy; but if the rails are in a dangerous condition, you are legally entitled to hold your course until they can be safely crossed, in which case you should signal to the driver behind to slow down by holding your right hand out and moving it up and down.

Keep to the right (or off) side of any traffic you overtake. This is a Rule of the road, but not Law. This means that you cannot be summoned for overtaking anything on the near side, which is a very common thing in London. But if you received any injury either while doing so or through doing so you could not recover damages; and if your breach of the Rule led to any injury to any person or property, damages would be obtainable from you. It is also common courtesy to obey a Rule even when it is not Law.

But if you are *overtaking a tramcar* always do it on the left or near side, keeping a sharp look-out for the passengers who may be either leaving or approaching it. Even if they have no sort of consideration for you, that is no reason why you should be a road-hog also.

The Law requires (Section 78 of the Highways Act) that people in charge of animals on the highway, *whether led or otherwise*, shall keep to the left side of the road when required, just the same as all other traffic. But a Custom of the Road requires you to pass led animals on the driver's side, so that he is between you and the animals: In practice, the conductor of led horses is nearly always on the wrong side of the road.

Whenever a dubious traffic situation arises, such, for instance, as led horses on the wrong side of the road and two motors approaching from opposite sides, the cyclist is not only wise, but dignified, who stops at once and looks on while the others muddle through. That is my own rule when either cycling or motoring, whenever a situation turns up which has elements of doubt about it; and the habit has often given me the superior Pharisaical satisfaction of seeing the others run into each other.

Whenever you propose to turn to the Right *hold out the right arm horizontally and never the left*. To hold out the left arm and then turn to the right, as I have seen both cyclists and motorists do, is a symptom of imbecility. Follow this Rule of the Road till you do it automatically even when alone on a country road. Signal in the same way with the left arm when turning to the left (particularly in London), but the other is the more important.

If you are going to *stop*, and there is following traffic, hold the right hand up vertically.

Cyclists can save themselves from much annoying hooting from overtaking motors if, as soon as they hear the first warning sound, they wave the right hand a few times to and fro, low down, as a signal that they have heard and are aware of the car's presence. In motoring practice, the sign means " Come on." There is courtesy in it as well as convenience.

In turning a blind *left-hand corner*, keep as close in as possible to the left all the way round, and slowly. If you meet a vehicle on the wrong side, remember that its driver will instantly turn outwards; *don't you do the same*.

In turning a blind *right-hand corner*, make a wide outward curve on your left side and never cut the corner.

When emerging on to a main road you cannot be too cautious, for by a Custom of the Road main-road traffic has precedence over by-road traffic.

Never on any account overtake and pass any sort of traffic *while turning a corner or curve round which you cannot see*. Let your permanent thought be : " There is a blithering idiot round that corner, and there's no knowing what he'll do. Safety First."

Although the Law requires you to keep to the left when required to by other traffic, you have a legal right to ride on any part of the road at other times. But modern conditions make it very risky to stand on one's legal rights in the matter. It strikes me as bad manners for cyclists to ride more than two abreast at any time or anywhere.

CYCLING FOR THE UNSOUND.

Cycling is quite a successful treatment for a much larger number of ailments than is generally realised. It is, unfortunately, not often prescribed by doctors, most of whom are now motorists—partly by the necessity for time-saving, and partly for social " swank." If your bicycle is dear to you, and a doctor tells you that you must give it up, do not rest until you have found another who is also a keen cyclist; then abide by his decision. The younger end of doctors to-day have no experience of cycling, and are, therefore, not qualified to give an opinion, while the older end have no experience of modern machines, and may allow their judgment to be warped by memories of machines which involved too much physical labour.

In cases of heart weakness, nothing but good can come from the sensible use of a good bicycle with a low gear, if no attempt is made to climb steep hills. But where there is organic disease of the heart there must be no cycling until an expert— preferably a cyclist—has pronounced judgment. Women with weak hearts should not cycle at all unless they are prepared to adopt the light masculine machine and a suitable dress.

VARICOSE VEINS in the legs, when they are of the usual kind resulting from loss of elasticity in the walls, and are *not* due to pressure elsewhere, can be cured by intelligent cycling, and often are. A *web* bandage should be worn, and it should be applied before the feet are put to the floor in the morning. It is better than the elastic stocking, because the pressure can be varied at different spots. This bandage should be applied tightly at the ankle, and less tightly in the ascent, *i.e.*, with just sufficient surrounding pressure to ensure comfort. Cycling on a good and reasonably-geared bicycle is then the right treatment, as the body's weight is taken off the legs during the exercise.

All forms of *rheumatic pain*, whether merely called rheumatism or disguised under fancy names like gout and lumbago, find an enemy in the bicycle. All these are manifestations of indigestion. The bicycle will not prevent these ailments in those unintelligent people who habitually eat too much, too often, or too fast; but cycling facilitates good digestion, and when pushed to the extent of slight perspiration it helps to get rid of rheumatic agents through the pores of the skin.

From time to time I come across people who suggest that

hæmorrhoids or piles are " caused by cycling." There is not a shred of truth in it. They are caused by constipation and an abundance of rich blood. Mild cases can be beneficially treated by cycling so long as the saddle is kept properly adjusted, or one of the saddles used which are specially designed to prevent the cyclist from sitting on his pubic arch, such as the Christy or Henson or Pattinson anatomical saddles (to be ordered from Brown Bros., *via* cycle agent). Bad cases can only be cured by operation. It is a major operation, and is quite successful when done by a good man; I know.

It must also be noted that piles can be very seriously irritated and aggravated by careless cycling. The saddle *must* be so adjusted (see pages 7 and 17) that the rider sits on those ischial tuberosities which are there for the purpose, and not upon the perineum or pelvic arch. The high saddle or long reach must particularly be avoided; and if one of these special anatomical saddles is chosen, the saddle pillar should be lowered, for they are all higher (or deeper) than ordinary saddles. These remarks apply also to urethral, prostatic, or bladder trouble; and additional care should be taken in these cases that the saddle is not only kept adjusted for tension, but also that the peak does not point upwards, and that the rider sits almost upright.

For insomnia, and many other forms of nervous disorder, it need hardly be said that cycling is a sovereign remedy.

SPARE SPOKES.

GUIDE-BOOKS.—Perhaps the best for the cyclist are the Roadfaring Guides, by Reginald Wellbye, and published by E. J. Larby, 30, Paternoster Row, London, E.C. 4. They are on novel, practical, and responsible lines, light in weight, and the right size for the pocket. The volumes are Northern England, Central England, Eastern England, Southern England (including the South-West), Wales and the Welsh Borderland, and Scotland; 2s. 6d. per volume.

GLOVES.—The only kind of glove worth having is the fingerless (or Canadian) type stocked by A. W. Gamage, Ltd.; but when a cape is being worn which covers the hands there is little need of gloves, even in cold weather. Gauntlet fingerless gloves in oilskin are sold by Barbour and Son, of South Shields.

SHOES.—Barbours are also the makers of the best cycling shoes I know—the Speedy, 18s. 6d., soles and heels of chrome leather.

STOCKINGS.—The hosiers offer the cyclist nothing but thick and heavy roll-top monstrosities which are not " rational dress " at all. This has driven many cyclists to wear women's black cashmere stockings, because of their light weight. But black is not practical on the road, and women's feet are smaller than men's. Result—immediate holes. I now get lightweight knitted stockings with 11-in. feet made for me in gray by E. L. Hunt, 5, Eastholm, Letchworth, for 4s. 9d. a pair. He will make any colour or any weight to order.

Mr. J. H. Greenwood, High Street, Hanley, Staffs., is also a maker who specialises in lightweight stockings for cyclists at 6s. 11d.

CAMPING.—The principal addresses of firms supplying tents and camping apparatus of special designs and light weight are, in alphabetical order :

Camp and Sports Co-operators, Ltd., 4, New Union Street, E.C. 2. This is an offshoot from the Camping Club, members of which are entitled to special terms.

The tents and other specialities designed by Mr. T. H. Holding, the father of light camping, are obtainable from 7, Maddox Street, W. 1.

The Lightweight Tent Supply Company, 70, High Holborn, W.C. 1.

Herbert Pocock, Park Mills, Salisbury.

CAMPING CLUB.—The address of the Camping Club of Great Britain and Ireland is 4, New Union Street, E.C. 2. Ordinary subscription rate for individual adult members, 10s. 6d. per annum ; 2s. 6d. entrance fee on joining. The Handbook of this Club is the best practical guide to lightweight camping now available.

C. T. C.—The address of the Cyclists' Touring Club is 280, Euston Road, N.W. 1. The annual subscription is 10s., with an entrance fee of 1s. Cyclists who join after September 15 in any year are covered by the one subscription to the end of the following year. For advantages from membership write the Secretary.

SLEEPING ROUGH.—The idea of sleeping out in a waterproof bag appeals to many in preference to either tents or resthouses. Wool-lined paramatta sleeping-bags are made by Taylor and Ross, Angel Row, Nottingham. A more luxurious (and costly) equipment, but lighter, would be the down-lined " Comfy " bag of the Lightweight Tent Supply Company (see ante), combined with the waterproof bag supplied to cover it.

T. C. F.—The address of the Touring Club de France is 65, Avenue de la Grande Armée, Paris, XVI. Annual subscription to foreigners is 15 francs.

FOOTPATHS.—Not only is cycling forbidden on footpaths alongside public roads, but it is also illegal even to wheel them on such paths. There is no law against cycling on footpaths which do not adjoin public roads.

FRAME HEIGHT.—Frame height is measured from the top of the seat-lug (at the point where the saddle-pin protrudes) to the centre of the crank-axle. Crank length is measured from centre of crank-axle to centre of pedal-axle.

CHAIN-LINE is the distance measured from the centre of the hub of the back wheel to the middle of the nearest tooth on the chain-ring of the back wheel.

ROMAN RIMS, made of an aluminium alloy which never rusts, are now made by Messrs. Kynoch, Ltd., Witton, Birmingham. The most satisfactory *brake-blocks* for use with these rims are the Hermetic, made by Self-Sealing Rubber Company, Ryland Street, Birmingham.

EXAMINE YOUR BRAKES periodically and carefully from end to end, especially before going on tour. See that the brake-blocks are not so worn that the metal shoes are in contact with the rims.

USE BOTH BRAKES evenly and at the same time. Do not let either of your brakes get out of use and action.

RAILWAY RATES for the conveyance of cycles as passengers' luggage at owner's risk :—

Distance in Miles up to	30	50	100	200	300
Bicycle Ticket.	1/2	1/11	3/-	4/6	6/-

and 9d. for each additional 50 miles or part thereof. Tandems are charged 50 per cent. more than singles.

Railway companies admit their liability for damage done to bicycles when the amount exceeds 10s. ; but not for a smaller amount unless the special insurance ticket is bought, which costs 1d. for any distance. In the latter case, take *special notice* that " No liability will be admitted unless the loss or damage be pointed out to a company's official before removal of the bicycle from the company's premises."

" KUKLOS " is correctly pronounced Kew-kloss. It is the Greek word from which our word " cycle " is derived. In the Greek it means (*a*) a circle or wheel ; and (*b*) a ring or circle of people.

———

PART TWO.

POTTED TOURS.

Section 1.—The English Lakes.

APPROACHES.—From the western half of England generally the most usual roads of approach are those which converge on Warrington and continue northwards through Wigan, Preston, Lancaster, and Carnforth.

From London and the South-East, this " North-West route " would be joined *via* Daventry, High Cross, Atherstone, Fazeley, Lichfield, Stone, Woore, and Nantwich to Tarporley, 18 miles south of Warrington.

Equal in distance from London, slightly more difficult (towards the end), but decidedly more interesting, is the route along the Great North Road all the way through Grantham and Doncaster until two miles short of Wetherby, where the Lakesbound traveller turns left and proceeds through Harewood, Otley, Skipton, Settle, Ingleton, and Kirkby Lonsdale.

If wanting to approach the Lakes from the North side, the traveller by either of these two routes would continue northwards from Kendal to Penrith, or even Carlisle. Or he might continue along the Great North Road through Wetherby to Boroughbridge, then along Leeming Lane, and over Catterick Bridge to Scotch Corner, there turning left for Bowes, Stainmoor, Brough, Appleby, and Penrith. Taken this way, it is an easy crossing of the Pennines; but in the reverse direction it is arduous.

My own favourite way of approach to the southern end of the Lake District begins at Milnthorpe, north of Carnforth and west of Kirkby Lonsdale. At Levens Bridge, 2¼ miles north of Milnthorpe, turn left on Grange road; 1½ miles farther, at Gilpins Bridge, turn right for Winster and Bowness, an easier and much more quiet route than the main road by Kendal.

Stouter footwear than cyclists usually have is advisable when mountain walks are intended, and even boots are excusable.

The best MAP is the Ordnance Survey, " The Lake District," two miles to the inch, large sheet series, 2s. on paper, 3s. on linen—copy all these details when ordering. It covers the whole of the routes to follow except the upper portion of Bassenthwaite Lake. Bartholomew's " Cumberland," Sheet 3 of his half-inch series, is also excellent, and in some respects better, but it cuts out the Furness District on the south.

Here are three routes of different mileage, which the reader must split into days just as things happen. In Lakeland, one wants to row a boat or climb mountains or watch waterfalls as well as ride a bicycle.

June and September are usually the best months for the Lake District, but a fine October beats them both.

TOUR A, 222 or 254 miles, which, if all the suggested mountain climbs are done, may easily occupy a fortnight : Lakeside to Cartmel, 6; Cark, Holker Hall, 2; Haverthwaite, 4½; Greenodd, 2; Lowick Bridge (which cross), 3; Nibthwaite, Brantwood, Coniston, 8 (climb Old Man); Barngates, Waterhead Hotel, Ambleside, 7½ (climb Wansfell); Skelwith (see fall a little above bridge), Elterwater, Great Langdale, Dungeon Ghyll Old Hotel, 8 (climb Bow Fell or Langdale Pikes, or walk to Blea Tarn, three or four miles return).

Ambleside, 8; Hawkshead, 4½; Esthwaite Water, Sawrey, Ferry, 3½; cross to Bowness (hard by Windermere Station), Ambleside, 6; Rydal Water, Grasmere, 4; Dunmail Raise top, 3. After descending a mile, turn left for west or left-hand side of Thirlmere Lake, by far the more picturesque as well as the easier route to Keswick. Helvellyn, however, is most easily and quickly climbed from the inn at Wythburn on the direct or east road; Keswick 10 by either road. Climb Latrigg or Skiddaw or both, and row on Derwentwater.

Round 1 from Keswick, fairly hard: Threlkeld, Troutbeck, Penruddock, 12; Penrith, 6; but as the first twelve miles are very hard, train might be taken to Penruddock. From Penrith to Pooley Bridge, 5; Glenridding, 8; back two miles, and turn left to Dockwray, Troutbeck, Keswick, 17.

Round 2 from Keswick, easy: Dancing Gate, Mire House Lodge, Bassenthwaite Vicarage, Castle Inn, Ouse Bridge, Pheasant Inn, Swan Inn, Portinscale, Keswick, 17. This is the circle of Bassenthwaite.

Round 3 from Keswick, hard: Portinscale, Hause End, Grange, Lodore, Keswick, 9. This is the circle of Derwent-water.

Lodore, Rosthwaite, Seatoller, 7; ask at last cottage on left for key of new road gate and pay 1d. for bicycles each, 6d. for motor-cycles; fairly easy climb and good road to top of Honister Pass, when *walk down* first half-mile at least; Buttermere, 6.

Scale Hill, 3½; Loweswater Village, Lamplugh Church, Kirkland, Ennerdale Bridge, 3; Anglers' Arms, 2; Ennerdale Bridge, Egremont, 8; Calder Bridge, 4; Gosforth, 2 (Seascale and back, 5); Wasdale, Wasdalehead, 10; climb Scawfell Pike; Santon Bridge, 7; Irton Hall, Muncaster, Ravenglass, 5; train to Ulverston or ride to Bootle, 7½; Silecroft, 4; turn left to Hall-thwaite and Broughton, 7; Grizebeck, Lowick Green, 6; Green-odd, 1½; Lakeside Station, 5½. (Ulverston to Greenodd, 3.)

TOUR B, 181 miles, which should be read in comparison with Tour A for detail suggestions: Lakeside to Bowness (hard by Windermere Station), 8; Ambleside, 6. Onward to Thirlmere and Keswick (see Tour A), 17. Round 2 from Keswick, 17; leave Keswick by route given after Round 3 all the way to Ravenglass, 61½; train to Furness Abbey (30 by rail); Dalton, Ulverston, 6; Greenodd, 3; Lowick Bridge (which cross), 3; Nibthwaite, Brantwood, Coniston, 8; Skelwith Bridge, Elter-water, Red Bank (beware descent), Grasmere, 8; Dunmail Raise and east side of Thirlmere (see note in Tour A), St. John's in the Vale, Threlkeld, 12; Troutbeck, 5; Dockwray, 4; Glenridding, 4; Kirkstone Pass, Windermere, 11; Bowness, Lakeside Station, 8.

TOUR C, 104 miles: Lakeside Station to Bowness (hard by Windermere Station), Ambleside, 14; Grasmere, Dunmail Raise, west side of Thirlmere (see note in Tour A), Keswick, 17;

Portinscale, Hause End, Grange, Rosthwaite, Seatoller, and back by Lodore to Keswick, 16; train to Penrith, Pooley Bridge, Glenridding, 13; Kirkstone Pass, Windermere, 11; Bowness, Ferry, 2; Sawrey, Hawkshead, 3½; Brantwood (no *need* to go into Coniston), Nibthwaite, Lowick Bridge, 10; Greenodd, 3; Haverthwaite, 2; Holker Hall, 4½; Cark, Cartmell, 2; Lakeside Station, 6.

Section 2.—The Yorkshire Dales.

The maximum total of the following tour is 287 miles, but it is distinctly hilly, and not one to be hurried over. Ladies and easy-goers generally might take twelve days over it. I think it should not be done in less than six, for there is much to see out of the saddle. The only important dale omitted is Teesdale, which lies equally in County Durham and naturally forms part of a more northerly round.

The following route lies in Airedale as far as Malham, crosses into Ribblesdale at Settle, includes Dentdale before Sedbergh and Garsdale after it; enters Wensleydale (or Yoredale, the valley of the River Ure) at the Moorcock, and follows it to Hardraw; crosses into Swaledale, and descends that valley for 30 miles. Wensleydale is re-entered at Leyburn, and followed on two sides until Bishopdale is entered from Aysgarth. Wharfedale is reached by Cray Ghyll, and left (after a run up Littondale and back) at Hebden. The journey above Pateley Bridge is in Upper Nidderdale. At Ripon the Ure is touched again and the Nidd at Knaresborough, but their deep valleys have flattened out. At Pool Bridge the Wharfe is again joined; from Ilkley to Burnsall is the prettiest part of this dale, and it is left at Linton for Skipton, where the starting-point is regained.

Skipton, on the Midland main line to Scotland, and Harrogate, now well-served by several companies, are the best starting-places, but the tour can, of course, be begun at any point on it and in either direction, according to individual convenience.

MAPS.—Order from local bookseller the Ordnance Survey Map of Yorkshire, four miles to the inch, Western Half, 1s. 6d. on paper, which covers all the routes. If the routes given are marked on this map in red ink, it will be obvious how the tour can be shortened at will. If the useful contour colouring of Bartholomew's half-inch (two miles to the inch) map is wanted, Sheets 4 and 6 include all but the Sedbergh corner. In the following itinerary only those distances that are printed in figures count towards the total.

From Skipton (see Castle) ride nearly to Gargrave, and turn to right through Eshton Park, Airton, and Kirkby Malham, to

Malham, 11 miles. See Malham Cove, 40 minutes' walk return, and Goredale Scaur, one mile distant, most of it riding. The latter must not be missed. Back to Kirkby Malham and over moor (rough walking first, fair riding on top, by Scaleber Force, a fine waterfall whose sound will betray it, final drop dangerous) to Settle, 6¼.

Clapham, 6; Ingleborough is best climbed from here. Ingleton, 4½; pay sixpence for scenery, well worth it, especially after heavy rain. If spending night in Ingleton, ride to Devil's Bridge, near Kirkby Lonsdale, and back, 12.

Weathercote Cave, 4, on left of Hawes road. "Chasm" is a better word. It is no longer shown, having become dangerous; Ribblehead, 2; Newby Head, 4; but just short of the inn turn left, and as soon as the railway viaduct comes in sight dismount and walk down into Dentdale. Sportsman Inn, 2½; Dent, 4; Sedbergh, 5½; Hawes Junction (on Midland main line) and Moorcock Inn, 11; follow Hawes road for four miles, but keep left then to Hardraw, 4½. See Hardraw Force by passing through Green Dragon Inn. (Hawes is nearly two miles away across the river, but need only be visited for rest-houses if Hardraw fails.)

Buttertubs Pass. This means 5½ miles mostly to walk, and it should not be left very late in the day. As you walk down the Swaledale side the road touches, on your left hand, the principal Buttertub (or pot-hole), and there are several just beyond it. Thwaite, 6; the Swaledale valley road is joined here. Two miles up the valley to the left is Keld, worth a visit for its own sake, and for Kisdon Force (Keld and back, 4).

Muker, 1; Gunnerside, 3; Reeth, 6; Richmond, 11. See view of castle from river bank; a mile walk by the river is to the ruin of Easby Abbey. Catterick, 5; Hackforth, Patrick Brompton, Constable Burton, Leyburn, 12; walk a mile along the Shawl and back if a fine day. Middleham Castle, 2, the astonishing stronghold of Warwick, the King-maker; back over river, and turn left to Wensley, 3½; Bolton Castle, 4; Carperby, Woodhall, Askrigg, 7; Bainbridge, 1½; Aysgarth, 4½; one hour or more here to visit falls, cross bridge, and turn right. West Burton, Bishopdale, Kidstones, Cray Ghyll, 7½; Buckden, 1½. Before descending the valley, the up-dale road should be followed through Hubberholme and Beckermonds to Oughtershaw, 6; no inn here; Buckden again, 6.

Kettlewell, 4, cross river and turn left; Skirfare Bridge, 2; Just past the bridge a road goes off to right up Littondale. It is well worth following through Arncliffe, 3, to Litton, 2½. (Litton and back to Skirfare Bridge, 11.) Kilnsey—bet yourself a shilling you can hit the crag with a stone thrown from the road and you will lose—Conistone, Grassington, 4.

Do not take the next stage very late in the day. Hebden, Greenhow, 7½; the descent into Nidderdale by Greenhow Hill is very long and very steep, but a good road; Pateley Bridge,

3. From here a sidelong excursion to the end of the valley should be made, viz., Ramsgill, 4½; Eugene Aram's school was here; Lofthouse, 2; new road to Angram; about two miles beyond Lofthouse the River Nidd falls into Goyden Pot; guides from farmhouse near will take you down with candles and magnesium ribbon, but you should have good nerves; rejoin road, cycle up dale as far as comfortable, and return to Lofthouse; return distance, say, 8. (A mile away up a steep hill is Middlesmoor, excellent for the night. A couple of hours may profitably be spent in the ravine of How Stean Beck.) Pateley Bridge, 7 or 8.

Leave by the Ripon road. Three miles out on the right are Brimham Rocks, which see; Studley Royal, 9; half-a-day may well be spent in visiting the park and the ruins of Fountains Abbey, 1s. admission; Ripon, 2; Ripley, 7½; Knaresborough, 5, visit castle; Harrogate, 3, bulk of town lies to right; Pool Bridge, Otley, 11. As the main road is very much motored, cross river-bridge and keep left to Askwith, 3; ignore suspension toll-bridge at Ben Rhydding and keep on to Ilkley, 4. If plenty of time or staying overnight, walk through Heber's Ghyll and up to the Old White House.

Addingham, Bolton Abbey, 6; enter grounds by gate near Cavendish monument, leave cycles at Strid Cottage, visit the ruined priory and the Strid, reckon two hours here at least. Barden Tower, 3, keep left; Burnsall, 3; Linton, Cracoe, Rilston, 6; Skipton Station, 5.

A SEAWARD EXTENSION.—Strong or leisured riders whose holiday is not filled by the previous routes, or who would like to include the best of the Yorkshire coast and the Cleveland and Hambleton Hills, may leave the previous route at Ripon, thus : Baldersby Gate, Thirsk, 11½; Tontine Inn, 11; just before it, on right, the unique Carthusian ruin of Mount Grace is passed; Stokesley, 8; Ayton, Guisborough, 8; Scaling Dam, Whitby, 21; High Hawsker, 3; Robin Hood's Town, 2; Fylingthorpe, Cloughton, Scarborough, 16; Brompton, Pickering, 17; Kirkby Moorside, 8; Helmsley, 6; Rievaulx Abbey, 3; Scawton, Sutton Bank Top, 5; better *walk* down, the steepest bit (one in four) is near the bottom; Thirsk, 6; Boroughbridge, 11; rejoining the Dales route at Knaresborough, 7.

YORKSHIRE DALES AND LAKE DISTRICT FROM AND TO YORK, 276 OR 315 MILES.—York to Boroughbridge, 17; Ripon, 7; Masham, 10; Middleham Castle, 9; Wensley, 3; Witton, Aysgarth, 6; Bainbridge, Hawes, 9; Moorcock, 5; Mallerstang, Kirkby Stephen, 11; Brough, Appleby, 12; Penrith, 13; Pooley Bridge, 6; Glenridding, 8; Dockwray, Troutbeck Station, Threlkeld, Keswick, 18.

Round One from Keswick : Seatoller, 7, see note on Lake District, page 39; Honister new road, walk down Honister

Pass, Buttermere, 6; Newlands, Keswick, 9, fully half of the last nine miles is unrideable.

Round Two from Keswick; Braithwaite, Bassenthwaite Lake Station, Bassenfell, Keswick, 17.

Leaving Keswick, turn right at two miles for west side of Thirlmere, Dunmail Raise, Ambleside, 17; Bowness Ferry, 6; cross lake, Sawrey, Hawkshead, Brantwood, Nibthwaite, Spark Bridge, Greenodd, 17; Haverthwaite, Newby Bridge, Lindale, Levens Bridge, Milnthorpe, Kirkby Lonsdale, 16; Ingleton, Settle, 17; Skipton, 16; Addingham, Ilkley, Otley, 15; Pool, Harewood, Collingham, Wetherby, 15; York, 14.

YORKSHIRE DALES, FROM AND TO PRESTON, 228 MILES.—Clitheroe, 17; Gisburn, 7; Long Preston, Settle, 11; Clapham, 6; Ingleton, 4 (pay 6d. to see falls); Ribblehead, 6; Newby Head, 4, turn left, dangerous drop into Dentdale; Dent, Sedbergh, 12; Hawes Junction and Moorcock, 11; Hawes road to Hardraw, 4 (see Force); Buttertubs Pass, Muker, 6; Reeth, 9; Richmond, 11; Catterick, 5; Hackforth, Patrick Brompton, Constable Burton, Leyburn, 12; Middleham Castle, 2; back over river to Wensley, Bolton Castle, 7; Carperby, Woodhall, Askrigg, 7; Bainbridge, Aysgarth, 6; Bishopdale, Kidstones, Cray, Buckden, 9; Kettlewell, 4; Kilnsey, Conistone, Grassington, 4; Burnsall, Barden Tower, Bolton Abbey, 9; Skipton, 6; Gargrave, Eshton Park, Airton, Malham, 11; Bell Busk, Coniston Cold, Hellifield, 8; Gisburn, 6; Clitheroe, Preston, 24.

FROM SEDBERGH BY YORKSHIRE DALES TO SCARBOROUGH AND BACK, 256 MILES.—Up Garsdale to the Moorcock and Hawes, 16; Bainbridge, Aysgarth, up Bishopdale, Cray, Buckden, 18; Kettlewell, Grassington, Burnsall, 13; Barden Tower, Bolton Abbey, Ilkley, 11; Otley, Harewood, Collingham, Boston Spa, 21; Tadcaster, York, 13; Malton, 18; Sherburn, Staxton, Seamer, Scarborough, 23.

Ayton, Snainton, Pickering, 17; Kirkby Moorside, Helmsley, 12; Rievaulx Abbey, Sutton Bank Top, 8, walk down; Thirsk, 5; Skipton-on-Swale, Leeming, Richmond, 24; Gilling, Greta Bridge, Barnard Castle, 14; Bowes, Stainmore, Brough, 17; Kirkby Stephen, 4; up Mallerstang to Moorcock, 10; down Garsdale to Sedbergh, 10.

Section 3. The Derbyshire Dales.

The small but mountainous district known as the Derbyshire Dales is, unfortunately, hemmed in by districts which are densely populated, dirty and ugly, or violently difficult. It is practically enclosed by Manchester, Huddersfield, Sheffield, Derby, and the Potteries. Sheffield is nearest to the dales proper, and with one long climb gives immediate access. In spite of these forbidding approaches, the country enclosed by that ring fence of black industrialism is among the most striking in these islands. Generally speaking, the roads are better engineered than in the Lake District and of good quality. Weak cyclists, however, should take a lot of time over it, and none of the tours here suggested should be undertaken *without a careful and responsible overhauling of the brakes.*

TOUR A, FROM AND TO SHEFFIELD, 128 MILES.—Rivelin Dams, Ashopton, 11; Bamford, 2; Hope, Castleton, 5; The Winnats, Sparrowpit, 5; Doveholes, Buxton, 5½; Millersdale, 6; Tideswell, 2; Eyam, 5; Grindleford Bridge, 2½; Hathersage, 3; Fox House Inn, Froggatt Edge, Calver, 7; Baslow, 2; Bakewell, 3½; Haddon Hall, 2; Winster, 4½; Hartington, 8; Hulme End, Ecton, Wetton Mill, Wetton, 6; Hopedale, Ilam, 4 (see Rushley Bridge); Dovedale, ½; leave machines at or near Izaak Walton Hotel, walk two or three miles up the valley and return; Mappleton, Ashbourne, 5; Bradbourne Lane-end, Grangemill, 9½; the Via Gellia, Cromford, 4; Matlock Bridge, 2½; Rowsley, 4½; Edensor (for Chatsworth Hall), 3; Baslow, 2; Owler Bar, 5; Sheffield, 7½.

TOUR B, FROM AND TO DERBY, 115 MILES.—Ashbourne, 13; Mappleton, Dovedale, 5; leave machines at or near Izaak Walton Hotel and walk two or three miles up the valley and back; Ilam, ½ (see Rushley Bridge), Hopedale, Wetton, 4; Wetton Mill, Ecton, Hulme End, Hartington, 6; Winster, 8; Haddon Hall, 4½; Bakewell, 2; Ashford, Taddington, Buxton, 12; Doveholes, Sparrowpit, 5½; The Winnats, Castleton, 5; Hope, Hathersage, 6; Fox House Inn, Froggatt Edge, Calver, 7; Stoney Middleton, Eyam, 2, back to same road; Tideswell, 5; Millersdale, 2; Taddington, Ashford, Bakewell, 8½; Pilsley, Edensor (for Chatsworth Hall), 3; Rowsley, 3; Matlock Bridge, 4½; Cromford, 2½; Ambergate, 5; train into Derby, 10.

TOUR C, FROM AND TO MANCHESTER, 132 MILES.—Train to Dinting Junction or Glossop; Snake Inn, 8 or 7; Ashopton, 6; Bamford, 2; Hope, Castleton, 5; The Winnats, Sparrowpit, 5; Doveholes, Buxton, 5½; Millersdale, 6; Tideswell, 2; Eyam, 5; Grindleford Bridge, 2½; Hathersage, 3; Fox House Inn, Froggatt Edge, Calver, 7; Baslow, 2; Edensor (for Chatsworth Hall), 2; Rowsley, 3; Matlock Bridge, 4½; Cromford, 2½; The Via Gellia, Grangemill, 4; Bradbourne Lane-end, Ashbourne, 9½; Mappleton, Dovedale, 5; leave machines at or near Izaak Walton Hotel, walk two or three miles up valley, and return; Ilam, ½ (see Rushley Bridge), Hopedale, Wetton, 4; Wetton Mill, Ecton, Hulme End, Hartington, 6; Winster, 8; Haddon Hall, 4½; Bakewell, 2; Ashford, Taddington, Buxton, 12; Chapel-en-le-Frith, 6; train to Manchester, about 20.

MAPS.—Sheet 9, called "Sheffield," and Sheet 13, called "Derby and Notts," of Bartholomew's two miles to the inch map of England, include all the above routes.

Section 4.—North Wales.

The Welsh mountain passes are mostly well engineered, and cyclists who inhabit the easier parts of the country and contemplate their first hill-country tour should do North Wales before the Lake District, the Yorkshire Dales or Derby Dales, Devon and Cornwall, or the Scottish Highlands.

Chester and Shrewsbury are the natural gateways to the road-system of North and Mid-Wales, and tours which begin and end at either are more or less obvious. It suits many, however, to make their start and finish at some popular seaside resort, to which end I include some round routes from Llandudno.

ROUTE 1, FROM AND TO LLANDUDNO, 127 MILES.— Conway, 3½; Trefriw, Llanrwst, 11½; Bettws-y-Coed, 4½; Conway Falls and back, 5; Swallow Falls, 2; Capel Curig, 3; Nant Ffrancon Pass, Bethesda, 9½; Bangor, 5; Menai Bridge, 2½; Beaumaris, 4; back over bridge; Carnarvon, 12; Llanberis, 7½; Pen-y-gwryd, 6½; Llyn Gwynant, Beddgelert, 7½; Pont Aberglaslyn, 1½, cross it; Penrhyn-deudraeth, 6; Maentwrog, Blaenau-ffestiniog, 5; Dolwyddelan, 5½; Bettws-y-Coed, 6; Llanrwst, 4½; Tal-y-cafn, Conway Bridge, Llandudno, 15.

NOTE.—Allow for five miles' walking up the mountain between Maentwrog and Dolwyddelan.

ROUTE 2, FROM AND TO CHESTER, 211 MILES.— Mold, 12; Bodfari, St. Asaph, 17½; Abergele, 6; Colwyn Bay, 6½; Llandudno, 5; round Marine Drive, 5; Conway, 3½; Penmaenmawr, Llanfairfechan, 8; Bangor, 8; Menai Bridge, 2½; Beaumaris, 4; back over bridge, Carnarvon, 12; Llanberis, 7½; Pen-y-gwryd, 5½; turn right, Beddgelert, 7½; Pont Aberglaslyn, 1½; cross it, as Route 1 to Bettws-y-Coed, 22½; Swallow Falls and back, 4; Conway Falls, 2½; Pentre Voelas, 4; Cerrig-y-druidion, 5½; Frongoch, 7½; Bala, 2½; Druid, Corwen, 11½; Llangollen, 10; Wrexham, 11, Chester, 11¼. See note to Route 1.

ROUTE 3, FROM AND TO SHREWSBURY, 206 MILES. —Oswestry, 17; Chirk, 6; Llangollen, 6½; Corwen, 10; Bala, 13; Dolgelley, 17½; Cross Foxes, 3; Tal-y-llyn, 6; Towyn, 10; Aberdovey, 3; Machynlleth, 14; Aberystwyth, 20; Devil's Bridge, 12; Ponterwyd, 3; Llangurig, 12½; Llanidloes, 5; Newtown, 13¼; Welshpool, 13½; Shrewsbury, 18¾.

ROUTE 4, FROM AND TO LLANDUDNO, 230 MILES.— Follow Route 1, excepting the Conway Falls visit, to Penrhyn-deudraeth, 80; Maentwrog, 4½; Harlech, 9; Barmouth, 11; Dolgelley, 10; Llwyngwril, 11½; Towyn, 8; Aberdovey, 4; Machynlleth, 10½; Corris, Minffordd, Dolgelley, 16; Drwsynant, Bala, 18; Frongoch, Cerrig-y-druidion, 10; Pentre Voelas, 5¼; Conway Falls, 4; Bettws-y-Coed, 2½; Llanrwst, 4½; Tal-y-cafn, Llandudno, 15.

ROUTE 5, FROM AND TO CHESTER, 240 MILES.—
Mold, 12; and, as Route 2, to Conway, 43, Llanrwst, 11½;
Bettws-y-Coed, 4½; Conway Falls and back, 5; Swallow Falls,
2; Capel Curig, 3; Nant Francon Pass top, 4½; Bethesda, 4½;
Bangor, 5; Menai Bridge, 2½; Beaumaris, 4; Carnarvon, 12;
Llanberis, 7½; Pen-y-gwryd, 6½; Llyn Gwynant, 3; Bedd-
gelert, 4; Pont Aberglaslyn, 1½ (cross it); Penrhyn-deudraeth,
6; Tan-y-bwlch, 4; Maentwrog, Harlech, 9½; Barmouth, 11;
Dolgelley, 10; Bala, 18; Corwen, 13; Llangollen, 10; Wrexham,
11; Chester, 11½.

ROUTE 6, FROM AND TO SHREWSBURY, 326 MILES.
—Oswestry, 17½; Llangollen, 12½; Corwen, 10; Cerrig, Pentre
Voelas, Bettws-y-Coed, 22; Conway, 15; Bangor, 15; Menai
Bridge, 2½; Beaumaris, 4; Bangor, 6½; Bethesda, 5; top of
Nant Francon Pass, 4½; Capel Curig, 5; top of Llanberis Pass,
6; Carnarvon, 13; Beddgelert, 12; Pont Aberglaslyn (which
cross), 1½; Penrhyn-deudraeth, 6; Tan-y-bwlch, 4; Maentwrog,
Harlech, 9½; Barmouth, 11; Dolgelley, 10; Cross Foxes, 3;
Tal-y-llyn, 6; Towyn, 10; Aberdovey, 3½; Machynlleth, 14;
Aberystwyth, 20; and, as Route 3, to Shrewsbury, 75.

ROUTE 7, TO AND FROM LLANDUDNO, 371 MILES.
—Follow Routes 1 and 4 to Maentwrog and Machynlleth, 153;
Aberystwyth, 20; Devil's Bridge, 12; Llangurig, 13; Llanidloes, 5; Caersws, 8; Cemmaes Road Station, 17; Mallwyd,
6; Cann Office, 11; Llwydiarth, Llanwddyn, 9½; round Lake
Vyrnwy, 10; hard going through Hirnant to Penybont-fawr,
7; Llanrhaiadr, 2½; to the fall and back, 8; Oswestry, 12;
Chirk, Llangollen, 12½; Corwen, 10; Llandrilo, Bala, 13; and,
as Route 4, to Llandudno, 42.

ANGLESEY.—The island is worthy of closer attention than
it usually gets, especially since it is much less be-motored than
the mainland, and, therefore, has better roads. It is very well
mapped on Bartholomew's " North Wales " sheet, and the
Telford highway from London runs in a straight line across
it—a distance of 21 miles. The town of Holyhead has little
attraction, but the Mountain beyond and the South Stack
lighthouse are interesting. The best ride in the island is on
the north-east side, from Pentraeth to Benllech Sands, Moelfre,
Amlwch, Bull Bay, and Cemaes Bay, not forgetting, of course,
that from Menai Bridge to Beaumaris and Penmon Priory. A
mile to the west from Menai Bridge is the Anglesey Column,
which you may climb for a small fee. Inland, the island is
rather tame, but the coast indicated is excellent. Fine views of
the Snowdon range are given by the by-roads to the south-west
from Menai Bridge.

A good pocket guide is " Road Touring in Wales," published
by E. J. Larby (see page 35).

MAP.—All the above routes are covered by Sheet 4 of the

new quarter-mile Ordnance Survey Map, large sheet series, 2s. on paper.

There is a fee (worth it) to Devil's Bridge grounds. Best castles : Harlech, Beaumaris, Carnarvon, Conway, Rhuddlan, Aberystwyth, Dolwyddelan, and Dolbadarn (at Llanberis). At Bettws-y-coed see the Conway Falls, Swallow Falls, and the Fairy Glen ; at Dolgelley, the Precipice Walk and the Torrent Walk. Snowdon can be ascended on foot from Pen-y-gwryd or by the railway from Llanberis.

Section 5.—The Western Rivers.

ROUTE 1 : WYE, SEVERN, AVON ; FROM AND TO BRISTOL, 230 MILES.—This route can obviously be begun and finished at Birmingham, Worcester, or Gloucester, as well as Bristol.

From Bristol take train through the Severn Tunnel to Portskewet or Severn Tunnel Junction, about 17 miles, and ride to Chepstow, 6 or 7 ; Tintern Abbey, Monmouth, 16 ; Whitchurch, 4 ; here turn R. for the ferry to Symond's Yat, 1 ; leave machines, cross ferry, climb to highest point (this is the climax of Wye scenery), return same way, reckon at least an hour from Whitchurch.

1½ miles farther, at Goodrich, turn R. to see Castle ; Ross, 4½ ; Harewood End, Hereford, 14½, Dinmore Hill (no need to avoid), Leominster, 13.

Ludlow, 11 ; visit Castle, leave machines, walk over Dinmore Bridge and round by the Whitcliff and Ludford Bridge back to the town ; Wooferton, Tenbury, 9 ; Witley, Ombersley, Droitwich, 22 ; Worcester, 6 ; Flyford, Alcester, Stratford-on-Avon, 25 ; Mickleton, Broadway (go to top of village), 15 ; Winchcomb, Cheltenham, 15 ; Painswick, Stroud, 13 ; Nailsworth, Dunkirk, Bath, 30 ; Bristol, 12.

ROUTE 2 : WYE AND USK ; 276 MILES FROM AND TO SHREWSBURY.—This round might also be entered at Worcester or Gloucester.

Shrewsbury to Cressage, 8½ ; Much Wenlock (do not be sent round by Ironbridge), 4 ; Bridgnorth, 8½ ; Birdsgreen, Kidderminster, 14 ; Ombersley, Worcester, 14 ; Malvern, 8 ; Wyche Cut, Camp Hotel, enquire way through Eastnor Park to Eastnor, 7½ ; Tewkesbury, 11½ ; Gloucester, 10 ; Dursley Cross, Lea, Ross, 25 ; Goodrich Castle, 4½ ; Whitchurch, 1½.

Turn L. to ferry for Symond's Yat, see previous route, back to Whitchurch, 2 ; Monmouth, 4 ; Tintern Abbey, Chepstow, 16 ; Llangwm, Usk, 14 (Usk need not be entered) ; Raglan Castle, 5 ; Abergavenny, 9 ; Crickhowell, 6 ; Bwlch, Brecon, 14 ; Bronllys, Hay, 15 ; Willersley, Hereford, 21 ; Dinmore Hill (no need to avoid), Leominster, 13 ; Ludlow, 11 (see previous route) ;

Stokesley Castle (on L. just before reaching Craven Arms, and should not be missed), Craven Arms, 8; Church Stretton, 8; Shrewsbury, 13.

Pronunciations on these routes: Simmons Yat, Lemster, Allster, Witch Cut.

MAPS.—These routes fall awkwardly on all maps. For Route 1, Sheets 23, called " Hereford," and 17, called " Shropshire," of Bartholomew's two miles to the inch map of England, will suffice, though a few odd corners are outside them. For Route 2, the same two are necessary, with Sheet 24, " Oxford," to cover the Alcester-Stratford-Broadway-Cheltenham portion.

Section 6.—South Wales.

Although well enough known to the roadfarers of Cardiff, Swansea, and the miners of Monmouth and Glamorgan, there is a corner of South Wales quite neglected by the usual tourist, though of quite uncommon beauty and interest. It may naturally and usefully come in to round off the orthodox tour down the Wye Valley, starting, say, at Hereford, and obviously it can be treated as an additional loop to the preceding tour (Section 5) by those who want additional mileage. After (or before) a tour in South-West England, also, the steamer service between Cardiff and Weston-super-Mare suggests another line of attack on the routes which follow. However you decide to approach them, be assured that they lie in richly beautiful country, almost innocent of disfiguring industrialism.

Caerphilly may be decided upon as the first objective. If you seek it from the lower end of the Wye Valley, the distance from Chepstow, *via* Caerwent, Newport, and Upper Machen, is 27 miles. From Usk to Caerphilly, *via* Caerleon, Newport, and Upper Machen, 22.

Caerphilly (see Castle ruins) to Nantgarw, Taff's Well, see Castell Coch, 5; cross river by road opposite; Pentyrch, 2½; Llandaff, 4.

Ely Station, 1; at two miles farther along Cowbridge road, turn left to St. Lythans and then round to St. Nicholas, 6; between the last two villages are two good dolmens.

Bonvilston, 2; turn left to Llancarfan, see Penmark and Fonmon Castles, then cross railway and River Daw (or Thaw) to St. Athan, 8.

Then northwards to St. Mary Church, see Beaupre (" Boper ") Castle ruins and St. Hilary Village, Cowbridge, 7; Llysworney, 2; Llantwit Major (full of interest), 3½; St. Donats (castle and churchyard cross), 2; Montnash, St. Brides Major, 5½; turn left to Southerndown, 1; and follow coast-road round to Ogmore Castle, Ewenny Priory, and Bridgend, 6½.

Coity (castle and church) and back to Bridgend, 4; Porthcawl, 6½; Pyle, 4; Margam Abbey, 3½; Aberavon, 3½; Neath, 5½; Glyn Neath, 11; Hirwain, 5; and over the moorland mountain (1,400 ft.) to Storey Arms, 15; Brecon, 8½; whence Hereford is 36.

Sheet 27, called "Swansea," of Bartholomew's half-inch map of England, includes all the above roads from Caerphilly and Cardiff to Storey Arms.

If landing at Cardiff from the Weston boat, I should go direct to Caerphilly, 7, in spite of the bad hill at the end, and then begin the route as above.

Section 7.—Cotswold Byways.

At the small cost of making your bicycle into a "push-cycle" now and again, you can see the best of the Cotswold scenery and villages (barring the Stroud end of the range) and have almost motorless trips by adopting the route suggestions which follow. They are quite practicable, also, for good cars with good and careful drivers; they are no use whatever to the motorist in a hurry. The plan is to make Stow-on-the-Wold a centre for, say, three trips of a day each, the mileage being kept purposely low on account of both difficulty and beauty.

Stow to Lower Swell, 1; Upper Slaughter, Lower Slaughter, 3; Bourton-on-the-Water, 2; Clapton, 3; Sherborne, 2½; Little Barrington, 2; Burford, 3; Taynton, 1½; Great Barrington, 1½; Great Rissington, 3; Little Rissington, 3; Church Iccomb, 3; Stow, 3; total, 31½.

Stow to Naunton, 5½; Guiting Power, 2; Barton, 1; Temple Guiting, 2; Ford, 1; down Stanway Hill to Stanway, 2½; Stanton, 1½; Broadway, 3; up Fish Hill and direct to Stow, 10½; total 29.

From Stow five miles back along road towards Broadway and turn left to Snowshill, 9; then cautiously down to Broadway, 2½; Willersey, Saintbury, Weston, Aston, 4; Chipping Campden, 2; Broad Campden, Blockley, 4; Bourton-on-the-Hill, 1½; Moreton-in-the-Marsh, 2; Evenlode, 3; Broadwell, Stow, 3; total 31.

Stow is 22 miles S. from Stratford-on-Avon; 30 W.N.W. from Oxford; 11 N. from Burford; 21 N.E. from Cirencester; 19 E. from Cheltenham; 17 S.E. from Evesham.

Sheet 24, "Oxfordshire," of Bartholomew's half-inch map, clearly indicates all these by-ways.

Section 8.—Devon and Somerset.

ROUTE 1: NORTH DEVON AND EXMOOR; 155 MILES, FROM AND TO TAUNTON.—Crowcombe, Williton, Washford (beautiful ruin of Cleeve Abbey here), Dunster (half-mile from road on left, but must not be missed), Minehead, 25; Porlock, 6. Push up old road. The new road (toll) misses best views. Just short of County Gate, six miles from Porlock, turn left to Oare, Brendon, Watersmeet (which visit on right), Lynmouth 12 from Porlock. By this route the precipitous descent of Countisbury into Lynmouth is missed.

Push up to Lynton or take the cliff railway. Through the Valley of Rocks to Lee Abbey (gates to open), Woods Bay, Hunter's Inn, Trentishoe, rough going for a few miles to Combemartin 12 from Lynmouth. This is much better than the inland or main road route, and not only because it dodges the wicked descent into Parracombe.

Ilfracombe, 5½; Morthoe Station, Morte Point, 7; Morthoe Station, Braunton, Barnstaple, 14.

Loxhore, Blackmoorgate, Challacombe, Simonsbath (this road is through the heart of Exmoor), 20; Exford, 5½; Wheddon Cross, 4½; Hole Bridge, Dulverton, 9; Exe Bridge, Tiverton, 13; Waterloo Cross, Wellington, Taunton, 21. This route is a stiff one, but includes some of the finest scenery in Britain. If time to spend at Dulverton, walk to Tarr Steps, nine miles return, and worth it.

All this route, except ten miles from and to Taunton, are on Sheet 35, called " North Devon," of Bartholomew's half-inch map.

ROUTE 2: DARTMOOR AND EXMOOR; FROM AND TO EXETER, 225 MILES; DIFFICULT.—Chudleigh, 10; Ashburton, 9; Dartmeet Bridge, Two Bridges, 11; Moreton Hampstead, 12; Whiddon Down, Sticklepath, 9½; Oke-hampton, 3½; Crediton, 17; Stockleigh Pomeroy, Cadeleigh Station, 8; Tiverton, 4; Bampton Road End in Exe Valley, 8; Dulverton, 5; Hole Bridge, Wheddon Cross, 10; Exford, 4½; Simonsbath, 5½; Challacombe, Blackmoorgate, 9; Loxhore, Barnstaple, 11; Instow, Bideford, 9; Appledore and back, 6; Clovelly via Hobby Drive and back, 22; Torrington, 7; Merton, Hatherleigh, 13; Okehampton, 8½; Sticklepath, 3½; Exeter, 19½.

ROUTE 3: " THE COMPLETE DEVONIAN "; FROM AND TO EXETER, 400 MILES.—Exminster, Dawlish,13; Teignmouth, 3; Newton Abbot, 6; Kingskerswell, Torquay, 7; Paignton, 3; Brixham, 5; Kingswear (at rival ferry notices at top of hill keep left), 4, ferry to Dartmouth; Stoke Fleming, Slapton Sands, Torcross, 8; Kingsbridge, 6½; Modbury, 8; Ermington, Ivybridge, 5; Ridgeway, 6; Plym Bridge, 2; George Hotel, 2; Horrabridge, 6; Tavistock, 4½.

North Brentor, Lydford, 9; Coryton, Lifton, Launceston, 12; Red Post, Stratton, Bude, 19; Kilkhampton, West Country Inn, Hartland, Hartland Point, 18; Clovelly, 7; through Hobby Drive (toll), Bideford, 11; Appledore and back, 6; Instow, Barnstaple, 9; Braunton, Ilfracombe, 13.

Combemartin, 5½; then rough going (see Route 1 reversed)

to Trentishoe and Hunter's Inn; Wooda Bay, Lee Abbey, Valley of Rocks, Lynton 12 from Combemartin. *Walk* down to Lynmouth or take cliff railway; Watersmeet, Brendon (very steep and long descent past Brendon Church), Oare; opposite Oare Church cross river, up to main road and turn right; at top of Porlock Hill *dismount and walk down to* Porlock 12 from Lynmouth.

Minehead, 6; Dunster, Wheddon Cross, 9; Dulverton, 9; Winsford Hill, Exford, 9 (see Route 1); Simonsbath, Challacombe, 11; Bratton Down, Brayford, South Molton, 12; Bampton Road End in Exe Valley, 15; Tiverton, 8; Cadeleigh Station, 4; Stockleigh Pomeroy, Crediton, 8; Okehampton, 17; Whiddon Down, Moreton Hampstead, 13; Two Bridges, 12; Dartmeet Bridge, Ashburton, 11; Chudleigh, 9; Exeter, 10.

He (or she) who would do this in ten days must be a tough rider.

MAPS.—Sheet 35, "North Devon," and Sheet 36, "South Devon," of Bartholomew's half-inch map of England.

Section 9.—Cornwall.

The scenic interest of Cornwall is almost exclusively confined to its coast-line. The roads, therefore, are not very easy, for if the hills are short—and there are none in any way resembling the freak-hills of North Devon—some of them are very steep. Most of the little fishing villages, the gems of Cornwall, have precipitous approaches on both sides, and these are usually a mass of loose stones.

There are two excellent main roads, both starting from Launceston, one going by Camelford and Wadebridge, the other going direct over Bodmin Moor. The tourist is usually told to avoid the latter, which touches nearly a thousand feet. I much prefer it, however, for its greater interest, while the gradients are not too steep and the surface is good.

These two roads come together at Blue Anchor and branch again at once, an excellent road going left to Truro and Falmouth, and a less good one going straight forward to the end of the county, being tram-lined and bad through Redruth and Camborne, and indifferent from Penzance to Land's End.

But these main roads are only for those going to some particular spot or taking some farther section of my "Complete Cornishman" routes. He who follows the latter right through will hardly touch the main roads.

The following routes total 230 miles, from and to Launceston, which is well served by both the Great Western and the South-Western railways. You start and finish in Cornwall and never leave it *en route*. The elderly or weak may take ten days over the round; I do not think it should be done in less than seven.

The most difficult part, which lies between St. Austell and Looe, is taken at the end of the tour, when you will be strong with clotted cream and sea air, and when the prevailing winds of the west are most likely to be in assistance.

MAP.—Sheet 37, "Cornwall," of Bartholomew's half-inch map of England. It includes the whole county, only excluding Launceston by four miles.

Launceston to Dolsdon Inn, Red Post, Stratton, 16; Bude, 1½.

North of this point, and not included in the mileage of these routes, is a little corner of the county containing Kilkhampton, with memorials of the Grenvilles, and Morwenstow, famous for the Rev. Stephen Hawker. Kilkhampton is on the road from Clovelly to Bude. Morwenstow is seven miles from Bude, *via* Stowe Barton, where is a dangerous descent. At the top of it are traces of the castle of Sir Richard Grenville, and at the bottom is Coombe Mill, nearly five from Bude, and a wonderfully pretty spot.

Bude to Wainhouse Corner, 8; Boscastle, 6½ (see harbour); Tintagel, 3. Bicycles should be left in the village while walking to King Arthur's Castle, reckoning an hour's absence. Three-and-a-half miles of very steep and baffling roads lead hence southward to the main road near Delabole Station.

Port Isaac, 8½; Endellion, St. Minver, Rock, 6; half-mile ferry to Padstow. If the ferryman is the other side, yell for him.

St. Columb Major, 8½; Mawgan, 12. (But the adventurous rough-rider, on leaving Padstow, may go to Trevose Head, five to the west, and then, with the help of the map, find his way by Penrose and St. Eval to Mawgan, making the distance from Padstow to Mawgan fourteen, and leaving out St. Columb, which is only included for better roads.)

Those who have come from St. Columb should not go round by Mawgan Porth. Return up the hill and turn right and then left for Tregurrian, St. Columb Porth, and Newquay, 6 from Mawgan. Then, Rejerrah, Goonhavern, Perranporth, 8; St. Agnes, 4; round Beacon Hill, Portreath, 7; Gwithian, Hayle, 8. Lelant, St. Ives, 5. Up past the "radium mine" to Zennor, Trereen, 6. See Gurnard's Head, leaving machines at hotel of the same name. (A short mile farther west, at the farmhouse labelled "Bosigran Castle," the cliffs again demand a walk across the obvious footpaths.)

Morvah, 3; Trewellard, 2. (A road on right leads in three-quarters of a mile to the Levant submarine mine. The northern end of the works, on the edge of the cliffs, make a remarkable picture.)

St. Just, 1½; Cape Cornwall and back, 2½; Sennen, Land's End, 6. The cliff walks best worth making are to Sennen Cove and the Logan Rock.

Land's End direct to Penzance, 10, keeping a sharp look-out for the motor-bus. (The strong rider may take the vastly more

picturesque and sportive lanes by the Vineries, the Merry
Maidens, Lamorna Cove, Paul, Mousehole, and Newlyn,
13 or 14 to Penzance. If you have ridden direct to Penzance,
you should ride and walk, before leaving, through Newlyn and
along the shore road to Mousehole and back.)

Marazion, 3. Follow Helston road to Breage, and one mile
farther turn right to Porthleven, 8; Helston, 2½. Follow
Lizard road two miles and turn right to Gunwalloe, Poldhu
(Atlantic wireless station), Mullion, 7; ride or walk down to
Mullion Cove and back.

Lizard Town, 5. Walk to Kynance Cove, 1½, if low water.
If the tide is up it is not worth while. Excellent walk by coast-
guard paths to Devil's Frying-pan and Cadgwith, about two
hours return.

Leaving Lizard, at two miles north on Helston road turn
right, over Goonhilly Down, to cross-roads at six from Lizard;
turn right, and right again at two miles farther, with a dangerous descent to Coverack 10½ from Lizard.

St. Keverne, 2. (An hour's walk gives a sight of Porthou-
stock Village and of the infamous Manacle Rocks, except at
high water.) Manaccan, Helford, 4 very hard miles. Ferry
over Helford River. Mawnan Smith, Swan Pool, Falmouth,
5¾. (If time to spare at Falmouth, take ferry to St. Mawes and
walk to Porthcuel, Porthscatho, and back, six miles return.)

Penryn, Truro, 10½; Probus, St. Austell, 14; St. Blazey, 4;
Lostwithiel (steep descent), 4; Restormel Castle, 1. Leave
machines at gates of farm on right and walk up opposite lane
on left to gate on right. Back through Lostwithiel to Fowey,
8; precipitous approach. The best view of Fowey is got by
taking the ferry to Bodinnick and walking to the top of the
street, half-an-hour's job. At the other end of Fowey, walk
to the mausoleum and back, one hour.

Leaving, ferry to Polruan, push up the "hill," and make
the best of your baffling way to Polperro, about 6. This, in my
opinion, is the most picturesque and interesting of Cornwall's
coast-line hamlets.

Barcelona, Wayland Cross, Looe, 4½; Sandplace, Liskeard, 9. (It is almost worth while to go to Liskeard on the
oddest of railways from Looe.) Callington, 9; Launceston, 11.
(The direct road, Liskeard-Launceston, saves four or five miles,
but is still hillier.)

The distances printed in *figures* are the only ones that count
in the total. Those given in *words* are for guidance only.

BRISTOL CHANNEL STEAMERS.—The Bristol Channel
lies awkwardly for cyclists, who often want to pass from South
Wales to the Somerset-Devon coast and *vice versâ*. By road, a
very long detour by Gloucester and Bristol is involved, the
34 miles between them being rather tedious also.

Two lines of steamers ply regularly between Cardiff and

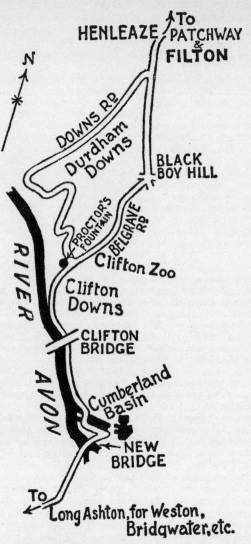

Avoiding Bristol; see next page.

Weston-super-Mare, and to a less extent between Cardiff and Minehead and Ilfracombe. Between Cardiff and Weston you get across for 2s. or 3s., *plus* 1s. 6d. for a bicycle. In the summer months there are as many as a dozen sailings each way daily. For monthly time-tables send stamp to Thos. Cook and Son, 2, Duke Street, Cardiff. Motor cycles are not conveyed on these boats.

AVOIDING BRISTOL BY ROAD.—The great, busy, and rather baffling town of Bristol stands across the path of the countless tourists making their way through Gloucester south-westwards towards Cheddar and Weston, for Somerset, Devon, and Cornwall generally. So it does for South Wales cyclists who are using the Severn Tunnel in preference to the steamers from Cardiff, alluded to in previous section.

Many of those westward-bound tourists, while not anxious to go through the middle of Bristol, would like to see the famous Suspension Bridge, the Downs, and the Zoological Gardens of the most beautiful suburb in Britain—Clifton. This may be easily done.

Dealing first with those cyclists who have come down through Gloucester and want the main road from Bristol towards Weston-super-Mare and the South-West, they should leave the main road to Bristol at Filton, four miles north of the city, and turn R. to Southmead (leaving Westbury on R.) and Henleaze, shown at top of map.

Here you have the choice of two ways. The most obvious is to follow the tram-lines forward to Black Boy Hill, where turn sharp R. along Upper Belgrave Road, past the Zoo to Proctor's Fountain. The other way leaves the first at the end of Henleaze Lane, and follows the other side of the Durdham Downs right round, descending steeply to Proctor's Fountain. This road, 40 ft. wide, gives a fine view of the river. The route then descends Bridge Valley Road to the bank of the Avon, passes *under* the Suspension Bridge, crosses the river by a new bridge at the Cumberland Basin, and then—well clear of the city—joins the main road to the south-west.

To cross Clifton Bridge itself means more traffic and trams, a severe climb, toll to pay, and a dangerous descent.

Cyclists who have toured down the Wye Valley to Chepstow, and South Wales cyclists generally, may take train from Severn Tunnel Junction to Patchway or Filton Junction, 11 or 12 miles, and make for the Southmead road from Filton Village, then as above.

Cyclists bound for Clevedon from the north side of the Severn take train to Pilning, 7 miles, and then ride by Compton Greenfield, Henbury, Shirehampton Park gates, and Shirehampton Village to Pill Ferry, 6½ from Pilning, ferry available at all states of the tide. The route is then Easton, Portbury, Clapton, Clevedon, 8. Do not go round by Portishead.

Section 10.—From London.

ROUTE 1 : KENT; FROM GRAVESEND TO MAID-
STONE, 178 MILES.—Gravesend to Cobham, 4, to see the
Leather Bottle, the Dickens inn to which the melancholy Mr.
Tupman fled from unrequited affection to seek gastronomic
solace. Through Cobham Park to Gadshill, 3, on main Dover
road to see the home of Charles Dickens.

Follow Dover road into Rochester, 2½, and visit cathedral
and castle. Follow Maidstone road southwards to Lower Bell
Inn, 5, near which will be found Kit's Coity House, a fine pre-
historic dolmen; Aylesford, 1½, see bridge; then, passing
Allington Castle (on right) into Maidstone, 3; Leeds Castle, 5;
Lenham, 3½; Charing, 4, where are ruins of an archiepiscopal
palace; Canterbury, 14.

Eastwards through Sturry and Sarre .to Minster, 11, you
are all the time in the country through which Smuggler Bill
was chased by an Exciseman on an infernal horse (see the
Ingoldsby Legends). Ebbsfleet, Sandwich, 3.

Richborough Castle (remains of Roman fortress) and back, 3.
Through Eastry to Tilmanstone, 5, where is the largest of the
Kent collieries. Through the lanes by Eythorne to Barfres-
ton, 3, which has a small but excellent Norman church. To
the Eagle Gate of Broome Park (Lord Kitchener's place), 3,
and along the main Dover road to Kearsney, 5¼. Turn aside
(right) to see the ruins of St. Radigund's Abbey, and ride into
Dover, 4.

Main road south-west, and beware the descent into Folkestone, 7; along the Leas, descend to Sandgate and see castle;
but on outskirts of Hythe turn right for Saltwood Castle, 5.

Round by Sandling Junction and the Royal Oak to Lympne,
3½, see castle and church. By West Hythe and Dymchurch to
New Romney, 8; and by Brenzett and Appledore to
Tenterden, 14.

Sissinghurst, Goudhurst, 11; Lamberhurst, 3; pretty ruin of
Bayham Abbey, 2; Tunbridge Wells, 6; Eridge Station, 4,
turn right; Groombridge, 2; Speldhurst, 3; Penshurst, 1½, to
see the lych-gate and Penshurst Place, the home of the Sidneys.
(Useless to go to Hever, as the castle is invisible.) Chiddingstone, 2½, which also should not be missed. Through Leigh
to Tonbridge, 8½.

Shipborne, 3¼; Budds Green, Ightham Mote House, 2 (the
best thing in Kent); Ightham, 2; Addington (just off main road
on left), 4½; cross high road again, and visit Offham and West
Malling (abbey ruins), 2½; Maidstone, 5¼.

MAPS.—Sheet 31, " Kent," of Bartholomew's half-inch map
of England, includes all the above routes except the Penshurst
country to the west of Tunbridge Wells, which is found on
Sheet 32, " Sussex," of the same series.

ROUTE 2 : CHILTERN HILLS; FROM WATFORD TO PINNER, 131 MILES.—Watford to Leavesden Green, Abbot's Langley, 4; Chambersbury, High Street Green, Redbourn, 8; Markyate, 4; Dunstable, 4.

Back to Kensworth, Whipsnade, Studham, Dagnall, Ringshall, Little Gaddesden, about 11. Some of these villages may take a lot of finding, but they are worth it. At Gaddesden you will want to explore Ashridge Park.

Great Gaddesden, Berkhamsted, 5; Tring, 5; approaching canal bridge near Aston Clinton turn left up to Cholesbury, Hawridge, Chesham, 10; Amersham, Great Missenden, 8; Wendover, Prince's Risborough, 9; Bradenham, West Wycombe, 6; the freak church and mausoleum on the hill should be visited.

Stokenchurch, Aston Rowan Station, Lewknor, Watlington, 11; Britwell Salome, Howe Hill, Assendon Stonor, Henley-on-Thames, 10. Medmenham, Marlow, 7; Bourne End, Wooburn Green, 4½; Littleworth Common, and round Burnham Beeches to Beaconsfield, 8.

Follow London road a mile, then turn L. to Jordans, 2, a Quaker shrine; the old meeting-house and the old barn believed to have been built from the " Mayflower's " timbers are at top of hill on R. going to Chalfont St. Giles, 2, where is Milton's cottage.

Chenies, 4; Chorleywood, Rickmansworth, 4; Northwood, Pinner, 5.

The beeches make this route especially attractive in late spring and late autumn.

MAPS.—Most of the above route lies on Sheet 25, " Bedford, Hertford, etc.," of Bartholomew's half-inch map. But after West Wycombe it runs on to Sheet 29, " Berks. and Wilts.," returning to Sheet 25 at Marlow. So much of this route being on by-roads, no map of more than 2 miles to the inch is advisable.

ROUTE 3 : THE RIVER THAMES, 213 MILES.— Kingston to Hampton Court, West Molesey, Walton, Shepperton, 8; Chertsey Bridge and along towpath to Laleham, Penton Hook, Staines, 5; Egham, Magna Charta Island, Bells of Ouseley, Windsor-Eton, 6-7; Clewer, Bray, Maidenhead, 6½; Boulter's Lock, Cookham Bridge, Cookham Dean, Marlow, 6½; Medmenham, Henley, 8.

Wargrave, Twyford, Sonning, Caversham, Reading, 11; Pangbourne, 5½ (turn aside to river); Streatley-Goring, 4; Wallingford, 6; Shillingford, Dorchester, 3½; Burcot, Clifton Hampden, Abingdon, 7; Fyfield, 5; Newbridge, Standlake, Cote, Aston, Bampton, 9; Clanfield, Radcot Bridge, Faringdon, 6½; Lechlade, 6. (William Morris pilgrims will want to ride to Kelmscot, six return.)

Fairford, 4; Marston Meysey, Castle Eaton, Seven Bridges,

Cricklade, 9; Ashton Keynes, Somerford Keynes, Ewen, Thames Head Bridge, Cirencester, 13.

Barnsley, Bibury, Burford (go down to bridge), 17; Witney, 7½; Eynsham, Swinford Bridge, 6½; Oxford, 5.

Wheatley, 6; Stokenchurch, 12; High Wycombe, 7; Beaconsfield, 5½; Uxbridge, 8; Ealing, 8½.

MAP.—Bartholomew's, "The River Thames," half-inch to mile, 2s. on paper.

ROUTE 4: THROUGH FENLAND TO THE SEA; FROM AND TO WOODFORD, 260 MILES.—Epping, 8; Bishop's Stortford, 13; Newport, 9; Chesterfield, 6; Cambridge, 11; Fenstanton, 10½; St. Ives, 2; Chatteris, 12½; March, 8; Guyhirne Station, 4½; Wisbech, 6; King's Lynn, 13½; Castle Rising, 4½; Dersingham, Snettisham, Hunstanton, 11½.

Docking, Syderstone, Fakenham, 19; Swaffham, 15; Fincham, Downham Market, 14; Littleport, 12½; Ely, 5; Soham, Newmarket, 13; Six-Mile Bottom, 6; Abington, 7; Linton, 2½; Saffron Walden, 6; Thaxted, 7; Dunmow, 6; High Roding, Leaden Roding, Chipping Ongar, 14½; Abridge, Chigwell, 9½; Woodford, 4.

MAP.—Except for the few miles south of Epping and Ongar, all the above roads appear on Sheet 7 of the Ordnance Survey quarter-inch map of England, large sheet series, 2s. on paper.

ROUTE 5: EASTER IN THE ISLE OF WIGHT; 180 MILES, KINGSTON TO BRENTFORD.—This is intended primarily for those who can comfortably do London to Portsmouth or Southampton in a day. At Easter, it is a prudent plan to get as far south as possible in the time. This suggestion, therefore, is for a quick run down to the Isle of Wight, two lazy days in the island, and a quick run back.

Kingston to Ripley, 11½; Guildford, 6; Godalming, 4; Hindhead, 8; Liphook, Petersfield, 12; Waterloo, Portsmouth, 17; steamer to Ryde.

Brading, Sandown, Shanklin, Bonchurch (see old church), Ventnor, the Undercliff, St. Lawrence (see old church), Chalegreen, Shorwell, Mottistone, Freshwater Bay, Yarmouth, Shalfleet, Carisbrook Castle, Newport, Cowes—a 50 miles round. Steamer to Southampton.

Winchester, 12; Kingsworthy, Itchen Abbas, Itchen Stoke, New Alresford, 8½; Alton, 10; Farnham, 9; Aldershot, Bagshot, 12; Staines, 10; Brentford, 9½.

MAPS.—The out and home routes being two great highways (and the main roads, being tarred, will give the best going at a wet Easter) no map is necessary for them. For the island, order Ordnance Survey one-inch map, Sheet 145, large sheet series, called "Isle of Wight," 2s. on paper

ROUTE 6: 142 MILES, MOSTLY IN SURREY; FROM HAMPTON COURT TO HOUNSLOW.—This route was drawn up and recommended by a reader who lives at Guildford, and the following is a copy of his manuscript:

From Hampton Court through East Moseley, past Esher
Station to the main Portsmouth road; turn right to Street
Cobham, follow main road past Painshill Park to the Hut Hotel
opposite Boldermere; Ripley, $11\frac{1}{2}$; turn aside R. to see Newark
Abbey ruin and old mill on Wey; Guildford, 6, visit Hospital
of the Holy Trinity (1619), Town Hall (1683), Grammar School
(1557), panelled hall of Angel Hotel and clock dated 1658, and
ruins of St. Catherine's Chapel (1317), about a mile south of
the bridge over the Wey; along Hog's Back to Farnham, 10,
see almshouses (1619) and castle; Waverley Abbey, $2\frac{1}{2}$
(Cistercian, 1128); Tilford, $1\frac{1}{2}$; Frensham Bridge, 2, visit church
and see Mother Ludlam's cauldron in basement of tower, also
visit Frensham Ponds; follow Haslemere road to Churt, $2\frac{1}{2}$,
walk up one of the three hills called the Devil's Jumps;
Thursley, $3\frac{1}{2}$; see church and murdered sailor's tomb in north-
west of churchyard; on to Portsmouth road again, and turn
right to Hindhead, 3; ask for road by Weydown Common to
Haslemere, $2\frac{1}{2}$; visit museum of peasant art and the weaving
industry; Chiddingfold, 5; Aldfold, 7, on Sussex border, see
stocks, turn left for Cranleigh, $4\frac{1}{2}$; Ewhurst, $2\frac{1}{2}$; Ockley, 5.

Capel, Newdigate, $3\frac{1}{2}$; through Charlwood and Povey Cross
to Horlev, $6\frac{1}{2}$; then *via* Harrowsley, asking as often as possible,
to Lingfield, 10; Crowhurst, Oxted, 6; Limpsfield and back to
Oxted, 3; Godstone, 3, see White Hart and Gilbert Scott's
almshouses; Bletchingley, 2; Nutfield, 1, where are famous
beds of fuller's earth; Redhill, 2; Reigate, 2, see castle and
Priory Park, and the southward view from the top of Reigate
Hill is worth while; Buckland, Betchworth (Box Hill on right),
Dorking, $6\frac{1}{2}$, leave by West Street for another view of Box
Hill from Milton Heath; Westcott, $1\frac{1}{2}$; Wotton Hatch, 1, the
birth and burial place of John Evelyn, the seventeenth-century
diarist; Gomshall, $2\frac{1}{2}$; Shere, 1, a happy hunting-ground of
artists; Albury, Newlands Corner, Merrow, $3\frac{1}{2}$; turn right, then
left, past Clandon Park on left, to Ripley, 5; Pirford, Addlestone, 7; Chertsey, 2; over bridge, turn left, follow towpath by Laleham and Penton Hook to Staines, $4\frac{1}{2}$; Hounslow, 7.

MAP.—Sheet 30, called "Surrey," of Bartholomew's half-
inch map of England, covers all the above route except Waverley
Abbey, near Farnham.

ROUTE 7: BYWAYS TO THE COAST; 235 MILES
FROM AND TO STREATHAM.—Mitcham, Carshalton, 5;
Woodmansterne, Chipstead, 5; Reigate Hill, Reigate, $4\frac{1}{2}$;
Leigh, 3; Charlwood, 4; Ifield, Crawley, 4.

Pound Hill, 2; Cowdray Arms, Balcombe, 4; Ardingley,
Lindfield, $5\frac{1}{2}$; Newick, 6; Peltdown golf-course (turn R.), 2;
Isfield, $3\frac{1}{2}$; Ringmer, 4; Laughton (turn R.), $3\frac{1}{2}$; Ripe, Chal-
vington, Berwick Station, Alfriston, $7\frac{1}{2}$.

Back and over river to Litlington, Eastdean, Beachy Head,
Eastbourne, 12.

Pevensey, 4½; Wartling, 3; Windmill Hill, 2; Bodlestreet Green, 2; Dallington, 3½; Brightling Beacon, 1½; Burwash, 2½; Wadhurst, 6; Tunbridge Wells, 6.

Frant Station, Bayham Abbey, Lamberhurst, 7; Goudhurst, 3; Cranbrook, 4; Benenden, 3; Rolvenden, 2½; Wittersham, 4½; Peasmarsh, Rye, 6.

Camber-on-Sea, Lydd, 9; New Romney, Littlestone-on-Sea, 4½; New Romney, Ivychurch, Ham Street, 8; Tenterden, 7; Biddenden, 4; Sissinghurst, Staplehurst, 7; Marsden, 3; Yalding, 4½; Wateringbury, 2; Mereworth 2½; Hadlow, Plaxtol, 6; Ivyhatch, 1; Ightham Mote House, ½; Budds Green, Tumbling Bay, Hildenborough Station, Leigh, 5; Penshurst, 2½.

Chiddingstone, Hever, Edenbridge, 7; Limpsfield, 5; Titsey Hill, Warlingham, 5; Sanderstead, Croydon, 5; Streatham, 9.

MAP.—Ordnance Survey, four miles to the inch, large sheet series, Sheet 10.

ROUTE 8: MOSTLY IN SURREY AND SUSSEX; 400 MILES FROM AND TO RICHMOND.

—Cross Richmond Bridge; Eelpie Island, Teddington Station, through Bushey Park to Hampton Court, 5; Garrick's Temple, Sunbury, Shepperton, 6; Chertsey Bridge and along towpath to Laleham, 3; towpath to Staines, 2; Egham, 1; Runnymede, Windsor-Eton, 5-6; through Windsor Park to Ascot, 6.

Virginia Water, 4, leave machines and visit; Bagshot, 6; Knaphill, Old Woking, 8; Newark Abbey and old mill, Ripley, 2½; Guildford, 6.

Godalming, 4; Milford, Hindhead, 8; Liphook, Petersfield, 12; South Harting, Marden, Lavant, Chichester, 15; Selsey, 8; Mundham, Bognor, 13; Arundel, 10.

Whiteways Lodge, 2½, take right-hand road through Houghton to see Amberley Castle, then round to Bury, 4½; Bignor, Duncton, Selham, Midhurst, 12; Fernhurst, Haslemere, 8.

Chiddingfold, 4½; Petworth, 9; Pulborough, 5; Billingshurst, Five Oaks, 7; Radgwick, Ewhurst, 8; Pitch Hill, Shere, 5; Newlands Corner, Merrow, 3½; Leatherhead, 10; Dorking, 5; ascend Box Hill.

By Chart Park to Blackbrook, Newdigate, Rusper, Horsham, 14; Nuthurst, Partridge Green Station, Ashurst, Steyning, 13; Upper Beeding, Henfield, 6; Hurstpierpoint, 5; Cuckfield, 6.

Balcombe, Worth, Horley, 12; Lingfield, 7; East Grinstead, 4; Wych Cross, 6; Sheffield Park, Chailey, Lewes, 15; Newhaven, 7; Seaford, 3½; Alfriston, 3½; cross river to Litlington, Eastdean, Beachy Head, Eastbourne, 12.

Pevensey Castle, 5; Hailsham, 6; Horsebridge, Mayfield, 14; Tunbridge Wells, 9; Southborough, Speldhurst, Penshurst, 5; Chiddingstone, Edenbridge, 7½; Oxted, 6; Godstone, 2½; Redhill, 5; Dorking (nearly), Leatherhead, 10; Surbiton, Kingston, 9; Richmond, 3½.

Same MAP as previous route.

Section 11.—The Norfolk Broads.

This tour, 224 miles from Grantham to Peterborough, is a compromise and almost a make-believe. The boat, rather than the bicycle, is the way to see the broads. But the bicyclist who does not like boating will find the route given a pretty tour, including many of the most famous resorts and many " water landscapes."

Grantham to Donington, Gosberton, Spalding 30; Holbeach, Long Sutton, King's Lynn, 27; Gayton, Litcham, 17; North Elmham, Bawdeswell, Reepham, Cawston, Aylsham, 22.

Felmingham, North Walsham, 6; Dilham, Stalham, 8; Hickling, Hickling Broad, 3; Catfield, 2; Rollesby, 5½; Ormesby St. Margaret, 3; Filby, Burgh St. Margaret, Acle, 7½; South Walsham, Ranworth, Horning Ferry, 6.

Horning, Hoveton St. John, Wroxham (see broad), 4; Norwich, 7; East Dereham, 16; Swaffham, 12; Downham Market, 14; Nordelph, Outwell, Wisbech, 13; Guyhirne, Peterborough, 21.

MAP.—Sheet 15, called " Norfolk," of Bartholomew's half-inch map of England, shows all the Norfolk Broads, and includes the above routes between King's Lynn and Downham Market, the rest being main roads.

Section 12.—The Scottish Border.

The Roman Wall, the River Tweed from sea to source, and the Scottish Border generally are the objectives of the following suggested tour of 314 or 337 miles. Good riders may do it in a week, but the majority should reckon on ten days, as some of the country is difficult. The longest climbs, however, are on well-engineered roads of good surface. For both natural beauty and for the interest of castles and abbeys more or less ruined, this tour is hardly inferior to any in the land. It is planned to start and finish at Carlisle on account of that town's great railway facilities, but obviously the route can be joined at any more convenient point in the circle.

Carlisle to Brampton, 10; Greenhead, 8; the Roman camp, wall, and castle of Housesteads, between Crag Lough and Broomlee Lough, 8 or 9. These are the most interesting parts of the Roman Wall between sea and sea.

Grindon, Haydon Bridge, 5; Hexham (see abbey), 6; cross River Tyne and turn left; Wall, Chollerford, 4; keep same side of river to Wark and Bellingham (see Hareshaw Linn), 12; Otterburn, 8½; Elsdon, Rothbury, 15; Long Framlington, Newton, Alnwick, 15½; Little Mill Station, Craster, 6½; Dunstanburgh Castle, Embleton, 5. Between Craster and Embleton the shore-road is hardly a road, and may have to be walked in wet weather.

Swinhoe, Beadnell, Seahouses, Bamburgh (castle), 10½; Belford, 5; at 6¾ on the road to Berwick a road on right leads to Beal and the shore opposite Holy Island, which can be reached on foot at low water, and contains the ruins of Lindisfarne Abbey, castle, etc.; back to the high road and Berwick, 10; Velvethall, Norham Castle, ¡7; Twizel Castle, 3½; Cornhill, 3. Then, either

(a) Coldstream and by the north side of the river to Kelso, 9½; or

(b) Mindrum, The Yetholms, 8; Morebattle, 4; inquire road to Cessford Castle, Crailinghall, and Jedburgh (abbey), 9; Kelso, 11.

St. Boswell's, 10; Dryburgh Abbey and back, 2; Me'rose, 2½; Abbotsford, 2½; ferry, 1 (after crossing river, Galashiels, 2 on right, is useful for hotels). Fairnilee, Innerleithen, Peebles, 19.

Neidpath Castle, 1; Stobo, Drummelzier, 8; Crook Inn, 6½; Devil's Beef-Tub, 11; Moffat, 4½.

St. Mary's Loch, 15; Yarrow Church, 9; Selkirk, 8; Hawick, 12; Mosspaul Inn, 13; Langholm, 10; Longtown, 12, Carlisle, 9.

MAP.—The whole of the above routes appear on Sheet 7, called "Border Country," of Bartholomew's quarter-inch map of Scotland, except the road from Morebattle by Cessford and Crailinghall to Jedburgh. The scale of such a map is rather small for the cyclist, but insistence on the usual half-inch map happens to mean several sheets for this tour.

Section 13.—Scotland.

ROUTE 1: GALLOWAY; 264 MILES FROM AND TO DUMFRIES.—This south-west corner of Scotland has been curiously neglected by the tourist. The only apparent explanation is that he " passes by on the other side "—hurrying to the Highlands. Yet Galloway has better roads and more reasonable hotels than the Highlands; it is rich in sea-edge roads, in lochs and rivers; while Merrick is nearly 3,000 ft. and Glen Trool is a rare jewel. The following tour is very easy compared with one of the same length in the Highlands. If Carlisle is used as start and finish, the total is increased by 68 miles, and, except for the interest of the new Gretna, it is hardly worth while. Several main lines of railway serve Carlisle.

(Carlisle to Gretna, Annan, and Dumfries, 34.)

Dumfries to New Abbey, Kirkbean, Lochend, Barnbarroch, Dalbeattie, 22; Palnackie, Auchencairn, 8; along Balcary Shore and back, 4.

Dundrennan Abbey, Kirkcudbright, 11; Drummore, Gatehouse, 8; coast road to Creetown, passing Dirk Hatteraick's Cave and Carlough Castle, 11; Newton Stewart, 6.

Wigtown, 7; Whithorn, 11; Port William, 8; Glenluce, 13½; Stranraer, 9½.

Cairnryan, Ballantrae, 17½; Lendalfoot, 6; Girvan, 6½; Pinwherry Station, 8; Barrhill, 4½; Bargrennan, 9.

On reaching Bargrennan Church, turn sharp left; a mile and a half farther, turn right and cross Water of Minnoch Bridge; keep straight on up Glen Trool, leaving the gates to Eschoncan Lodge on your right, as far as Buchan Farm, where see Falls of Buchan, and return same way to Bargrennan Church, nearly 12 total.

Newton Stewart, 8½; New Galloway, 17; New Galloway Station, Woodhall Loch (also called Loch Grenoch), Laurieston, 9; Ringford, 5; Castle Douglas, 6; Parton, Spalding Arms, 13; Corsock, Crocketford, Dumfries, 23.

MAP.—All this route (from and to Dumfries) is clearly shown on Sheet 6, called "Galloway and Lower Clyde," of Bartholomew's quarter-inch map of Scotland.

ROUTE 2 : HIGHLANDS, 200 OR 208 MILES, GLASGOW TO EDINBURGH OR *VICE VERSA*.—By rail from Glasgow (Queen Street) to Craigendoran; or, if coming up the Ayr Coast, take steamer from Greenock to Helensburgh, which is close to Craigendoran.

Craigendoran to Helensburgh, Luss, Tarbet, Arrochar, 19; Glencroe, Inveraray, 22; Cladich, Dalmally, 16; Tyndrum, Crianlarich, 16; Luib, Killin, 13; Lawers, Fearnan (turn left), 13; Fortingal, Coshieville, 5; Tummel Bridge (cross and turn right), 8; Queen's View, Fincastle Post Office, Garry Bridge, 11½, but just before reaching the bridge a footpath on right (leave machines behind) leads in a short mile to the Falls of Tummel, which must not be missed.

Pitlochry, 2½; Ballinluig, Dunkeld, 12; Blairgowrie, 12; Meikleour, Perth, 15; Bridge of Earn, 4; Glenfarg, Kinross, 13½.

Cowdenbeath, 8; Burntisland, 6½, for Granton Ferry, Edinburgh, 3; or, if the cyclist wishes to see the Forth Bridge, from Cowdenbeath to Inverkeithing and North Queensferry, 8; South Queensferry to Edinburgh, 9.

MAPS.—As this tour falls awkwardly on the half-inch sheets, it will be easier to use Sheet 4, called "Glasgow and Oban," and Sheet 5, called "Forth and Tay," of Bartholomew's quarter-inch map of Scotland.

CLYDE STEAMERS.—For time-tables of steamers from Glasgow, Greenock, Gourock, etc., to Helensburgh and many other places on the Clyde coast and the western lochs, write the Marine Superintendent, North British Railway Company, 48, Dundas Street, Glasgow; and to David MacBrayne, Ltd., 119, Hope Street, Glasgow.

C

" TROSSACHS " NOTE AND ALTERNATIVE ROUTE.

—The cyclist who has reached Tarbet Pier in preceding route may find himself looking across Loch Lomond to the famous " Trossachs " route to Callander. But it is an irksome job for the cyclist, and I personally prefer to leave it to the steamer and coach tourists. It involves steamer across to Inversnaid; then five miles of steep and bad road to Stronachlacher Pier; then steamer again along Loch Katrine; then nine miles of short steep hills to Callander.

But if the spell of Walter Scott is too strong to be flouted, the preceding route reads thus :

Helensburgh to Luss, Tarbet, 17; steamer to Inversnaid, Stronachlacher, 5; steamer to Loch Katrine Pier, Callander, 9½; Strathyre, Lochearnhead, 14; Killin, 7, where the previous route is joined. There are thirty miles more to cycle on the previous route, but they are worth while.

TO DODGE GLASGOW.—Cyclists (and motorists) proceeding northwards from the Border and aiming at Loch Lomond and the Highlands may wish to leave the unpleasantness of Glasgow out entirely, as well as that long bad stretch of the Carlisle-Lanark-Stirling highway where it passes to the east of Glasgow.

Having reached Hamilton, then, which is 11½ from Glasgow, they should keep more west to High Blantyre, East Kilbride, Busby, Paisley, 17; Erskine Ferry, 5, cross to Old Kilpatrick, Bowling, 2; a mile farther turn right over railway (direction post " to Stirling "), Bonhill, 5; cross river, Alexandria, 1; Luss, 9; Tarbet, 8½.

Cyclists who have followed the coast roads of Ayr and Renfrew up from Galloway, *via* Girvan, Ardrossan, and Wemyss Bay to Greenock, may take steamer from Greenock over to Helensburgh, 3½ miles, whence Luss is 9 and Garelochhead, 7. Thus Glasgow is avoided. See " Clyde steamers," page 63.

ROUTE 3: HIGHLANDS; FROM AND TO EDINBURGH, 520 MILES.—Edinburgh to Granton Ferry, 3; Burntisland to Cowdenbeath, Kinross, 15; Glenfarg, Perth, 17½; Cargill, Blairgowrie, 15½; Dunkeld, 12; Ballinluig, Pitlochry, 12½.

Cross Clunie Bridge, see Falls of Tummel; Foss, Tummel Bridge, 13; Queen's View, Fincastle Post Office, Garry Bridge, 10; Pass of Killiecrankie (go down to river), 1; Blair Atholl, 3; Dalnacardoch, Dalwhinnie, 23½; Kingussie, 14; Aviemore, 12; Carrbridge, 7; Moy, 13; Inverness, 11½.

Lochend, Drumnadrochit, Invermoriston, Fort Augustus, 34 (a distance in which no resthouse can be counted on till F.A. is reached); Spean Bridge, 22½; Fort William, 9½; Ballachulish Ferry, 12½; Duror, Appin, Creagan, Inver, Connel Bridge, 29; Oban, 5.

Taynuilt, 12; Pass of Brander, Dalmally, 13½; Cladich, Inveraray, 16.

Cairndow, 10; " Rest and be Thankful " Stone, Glencroe, Arrochar, 12; Tarbet, 1½; Ardlui, 8; Crianlarich, 8½; Luib, 7½; Killin, 6; Lawers, 8½; Fearnan, 4; Kenmore, 3½; Aberfeldy, 6; Grantully, 5; Dalguise, Birnam-Dunkeld, 12; Amulree, 9½; Sma' Glen, Crieff, 12; Muthill, Dunblane, 16½; Bridge of Allan, Stirling, 6; Alloa, Clackmannan, Bogside, Dunfermline, 21; Queensferry, 7; South Queensferry to Edinburgh, 9.

MAPS.—To include all the above routes in one sheet, get Bartholomew's Road Map of Scotland, ten miles to one inch. If greater detail is required, get Sheets 2, 3, 4, and 5 of Bartholomew's four miles to one inch Map of Scotland.

———————

Section 14.—Ireland.

If the success of road-touring depended on road-surfaces, there would be a lot of grievous disappointment in Ireland; but there are only a few " tourists " of that sort. Most of us travel to see places, people, landscapes. The Irish are the most charming, generous, warm-hearted, and courteous people in the world. Great Britain has nothing quite so beautiful to show as the west of Ireland, while Erin is singularly rich in historic architecture. The best roads are in the north-east. Those who can only tour with light wheels, tyres, and saddles should go to no other part of Ireland. I do not advise riding direct from Dublin to the south-west—I found dreadful roads in Carlow, Kilkenny, and Tipperary counties. In the districts of greatest fame and beauty the roads are good enough for good bicycles. The standard of cleanliness in England and Scotland is rather higher than in Ireland.

Mecredy's Road Books of Ireland are of quite unique value to the road tourist in Ireland. They are in two volumes, " Northern " and " Southern," but, unfortunately, the former is out of print at present. The Southern volume, 1s. net, *plus* 2d. postage, can be had from Mecredy, Percy, and Co., Ltd., 54, Upper Sackville Street, Dublin. The routes I am giving are partly based on those books; and my Routes Nos. 1 and 2 (and 3, with the exception of Connemara) will be found with much useful detail in the Southern volume.

ROUTE 1 : SOUTH AND SOUTH-WEST; FROM AND TO DUBLIN; ABOUT 450 MILES :

STEAMERS from Holyhead, Heysham, and Liverpool; for sailings see Bradshaw's Guide.

Milltown, Dundrum, Stepaside, The Scalp, Enniskerry, 13; Tinnahinch Bridge, Rocky Valley, Calary Bog, Roundwood, 10; Annamore, Laragh, Glendalough, 7.

Laragh, Rathdrum, 7½; Ovoca, 4, Woodenbridge, 4; Arklow,

4; Gorey, 10; Camolin, Ferns, 11; Enniscorthy, 7; Clonroche, New Ross, 23.

Waterford, 14; Kilmacthomas, 15; Dungarvan, 12; Kelly's Cross Barracks, 8; Ardmore, 4; Youghal, 7; Castlemartyr, 10; Midleton, 6; Cork, 13.

Dripsey, 14; Macroom, 11 (but Cork to Macroom is profitably done by train); Inchigeelah, 8; Bealnageary, 5; Gougane-barra Hotel, 4; Keimaneigh Pass, Snave Bridge, 16; Bantry and back, 8; Glengarriff, 7; Kenmare, 17; Templenoe, Black-water Bridge, 8; Sneem, 9; Cahirdaniel, 4; Darrynane, 2.

Waterville, 6; Balloughosheen Pass, 14; Bealalaw Bridge, 4; Loch Acoose, 4; Kilgobnet, Beaufort Bridge, Killarney, 10.

NOTE that the direct road from Kenmare to Killarney, 18 miles, gives the cycling tourist the better views of Killarney scenery, but cuts out most of the best of Kerry.

Barraduff, Duncannon Bridge, Millstreet, 22; Banteer, 9; Mallow, 12; Killawillin, Ballyhooley 12; Fermoy, 5; Ballyduff, 10; north side of river to Lismore, 6; Cappoquin, 4; The Gap, Clogheen, 13; Ardfinnan, Clonmel, 15.

I advise taking train to Dublin from Clonmel. The road-route is Callan, 22; Kilkenny, 9; Leighlinbridge, Carlow, 23; Castledermot, Kilcullen, Naas, Rathcoole, Dublin, 50.

MAPS.—Sheets 5, 6, and 7, called respectively " Killarney and Cork," " Dublin and Athlone," and " Wexford and Water-ford," of Bartholomew's four miles to the inch Map of Ireland.

ROUTE 2: SOUTH-WEST; FROM AND TO CORK, ABOUT 350 OR 400 MILES:

STEAMERS from Fishguard and Liverpool; for sailings see Bradshaw's Guide.

As in Route 1 from Cork to Kenmare. Then, Windy Gap, Muckross, Killarney, 20; Farrinfore, 9; Tralee, 11; Castle Gregory, 15; Stradbally, Connor Pass, Dingle, 14.

Ventry, round Mount Eagle to Slea Head and back to Dingle, 20.

Anascaul, 11; Inch, Castlemaine, 16; Killorglin, 6; Caragh Bridge, Glenbeigh Hotel, 7; Cahirciveen, 18; Valentia Ferry, 2, cross to Knightstown; ride to the Quarries and Bray Head, then back by south road to Knightstown and ferry. Bear left on to main road from Cahirciveen to Waterville; turn towards Waterville, and after one mile leave it, turning right to The Glen, 11; keep south along bay and over hill to Ballinskelligs, 5; Inny Bridge, Waterville, 9; Coomakista Pass, Darrynane, 6.

Cahirdaniel, 2; Sneem, 12; Blackwater Bridge, 8; Tem-plenoe, 4; Kenmare, 3; then either.

(a) Kilgarvan, Loo Bridge, 14; Ballyvourney, Macroom, 20; Cork, 25; or

(b) Castletown-Berehaven, 33; Glengarriff, 21; Snave Bridge, Keimaneigh Pass, Bealnageary, Macroom, 37; Cork, 25.

MAP.—Sheet 5 called " Killarney and Cork," of Bartholomew's four miles to the inch Map of Ireland, contains all the above routes.

ROUTE 3 : FROM AND TO DUBLIN, 500 OR MORE ; CROSSING THE BOG OF ALLEN TO CLONMACNOISE AND THE SHANNON, ROUND THE CLARE COAST TO CONNEMARA.—Dublin to Lucan, Maynooth, 15 ; Kilcock, Enfield, 11 ; Carbury, Edenderry, 12 ; Mount Lucas, Philipstown, 12 ; Ballinagar, Tullamore, 10 ; Clara, 7½ ; Ballycumber, Togher, Clonmacnoise, 16 ; you have come here to see the " Seven Churches."

Shannonbridge, 4 ; Cloghan, 8 ; Parsonstown (or Birr), 9 ; Nenagh, 20 ; Portroe, 7 ; Killaloe, 8 ; follow road to Scarriff for six miles, as far as the top of Ogennolloe Hill, and return to Killaloe, 12 ; O'Briensbridge, 5, cross it ; Castleconnell, 3 ; Limerick, 8.

Patrickswell, 6 ; Adare, 4 ; Askeaton, 9 ; Foynes, 7 ; Glin, 9 ; Tarbert, 4 ; steamer to Kilrush.

Kilkee, 8 (if time for a 33 miles' ride in the peninsula south of Kilkee, go to Carrigaholt, Cross, Loop Head, and back by Cross and Doonlicha Castle to Kilkee).

Doonbeg, 7 ; Kilmurry, 8 ; Spanish Point, 4 (two miles inland Milltown-Malbay hotels) ; Lahinch, 8 (two miles inland Ennistimon hotels) ; Liscannor, Hog's Head, 6 ; footpath above cliffs of Moher exceptionally fine ; Roadford, 7 (if a resthouse is wanted, keep right to Liodoonvarna, 4 ; if not, keep straight on from Roadford to the coast again).

Black Head, 12 ; Ballyvaughan, 6 ; Kinvara, 12 ; Clarinbridge, 8 ; Oranmore, 4 ; Galway, 5½. (From Ballyvaughan to Galway is less profitable. There is a steamer service between the two, of which time-tables can be had from the Galway Bay Steamer Company, New Dock, Galway.)

Salt Hill, Barna, Spiddle, 11 ; Moycullen, 9 ; Oughterard, 11 (Lough Corrib is half-mile on right).

Maam Cross, 10 ; Recess, 7 ; turn south beyond Glendalough Lake to Cashel Hotel, 7 ; Toombeola Bridge (cross and keep right), Ballinaboy Bridge, Clifden, 13.

Ballinahinch, Recess Station, 12 ; turn north, Kylemore Lake, Letterfrack, 15½ ; Rinvyle Hotel, 5 ; Tully Cross (keep left), Salrock, 8 ; Bundorragha Ferry, 3, cross ; ride five miles north to Glencullin Lake, return same way to ferry, 10 ; Leenaun, 3.

At this point—up to which about 460 miles have been covered —choice may be taken between three alternatives :

    (a) Leenaun to Maam Bridge, 8½ ; Cornamona, Cong, 14 ; Neale, Ballinrobe, 7½ ; train to Dublin, 140.

    (b) Leenaun to Erriff Bridge, Westport, 20 ; Newport, 7 ; Achill Sound, 20 ; across Achill Island to Doogart, 8 ; train to Dublin from Achill Sound or Westport.

    (c) As in (b) to Westport, 20 ; Partry, 13 ; Ballinrobe, 6 ; Tuam, 20 ; Mount Bellew, 13 ; Ballinamore, 10 ; Bally-

foran, 5; Athlone, 14; Moate, 10; Kilbeggan, 10; Tyrrell's Pass, 5; Rochford Bridge, 4; Kinnegad, 9; Clonard,
4; Enfield, 7½; Kilcock, 7; Maynooth, 4; Lucan,
Dublin, 15.

MAPS.—Sheets 3, 4, and 6 of Bartholomew's four miles to the
inch Map of Ireland.

ROUTE 4: FROM AND TO BELFAST OR LARNE, 400
MILES OR LESS; LOUGH ERNE, DONEGAL, AND
ANTRIM:

STEAMERS to Belfast from Liverpool, Heysham, Fleetwood,
and Glasgow.

Steamers to Larne from Stranraer.

Steamers to Londonderry from Heysham.

See Bradshaw's Guide.

(By road from Larne to Belfast through Carrickfergus,
25 miles.)

Belfast to Lisburn, 9; Lurgan, 13; Portadown, Armagh, 16½;
Monaghan, 16; Clones, 12; Lisnaskea, 13; Enniskillen, 11½,
where a day boating on Lough Erne would be well spent.

Silver Hill, Ely Lodge (private drive open to public), 5;
Church Hill, 7; Belleek (pass through town and over river),
11½; Ballyshannon, 4½; Ballintra, 6½; Donegal, 6½.

Mount Charles, 3; Inver, Bruckless, Killybegs, 16; Kilcar, 8;
Carrick, 3. At least half-a-day should be devoted to seeing the
2,000 ft. cliffs of Slieve League, two or three miles south-west
from Carrick. The trip should be done on foot, taking Car-
rigan Head and Bunglas Point first. On a still day, the clear-
headed may traverse the One Man Path.

Carrick to Glencolumbkille, 5½; Pass of Glengesh (danger),
10; Ardara, 5; Glenties, 6; Gweebarra Bridge, Dungloe, 14;
Gweedore, 10.

Ride about seven miles eastward, past Dunlewy Chapel to
Mount Errigal, leave machines and climb it from south-east
side; on to Calabber Bridge, cross it, keep left, over Muckish
Gap to Falcarragh, 20 from Gweedore.

Dunfanaghy, 7; Creeslough, 5½; Carrigart, 7; Milford, 9;
Ray, 4½; Rathmullan, 3; ferry (2½) to Fahan, Londonderry, 10.

Limavady, 17; Coleraine, 13; Portrush, 5; Bushmills, 5½;
Giants Causeway, 2½; Ballintoy, 7½; the famous swinging bridge
of Carrick-a-rede is on the left just beyond Ballintoy.

Ballycastle, 5; Cushendall, 16; Glenarm, 13; Larne, 11½;
shore road to Carrickfergus, 14; Belfast, 10½.

MAPS.—Sheets 1 and 2 of Bartholomew's four miles to the
inch Map of Ireland.

If the return route must be shortened and the Antrim coast
left for another time, leave above route at Londonderry and go
direct to Belfast as follows: Cumber Presbyterian Church, 8;
Cross View Inn, 7½; Dungiven, 4; Carn, Glenshane Pass,

Maghera, 13; Toome, 11; Randalstown, 6; Antrim, 5; Temple-patrick, Glengormley, Belfast, 17.

The combination of this route with the Londonderry-Bally-castle-Belfast route above would make an excellent short tour from and to Belfast of 190 miles, for which only Sheet 2 (see above) would be required.

Section 15.—London.

The problem presented by London to the touring cyclist or motor-cyclist is considerable. The " London " of the Metro-politan Police District contains 690 square miles and over seven million people. It is 16 miles through the area of dense popu-lation in any direction.

In the actual centre of London, apart from the few central roads on which are tramways, cycling is safer than in any other city in the world, because of the traffic's perfect order and con-trol, and in spite of the heavy motor traffic. It is outside the central area that London becomes risky for those who are not well used to it. The prime danger is the tramways, which are everywhere, and are always the cyclist's worst enemy. Where the police are fewer, too, the taxi-drivers have a bad habit of cutting corners on the wrong side of the road.

I am confident that very many provincial cyclists with trips to London in view would prefer to do the journey by road but for their natural fear of London's huge size, complexity, and traffic.

My suggestion to such is that they ride as far as the outer-most station on the electric railways or " tubes " and no farther; that, having left their machines at the nearest cycle-shop or in other safe custody, they detach their luggage and waterproofs and make for the electric trains, which will take them anywhere for a few pence. You can be booked through to any station on the system, and your ticket tells you where to change if it is necessary. The cloak-rooms at the outer stations will generally take bicycles.

For example, my own usual approach to London is by the *Great North Road* through Barnet and on to the Tally-Ho Corner at Finchley, where the tramway divides. Keeping to that on the right there is still easy riding forward to *Golder's Green Station*. I put my bicycle up at the special cycle house in the station yard, and the " tube " takes me in a few minutes into Central London.

This applies also to the *Coventry Road* (coming in through St. Albans), which joins the Great North Road at Barnet. Golder's Green is the station to make for.

Coming in by the *Banbury Road*, through Aylesbury and Berkhamsted, stop at *Watford*, and proceed by the Bakerloo line. This is 15 miles from Charing Cross, but it saves some bad road and heavy motor-bus traffic. If there is any special reason why you should ride farther in, proceed to Stanmore, Edgware, and up the Edgware Road as far as *Kilburn Park Station*.

Coming in by the *Oxford* and *Worcester Roads*, through High Wycombe, there is a terminal station of the electric railways at *Uxbridge*, also 15 miles from Charing Cross; but if the roads are dry, the cyclist may continue along the London road as far as *Ealing Broadway* or *Ealing Common* Stations, which are close together.

Coming in on the *Bath Road*, through Slough and Colnbrook, stop at *Hounslow Barracks Station*, a mile past Cranford.

Coming in on the *Exeter-Salisbury Road*, through Bagshot and Staines, go to *Heston-Hounslow Station*, turning to left in Hounslow at the Windsor Castle Hotel just where the Bath Road comes in.

Coming in on the *Portsmouth Road*, through Ripley and Kingston, stop at *Putney Bridge Station*, on the right just over the bridge.

Coming in on the *Brighton Road*, give a miss to the Redhill-Croydon route, and proceed through Reigate to Burgh Heath, turn left to Ewell, over Cheam Common to Merton, turn left at the Grove Hotel, and then right at Merton Park Station to *Wimbledon Station* or *Putney Bridge Station*.

Coming in on the *Eastbourne Road* through East Grinstead, leave it at Purley (in order to avoid Croydon), and go on through Wallington and Mitcham to *Wimbledon Station*, having turned acutely left just past Merton-Abbey Station.

Coming in on the *Hastings Road* through Tonbridge and Sevenoaks, there is no station on the electric railways until New Cross is reached, where traffic is dense. It would be more comfortable to " chuck it " at *Bromley South Station*, whence there is a good service to Victoria by the South-Eastern and Chatham Railway. At Victoria the " Underground " can be taken for all parts.

Coming in on the *Folkestone Road* through Maidstone and Wrotham, there is the same absence of a convenient station on the electric railways. Stop at *New Eltham Station*, on the South-Eastern and Chatham Railway, and take train to either Charing Cross or Cannon Street for the Underground.

Coming in on the *Dover Road* through Gravesend and Dartford, stop at *Welling Station*, a mile past Bexleyheath, and take train as in previous case.

Coming in on the *Ipswich Road* through Chelmsford, stop at *Ilford Station*, and proceed by train to Liverpool Street.

Coming in on the *Norwich Road* through Newmarket and Epping, keep to the left just south of the Wilfrid Lawson on Woodford Green and stop at *Snaresbrook Station*, on the left, just south of the Eagle Hotel. Take Great Eastern train to Liverpool Street, where change to Underground.

Do not try to take bicycles on the Underground.

A pocket *Map of the Underground Electric Railways* is supplied gratis on application to Electric Railway House, Broadway, Westminster, S.W. 1, or to the station staffs.

An excellent " Pocket Atlas and Guide to London " is published by John Bartholomew and Son, Ltd., Duncan Street, Edinburgh, 2s. post free.

THROUGH LONDON.—But there are cyclists who *want* to ride right through London, for various reasons, and have no strong objections to traffic riding. It is worth remembering, too, that on Sundays the complete transit of London is easy. The routes given below are chosen chiefly on the ground of being easy to find.

ROUTE 1 : NORTH TO SOUTH, coming in from Hertford, Ware, Hoddesdon, etc.—Along Tottenham High Street, turn R. into Seven Sisters Road, L. into Green Lanes, along Highbury New Park to Highbury Corner, all along Upper Street to the Angel, St. John Street, Rosebery Avenue.

Theobald's Road, Hart Street, cross over Oxford Street, along Great St. Andrew Street, St. Martin's Lane, Trafalgar Square, along Whitehall, leave Abbey on left, Victoria Street, turn L. into Regency Street, over Vauxhall Bridge, along South Lambeth Road to the Swan, along Clapham Road to the Plough, keep L. and straight on for four miles along South Side, Balham Road, Tooting Road, over the River Wandle at South Wimbledon, and half-a-mile farther turn L. along Morden Road, for Morden, Reigate, and Brighton.

If coming in from the north through Barnet, follow the tramway for three miles to Tally-Ho Corner, where keep R. through Finchley, past Golder's Green Station, continue along Finchley Road to Swiss Cottage Station, then Avenue Road, cross Regent's Canal and turn R., keep Regent's Park on L. as far as Clarence Gate, where sheer off R. along York Place and Baker Street into Oxford Street, turn R., then L. through Marble Arch, straight on to Hyde Park Corner, cross straight over, down Grosvenor Place, and Grosvenor Gardens to Victoria, keep station on R., and turn into Vauxhall Bridge Road, the previous route being joined here.

ROUTE 2 : NORTH-EAST TO SOUTH-WEST.—Coming in from Epping and Woodford, go along Lea Bridge Road (Leyton) to its end, cross Clapton Road, turn L. along Powell Road, Cricketfield Road, and Pembury Road, cross Amhurst Road, along Dalston Lane to Dalston Junction Station, cross to Balls Pond Road, St. Paul's Road, to Highbury Corner, turn L. along Upper Street to the Angel, along Pentonville Road to

King's Cross, along Euston Road and Marylebone Road to Baker Street Station, turn L. along York Place and Baker Street into Oxford Street, turn R. and then L. through Marble Arch, straight on to Hyde Park Corner, turn R. along Knightsbridge, then L. down Sloane Street to King's Road, follow King's Road all the way to Putney Bridge—for Kingston, Guildford, Portsmouth, etc.

ROUTE 3: NORTH-WEST TO SOUTH-EAST.—From Watford or St. Albans to Edgware and along the full length of the Edgware Road (eight miles), cross Oxford Street, through Marble Arch to Hyde Park Corner, Constitution Hill, Birdcage Walk, Great George Street, over Westminster Bridge, along Kennington Road to the Horns, cross Kennington Park Road, follow Camberwell New Road to its end, along Church Street, Peckham Road, High Street, Queen's Road, New Cross Road, cross Deptford Bridge and keep R.; then, for Canterbury, Margate, Ramsgate, Dover, etc., keep straight on over Shooter's Hill; for Folkestone, Hastings, and Eastbourne turn R. to Lewisham.

AVOIDING LONDON.—When London stands across the cyclist's route, he nearly always prefers to avoid it. That being so, it is best to give it as wide a berth as possible. To go any nearer to it than the following routes means greatly increased difficulty in finding the way. As most of this traffic is north and south in direction, I give the circuit in two sections—on the west side and on the east side. These avoiding routes are, of course, constantly crossing the great main roads into London, and these are indicated *in italics* so as to suggest where the circuit may be joined or left.

1.—WEST CIRCUIT, *Hatfield to Reigate:* Hatfield (on *Great North Road*) to St. Albans (*Coventry Road*), 5½; Watford, 7½; Rickmansworth, 3½; Uxbridge (*Oxford Road*), 7½; Cowley, West Drayton, 3; Harmondsworth, emerge on *Bath Road*, turn R., cross railway at Colnbrook Station, and turn L. 400 yards farther at Punch Bowl Inn for Staines (*Exeter Road*), 7; cross Thames and turn L., Chertsey, 3; Addlestone, turn L. past station, Weybridge, 3; Church Cobham (*Portsmouth Road*), Stoke, Leatherhead, 10; Dorking (*Worthing Road*), 4½; Reigate (*Brighton Road*), 6.

Reverse: Reigate to Dorking, 6; Leatherhead, 4½; Stoke Church Cobham (*Portsmouth Road*), Weybridge, 10; Addlestone, turn R., Chertsey, 3; Staines (*Exeter Road*), 3; cross bridge, leave London Road on R. and go on by waterside and past Great Western Station; over railway and straight ahead until you emerge on the *Bath Road* at the Punch Bowl Inn, turn R., cross railway at Colnbrook Station, and a mile and a half farther turn L. to Harmondsworth, West Drayton, Uxbridge (*Oxford Road*), 10; follow Oxford Road two miles, then turn R. to Rickmansworth, 7½; Watford, 3½; St. Albans, 7½; Hatfield, 5½ (*Great North Road*).

2.—EAST CIRCUIT, *Hatfield to Reigate:* Hertford, 7;

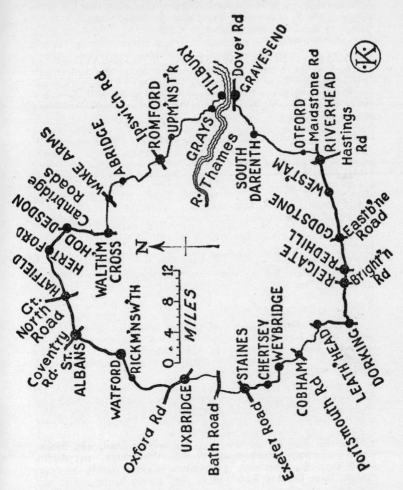

Hoddesdon (*from Cambridge*), 4; Cheshunt, Waltham Cross, 5½; turn L., Wake Arms in Epping Forest (*from Cambridge*), 4½; Theydon Bois, Abridge, Chigwell Row, Collier Row, Romford (*Ipswich Road*), 11; Hornchurch, Upminster, 3½; South

Ockendon, 4; Stifford, Grays, Tilbury, 6. There are several alternative ways from Upminster to Tilbury, all about the same distance. From Grays the way is well sign-posted.

Ferry to Gravesend (*Dover Road*); ferry runs from 8 a.m. to 9 p.m. (9 to 9 Sunday) from May to September; 8 a.m. to 6 p.m. (9 to 6 Sunday) October to April.

Southfleet Station, Betsham, Green Street Green, South Darenth, 7; Farningham, Eynsford, Shoreham Station, Otford, 7½; Riverhead (*Hastings Road*), 2½; Westerham, 4½; Limpsfield, Oxted, Godstone (*Eastbourne Road*), 6½; Redhill, Reigate, 6½.

Reverse: Reigate to Redhill, Godstone (*Eastbourne Road*), 6½; Oxted, Limpsfield, Westerham, 6½; Riverhead (*Hastings Road*), 4½; Bat and Ball Station (turn L.), Otford, 3; Shoreham Station, Eynsford, Farningham, South Darenth, 7½; Green Street Green, Betsham, Gravesend, 7; ferry to Tilbury (for Chelmsford on *Ipswich Road*), Grays, Stifford, South Ockendon, 6; Upminster, 4; Hornchurch, Romford, 3½; Collier Row, Chigwell Row, Abridge, Theydon Bois, Wake Arms (*Cambridge Road*), 11; Waltham Abbey, Waltham Cross, 4½; Cheshunt, Hoddesdon (*Cambridge Road*), 5½; Hertford (for *Great North Road* at Stevenage), 4; Hatfield, 7.

LONDON RESTHOUSES.—The best London district for quickly securing accommodation at moderate prices is that bounded on the north by Euston Road (where the great railway termini, King's Cross, St. Pancras, and Euston are found), on the east by Gray's Inn Road, on the south by Hart Street and Theobalds Road, and on the west by Tottenham Court Road. The principal electric railway stations within this area are Euston Square, Euston, and King's Cross on the north edge; Tottenham Court Road, Museum, and Chancery Lane on the south edge; Warren Street and Goodge Street on the west edge, and Russell Square in the middle of it. All these are easily and quickly reached from any of the stations to which cyclists approaching London have previously been recommended to stop riding. (See map next page.)

All the district thus indicated abounds in hotels and houses where the bed-and-breakfast traveller is catered for. Many of them are undesirable—and look it. Many of them still advertise the pre-war charge of 4s. 6d. for bed and breakfast on their fanlights and lamps—and charge more. I doubt if it is now safe to pay less than 6s. for bed and breakfast. At 6s. 6d. I can recommend Seabrook House, 28, Cartwright Gardens, W.C. 1, off Euston Road, near St. Pancras; and 37, Argyll Street, near King's Cross; and Mills's Hotel, 107, Gower Street, W.C. 1.

At Turner's Hotel, 73, Guilford Street, W.C. 1, the charge is 6s. 6d. to 7s. 6d., according to floor.

At the Kingsley Hotel, Hart Street, W.C. 1, and at the Thackeray Hotel, opposite the British Museum, in Great Russell

Street, both first-class hotels, the charge is 8s. 6d. for bed and breakfast. These five addresses are known to me personally.

Others in the same area are Taverner's Hotel, Hunter Street, Brunswick Square; Johnston's Euston Hotel, 70, Euston

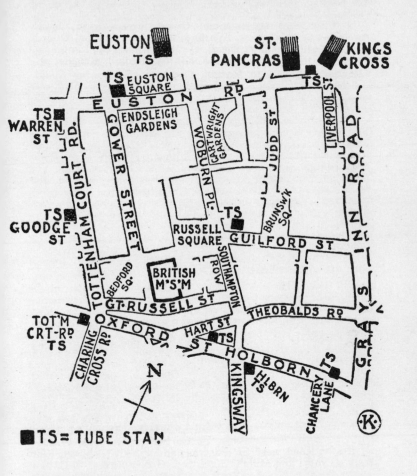

Square; Northern Hotel, 59, Liverpool Street, King's Cross; Bristow's Hotel, 6, Chesterfield Street, King's Cross; and Palmeira House, 11, Woburn Place, Russell Square. All these and the previous addresses are unlicensed houses.

Section 16.—France.

This section is chiefly intended for those who know nothing of the French language. That ignorance need not prevent any one from going to the best road-touring country in the world. Certainly, French roads are not what they used to be; but the cyclist, with only one track to find, can go comfortably where the motorist cannot. What helps to make France the road-touring country *par excellence* is the presence everywhere of modest and satisfactory hotels which exist for the purpose of providing meals and bedrooms.

Prices in France are about double what they were, but even then, touring is no more expensive than in England, especially now that the rate of exchange is in favour of English money.

But you must make up your mind to live as the French do. You cannot have eggs and bacon for breakfast. But you can have café-au-lait, with bread and butter, as early as you like—and be off by 7.30 if you choose. Lunch is ready at any hotel or restaurant by twelve noon and for an hour or two. You must not count on afternoon tea, but it is generally obtainable in the best confectioners' shops of the larger towns in the North of France. Everywhere, at hotels, inns, restaurants, a good dinner is ready at seven p.m. and available for two or three hours. If you want a heavier breakfast than that mentioned, ask for an omelette. Omelettes can also be had in a few minutes between the regular meal-times at any hotel or restaurant. If the table is set with bottles of wine or jugs of cider at lunch or dinner, there is no extra charge for it.

ASKING THE WAY.—Point to the place you want on the map. But look out for the iron direction plates, white letters and figures on blue ground which are found fixed to buildings at street-corners, and on the first and last buildings in villages.

ACCESSORIES.—As you should finish your riding every day not later than 6.30, it is hardly worth while to take a lamp. The French take little notice of bells on bicycles. Small horns are more effective, and cheap. They can be thrown over-board on the way back. *Ride on the right-hand side of the road and overtake other traffic on its left-hand side.*

PASSPORTS.—It is still necessary to provide yourself with a passport before you can enter France, and for this you will require two photographs of yourself, carte-de-visite size. Write Passport Office, 1, Queen Anne's Gate Buildings, Westminster, S.W. 1, or Branch Passport Office, 36, Dale Street, Liverpool.

If your journey to the English coast is to be done by rail, you will save trouble by letting Thos. Cook and Son, Ludgate Circus, E.C. 4, get your tickets and passports and change your money; and especially so when you contemplate an initial rail journey in France.

Information about touring in France is courteously given at the Office Français du Tourisme, 56, Haymarket, S.W. 1.

In Southampton you may confidently change money also at Jackson and Sons, Canute Road, opposite South-Western Hotel, with a branch in Oxford Street.

If you take any quantity of English money into France, it should be in Bank of England £5 notes. If you want to change these in France take them to either the Crédit Lyonnais or the Société Générale, with branches in every town. Hotel people and shopkeepers will not change English Treasury notes.

There are *local* notes circulating in France which are of little value outside the place of issue. Banque de France notes are good everywhere.

" Will you change me this note, please? "—" Voulez-vous bien me changer cette note, s'il vous plaît? "

Coming *back* from France, have as little French money as possible. It is illegal to bring away more than 10 francs in French silver.

COST.—Normandy is more expensive than Brittany. At very nearly all the French hotels in my list the charge is from 15 to 25 francs a day. At the best hotels in the larger towns it is 25 to 35 francs a day. Paris is expensive, and the seaside resorts on the Normandy coast in July and August may charge anything. If you speak French, always *ask*, which is quite usual in France. West of St. Malo the seaside places are reasonable even in July and August.

STEAMER SERVICES.—Time-tables are found in Bradshaw's Guide. For other information respecting the boats write Marine Superintendent, L. and S.W. Railway, Southampton. Arrived at Southampton, go into dockyard and leave bicycles at the South-Western office, where you also get tickets.

FRENCH CUSTOMS DUES.—*New* bicycles taken into France for either short or long periods are liable to the import duty. If your bicycle is new, or looks new, rub it over with mud. Under date, February 11, 1920, the Director-General of French Customs assured me once more that English tourists with " used " bicycles and return tickets of limited availability will not be required to deposit the duty on imported bicycles. Thus there is no need to belong to any club so far as the northern ports are concerned. On landing in France, your bicycle will probably be taken away to one shed while you yourself are shepherded into another. You may pass through this latter at once, since all your luggage is probably on the bicycle, but if carrying a camera case show it to one of the counter officials along with any tobacco, cigarettes, or matches you may have. Be sparing under these heads; an unbroken packet or box is liable to be charged heavy duty. Petrol lighters are forbidden.

You pass then to the shed where the bicycles (bicyclettes) are, and an official is making out the papers, called " permis de circulation," now two francs each, which free you from the annual tax on bicycles. Have your return ticket (billet de retour) ready for him along with a paper you have made out at home as follows :—

RENSEIGNEMENTS POUR LA DOUANE.

Nom: Smith.
Prénoms: John William.
Nationalité: Anglais.
Marque du Vélo: B.S.A. (for example).
Numéro du Vélo: 53,021 (for example).
N.B.—Retour dans 8 jours.

Write all this *very* plainly. If there is *no* number stamped on your bicycle that you know of, paint or scratch any old number you like anywhere on the machine, or paint it on a bit of tin and tie it on. This is not very important. Twenty tours at least have I made in France, and not once have I carried a visible number or had one on my " permis de circulation," or been asked for one. Generally my " permis " have been marked " Sans numéro "—no number. When you have got this " permis " you are free to depart ; and if there is a fierce-looking person in dirty blue trousers hanging on to your bicycle give him 3d. to let go. Keep your " permis " carefully, and in the highly unlikely event of your being challenged by the police subsequently, produce it.

ESSENTIAL WORDS.—This list is intended for " pointing " purposes. Breakfast (at almost any time you like) may be ordered as " un café-au-lait complet," with the number of your party in place of the " un "—deux, trois, quatre, etc.

> Dining-room—salle-à-manger.
> Bedroom—chambre.
> Bedroom with one double bed—chambre à un grand lit.
> Bedroom with two single beds—chambre à deux petits lits.
> The bill—la note.

W.C.—les cabinets. Ask *anybody* on the staff for it, man or woman—the French have not the disease of false modesty. Often you will find " No. 100 " on the door, and sometimes " Ici." Often they leave something to be desired.

If you want something more than this in the way of phrases

and useful information, order from your bookseller " The Continong," published by J. M. Dent and Sons, 2s., a very practical, useful, and amusing booklet.

Last word : Take your own soap.

ROUTE 1 : THREE DAYS FROM ST. MALO.—First day, Paramé, Dol, Pontorson (turn left), Mont St. Michel, 34 miles. Parties are conducted over abbey and fortress by uniformed guides (tip at end), and it takes about an hour. Leave not later than five, and ride back through Pontorson to Antrain, 13, for the night. Second day, Combourg, 14; Dinan, 15 (see high bridge over Rance river), Jugon, 14. Third day, Lamballe, 10; Plancoet, 15; Ploubalay, Dinard, 12; ferry to St. Malo—" bac à St. Malo."

ROUTE 2 : FROM AND TO ST. MALO, 222 MILES.— Chateauneuf, 7; Tinteniac, 17; Hédé, 3; Rennes, 14; l'Hermitage, Montfort, 13; Iffendic, St. Malon, Paimpont, 14; Ploermel, 12; la Chapelle, Roc, Serent, Elven, 17; Vannes, 10; Meucon, Locminé, 17; Josselin, 15; les Forges, Rohan, 13; Loudéac, 8; Plouguenast, 8; Moncontour, 7; Lamballe, 10; Noyal, Jugon, 10; Dinan, 14; Pleslin, Dinard, 13; ferry to St. Malo.

ROUTE 3 : FROM AND TO ST. MALO, 445 MILES.— Ferry to Dinard (" Bac à Dinard "), Ploubalay, Plancoet, Lamballe, 27; St. Brieux, 13; Pordic, Binic, Etables, 9; St. Quay, Plouha, 7; Plouézec, Paimpol, 10; l'Arcoest, 3; motor-boat to Ile Bréhat; there is little or no riding on the island, and unless you are staying on it overnight, bicycles may be left at l'Arcoest; Paimpol, 3.

Lézardrieux, Tréguier, 9; Perros-Guirec, Ploumanach, 13; Lannion, 7; Plouaret, 9; Belle-Isle, 8; Callac, 10; Mael-Carhaix, 8; Rostrenen, 6; Goarec, 7; Mur, 10; Pontivy, 10; Silfiac, Rostrenen, 21; Carhaix, 13; Gourin, 12; le Faouet, 10; St. Fiacre, Quimperlé, 13; l'Orient, 12; Hennebont, 6; Merlevenez, Erdeven, Plouharnel, Carnac, 18 (visit " les pierres alignées ").

La Trinité, Lokmariaker, 7 (get small boy to guide you to the Table des Marchands), Crach, Auray, 7; Vannes, 12; Elven, 10; Roc St. André, 12; turn left, Josselin, 9; Ploermel, 7; Campenéac, Paimpont, 12; St. Malon, Iffendic, Montfort, 14; St. Méen, St. Jouan, Broons, 12; Lamballe, 16; Jugon, 10; Dinan, 14; Chateauneuf, St. Malo, 19. Between Lannion and Plouaret are many old castles not far from the roads; the chief are Coetfrec, Tonquedec, Kergrist, Kerfaouez, and Ploubezre.

EXTENSION WESTWARDS OF ROUTE 3, ADDING 288 MILES.—From Lannion to Plestin, 10; Lanmeur, 4; Morlaix, 8; Taulé, St. Pol de Léon, 13; Roscoff and back, 5; Plouescat, 9; Goulven, Brignogan, 8; Kerlouan, Guisseny, Lannilis, 14; Ploudalmézeau, 7; St. Renan, 8; le Conquet, 9; Brest, 13;

le Passage, 5, ferry over; Plougastel (see calvary), 1; Daoulas, 5; le Faou, 7, turn right, Térénez Ferry, 5; Crozon, 10; Morgat and back, 2½; Telgruc, Ploéven, Plonevez, Douarnenez, 26, and hard going.

Pont-Croix, 10; Audierne, Pointe du Raz, 14; (see Bay of the Dead on right); Audierne, 11; Plozevet, Plonébur, Pont l'Abbé, 20; Penmarch, 7; lighthouse, St. Guénolé, Penmarch, 5; Plobannalec, Loctudy, 9; ferry to Ile Tudy, Combrit, Bénodet Ferry, 7; Quimper, 9; Concarneau, 13½ (see Chateau Keriolet, 1½ miles away); Pont Aven, Quimperlé, 10, where Route 3 is rejoined. This extension covers the coast line of Finistère, and the two omitted inland places of chief interest are Huelgoat and le Faouet, of which the latter is the more interesting. When you have carried out Route 3, with the extension, Brittany has little left to show you.

ROUTE 4: FROM AND TO CHERBOURG, 323 MILES, MOSTLY IN NORMANDY.—This may well be arranged to spend nights at Carentan, Mortain, Antrain, Jugon, Dol, Genest, and Port-Bail.

Cherbourg to Valognes, Carentan, 30; St. Lo, 16; Torigny, 7; Vire, 15; Mortain, 14; St. Hilaire, 9; Ducey, Mont St. Michel (see Route 1), 15; Pontorson, Antrain, 13; Bazouges, Combourg, 13; Dinan, 15; Jugon, 14; Plancoet, 10; Ploubalay, Dinard, 12; ferry to St. Malo, Dol, 16; Pontorson, 12; Avranches, 15; Genest, 5; Carolles, Granville, 13; Bréhal, Coutances, 15; Lessay, 12; la Haye, 4; Port-Bail, 8; Barneville, Carteret, 6; les Pieux, 12; Cherbourg, 15.

ROUTE 5: THE CHATEAUX OF THE LOIRE, 480 MILES.—This route is shaped like a top lying on its side and with the point on Nantes. The nearest French seaport is St. Malo, from which it is 100 miles by rail to Nantes. If cycling all the way, ride from St. Malo to Rennes, Chateaubriant, la Chapelle, St. Mars, Ancenis, 115 miles, see route below. The principal chateaux are printed in capital letters. Those of them which are in private hands may have raised their prices of admission since my last information.

Nantes to Ancenis, 24 miles; Varades, St. Georges, 21, inquire for chateau of SERRANT, a mile away; it is visitable in the absence of the proprietor, otherwise and sometimes on presentation of private card.

ANGERS, 11. The chateau's principal interest is outside, but there is much also to see in town; les Ponts-de-Cé, 4; cross river and seek finger-plate on left to BRISSAC, 6, to visit chateau apply concierge; Gennes, 12; SAUMUR, 10, chateau now public museum; Saúzay, Candes, Thizay, CHINON, 20, chateau is public property and open daily from nine to six; Huismes, USSE, 8, chateau visitable on Sunday, Tuesday, and Friday after midday from March to July, and from August to February on Sundays only from two to four.

AZAY-LE-RIDEAU, 8, open daily from 9 to 5.30, June to September, 10 to 4 from October to May; Bréhémont, 3; turn right for chateau of VILLANDRY, grounds open daily, admission to chateau one franc from nine to six; back to Bréhémont and over rivers to LANGEAIS, 8, one franc, daily, 9 to 11 and 1.30 to 6.

Cinq-Mars, 4, chateau on left; LUYNES, 5, chateau may be partly visited daily, ascend old steps; Tours 7, see cathedral, Hôtel de Ville, and old houses, museum open to foreigners every day; one mile away is chateau of Plessis-les-Tours, ring for concierge; cross River Cher on south and turn left to Bléré; re-cross river and turn right to CHENONCEAUX, 20, open daily, one franc, 10 to noon and 2 to 6.

Forward nearly to Chisseaux, turn right over river through Francueil and Luzillé and St. Quentin to LOCHES, 16, one franc daily, 9 to 6, half-price Sundays and holidays; Beaulieu, MONTRESOR, 10, open daily 9 to 6; Nouans, Lucay-le-Mâle, VALENCAY, 20, chateau not visitable, but grounds open; Selles, 8; St. Aignan (chateau), 9; re-cross river and turn left for Thezée, Montrichard (chateau), 12; AMBOISE, 11, open daily, 10 to 6.

Chargé, CHAUMONT, 12, open daily, 9 to 6, from January to July, on Thursday afternoon only from August to December; Candé, les Moutils, Ouchamps, Fougères, CHEVERNY, 16, open daily.

Bracieux, 5; CHAMBORD, 5, visitors conducted daily through chateau; Huisseau, BLOIS, 9, open daily, very fine town; VENDOME, 20, courtyard of chateau is public promenade; re-cross river and turn right; les Roches, 9; Montoire, 2; LAVARDIN and back, 4, guide can be got at inn.

St. Jacques, Trôo, Pont-de-Braye, Poncé, 10 (half-way between last two places, two miles to south over railway and river, is the Chateau de la Poissonnière); la Chartre, Marcon, Chateau-du-Loir, 14; LE LUDE, 14; Baugé (chateau), 15; Jarzé (chateau), 6; Seiches, 6; ANGERS, 12; and as before to Nantes, 56. But if riding back to St. Malo from Angers go through Candé, Chateaubriant, and Rennes to St. Malo, 122.

ROUTE 6: FROM AND TO DIEPPE, 182 MILES IN NORMANDY.—Dieppe to Neuville, Envermeu, Londinières, 16 miles; Neufchatel, 8; St. Saire, Forges-les-Eaux, 10; Argueil, 5; le Feuillie, Lyons-la-Foret, 11; les Andelys, 12, see Chateau Gaillard, Heudebouville, 9; Pont de l'Arche, 9; Rouen, 10; Canteleu, Duclair, 12; Yainville, 3; Jumièges Abbey and back, 4; Caudebec, 7; Lillebonne, 10; Bolbec, 5; Goderville, 7; Fécamp, 7; Cany, 12; St. Valéry, 8; Quiberville, Dieppe, 18.

ROUTE 7: FROM AND TO LE HAVRE, 320 MILES IN NORMANDY.—Le Havre to Octeville, Etretat, 16½ miles, Fécamp, 9½; Ecretteville, Veulettes, St. Valéry, 22; Veules, Quiberville, Dieppe, 18½; Neuville, Envermeu, Londinières, 16;

Neufchatel, 8; St. Saire, Forges-les-Eaux, 10; Argueil, 5; la
Feuillie, Lyons-la-Forêt, 11; les Andelys, 12; Heudebouville, 9;
Pont de l'Arche, 9; Rouen, 10; Canteleu, Duclair, 12; Yainville,
3; Jumièges Abbey and back, 4; Caudebec, 7; ferry over river;
Pont-Audemer, 18; Cormeilles, 11; Lisieux, 12; Vimoutiers, 6;
Trun, 12; Falaise, 13; Caen, 17; Cabourg, 16; Dives, Trou-
ville, 14; Honfleur, 9; ferry to le Havre.

Don't stay at Pont-Audemer. Don't try to " get in " at
Trouville in July and August.

ROUTE 8 : THE WAY TO PARIS.—I am frequently asked
for routes from the French coast to Paris, although I have
found no pleasurable cycling myself in or near the French
capital.

From Dieppe the distance is 21 miles less than from le Havre,
but the latter route is much more picturesque, largely following
the valley of the Seine. Both routes given herewith come
together at St. Germain-en-Laye, well to the west of Paris, the
intention being to avoid the bad paving on all the more direct
and northerly routes into the city.

(1) From le Havre to Harfleur, St. Romain, 19 kilometres;
Lillebonne, 16; Caudebec, 16½; Duclair, 16½; Rouen, 20; Pont
de l'Arche, 18½; Heudebouville, 14½; Gaillon, 8; Vernon, 14;
Bonniéres, 10½; Mantes, 13½; Mezières, St. Germain, 31.

Through this town and onwards I give the best route in
detail : Place de Pontoise, Rue de Pontoise, Rue Louis-Cagnard,
Rue de la Surintendance, Place du Château, turn left to Place
Thiers, Rue Thiers, turn right, Avenue Gambetta, turn left to
Place Royale.

Le Pecq, 1½; cross the bridge; at branch roads take that on
right to

Le Vésinet, 2; Chatou, 1½; cross River Seine; at fork leave
the paved road to the left and take that on right to

Rueil, 2½; turn right when leaving Rueil, then left to

Suresnes, 5; cross the Seine to the Bois de Boulogne; a
quarter-mile farther, at the Cascade, follow the Allée de Long-
champ to the Porte Maillot, 6. Total, 216 kilometres, or 135
miles.

(2) From Dieppe to Bouteilles, Archelles, St. Aubin,
Dampierre, Neufchatel, 34 kilometres; Gaillefontaine, Songeons,
41; Beauvais, 21; Allonne, Ressons, Méru, 26½; Pontoise, 22½;
Eragny, St. Germain, 19; and as in previous route to the
Porte Maillot, 18¾. Total, 182 kilometres, or 114 miles.

ROUTE 9 : THE BATTLEFIELDS.—Probably only a very
few of the British soldiers who crossed the Channel to France
know that the war-area is the least interesting and least picturesque part of that great country; that it is the only part
where most roads are stone-paved, and that, compared with
the whole of France, the war-area is just one part in 500.

North of a line drawn from Paris through Reims to the

frontier, and east of a line drawn from Paris to Dunkerque, paved main roads must be expected, though there are often paths of a sort alongside for the use of cyclists.

War damage to roads has already been largely repaired. Hotels also are being contrived in the half-ruined towns of famous history.

In view, then, of the indifferent roads and of the fact that outside war associations and a few cathedrals, this country is deficient in interest, I have taken it that only young and strong ex-soldiers are likely to make the following tour. It totals 745 miles, which such would do in a fortnight; but slight study of the map will show how it can be shortened at will. Do not try any road marked " Route Interdite."

The route is arranged to start and finish at Ostend in Belgium. (Fourteen miles away, in the opposite direction to this route and along the coast all the way, is Zeebrugge, passing through Blankenberghe *en route*.)

BELGIAN CUSTOMS-HOUSES.—Ordinarily, the Belgians are exacting in the matter of frontier formalities, and any cyclist who is making a detailed visit to such sections as Menin-Armentières-Poperinghe or Mons-Maubeuge is likely to be continually crossing the Franco-Belgian frontier. I, therefore, approached the Director-General of Belgian Customs in the matter, and have his assurance, under date, February 19, 1920, that " the collectors at points of entry into Belgium are authorised to admit freely and without formalities, when there is no ground for suspicion, bicycles imported by people who are in a position to prove that they are crossing the country direct or can only make a very short stay in it. In this matter, such proof is admitted as circular-tour railway tickets, steamer return tickets, etc." If the officials at some inland frontier station are disposed to be awkward, point to this sentence : " Je suis ancien combattant, et je fais la visite des champs de bataille—séjour de quinze jours seulement."

The following figures of distance stand for kilometres; a kilometre is five-eighths of a mile :

Ostend to Dixmude, 27 ; Ypres, 22 ; Menin, 20 ; Lille, 20 ; Armentières, 14 ; Laventie, Neuve Chapelle, La Bassée, 22.

Lens, 12 ; Vimy Ridge, Arras, 17 ; Cambrai, 36 ; Bapaume, 28 ; Albert, 19 ; Péronne, 24 ; St. Quentin, 29 ; Ham, 20 ; Roye, 23 ; Noyon, 20 ; Chauny, 17 ; La Fère, 13 ; Laon, 23.

Soissons, 32 ; Fismes, Reims, 57 ; Suippes, 42 ; Ste. Ménéhould, 29 ; Verdun, 44 ; Ste. Ménéhould, 44 ; Vitry, 50 ; Châlons, 32 ; Epernay, 30 ; Château Thierry, 47.

La Ferté-sous-Jouarre, 30 ; Meaux, 18 ; St. Soupplets, 11 ; Ermenonville, Senlis, 28 ; Creil, 10 ; Clermont, 15 ; St. Just Breteuil, 33 ; Amiens, 30.

Doullens, 30 ; St. Pol, 28 ; Fruges, 22 ; St. Omer, 30 ; Dunkerque, 37 ; Furnes, 21 ; Nieuport, 11 ; Ostende, 17. Total, 1,184 kilometres, or 745 miles.

A remarkable series of illustrated *Guide-Books to the Battlefields* has been issued by the Michelin Tyre Company, Ltd., 81, Fulham Road, S.W. 3. There are about ten books, ranging in price from 1s. 6d. to 5s. 6d. All ordinary interests are dealt with, as well as the local associations with the war.

MAPS FOR FRENCH TOURS.—I advise sending to the Librairie Hachette, 18, King William Street, Strand, W.C. 2, for the necessary sheet or sheets of the Carte Taride. These are sent (at present) for 1s. 9d. each on paper, post free, or 4s. 6d. on cloth.

For Routes 1 and 4 you need Sheet 5 of the Carte Taride.

For Routes 2 and 3, Sheets 5, 5 *bis*, and 9.

For Route 5, Sheets 8, 9, and 12.

For Routes 6, 7, and 8, Sheet 4.

For Route 9, Sheets 1, 3, and 4, which cover all the places named except Verdun, which is just outside Sheet 3, due east from Reims.

Excellent road-maps of France are also sold by the Michelin Tyre Company, see *ante*.

NOTE ON BELGIUM.—I have had one cycle tour along the Belgian coast and to Bruges, Ghent, Antwerp, Brussels, etc., and I do not advise cycling in Belgium north of a line drawn from Valenciennes through Namur to Liége. Apart from the beautiful old Flemish towns, the country is worse than monotonous, and all roads are roughly stone-paved.

South of that line the conditions are quite different. It is the country of the Belgian Ardennes, with macadam roads and rather hilly character, resembling the Yorkshire dales, with the valley of the Semois as the tit-bit. Better take train from the coast to Namur or Liége.

NOTE ON HOLLAND.—I have no personal experience of cycling in Holland. The following, taken from a letter in the C. T. C. *Gazette* last year, may be useful : Route, Harwich and Hook of Holland ; fare for cycle, 7s. 6d. each way, and duty-free into Holland. Roads mostly excellent. Motor nuisance infinitesimal compared to what it is with us ; dust trouble only slight, and thorn trouble non-existent. The great main highways are surfaced with hard bricks, placed edgewise, affording quite good running ; they are non-slipping, soon dry after rain, non-puncturing, not too flat, and are picturesque with miles of fine avenues, one, the Midachter Allee, between Arnhem and Zutphen, with immensely tall beeches reputed the most impressive in Europe. All main roads have capital smooth side-paths for cyclists only. Secondary roads (heavy motors mostly forbidden) are often splendid going both for the tourist and the speedman. Hotel and living prices are slightly higher than in England. Restaurants in towns and villages good, the latter with gardens and fine views, particularly attractive to cyclists. Food and cuisine mostly good, often excellent. Alcoholic refresh-

ment obtainable any time, of course including Sundays all day.
The scenery is more attractive in the east, *e.g.*, around Arnhem and Nymwegen, and the Dutch landscape everywhere has a
fascination all its own. French is spoken in hotels, English not
much used. Failing Dutch, German is the most useful. Sign-
posts are so numerous and thorough that a good map reader
can find his way easily without inquiry. The touring club is the
A.N.W.B. (Algemeene Nederlandsche Wielrijders' Bond), 590,
Keizersgracht, Amsterdam, 8s. per year, and it supplies to
members hotel, etc., handbook, gazette, and excellent district
maps of three miles to the inch scale at 8d. per section.

PART THREE.

RESTHOUSE DIRECTORY.

FOREWORDS.—This list, though it contains nearly 3,000
addresses, is only a beginning. It is based, primarily, on the
list which I have myself carefully kept during 30 years of road-
travel. The recommendations of my readers in *The Daily News*
—all filed and often checked—have materially extended it, and
they can quickly double it if they like. Whenever and wherever
you pay for a night's lodging and can recommend the house
for reasonable charges, cleanliness and civility, send the bill
to me with any comment you may care to add.

My list was nearly ready for publication in 1914, and was
shelved for obvious reasons. A great deal of revision has been
done, and any remaining inaccuracies should disappear after the
first year of use. Changes are constantly taking place for either
better or worse.

PRICE BASIS.—I have tried to exclude from this list any
address where the charge for bed and breakfast exceeds 6s. 6d.
The average charge in it is perhaps 5s. 6d. in England, Wales,
and Ireland, and 6s. in Scotland. After all, charges for meals
depend on what you want. The Scottish Highlands are dearer
than the Lowlands, and resthouses much less frequent. In the
Highlands, too, prices are often advanced in July and August.
It is a country where the camping tourist scores heavily. The
case of Ireland has altered curiously, for prices have hardly
risen since 1914, and it is now much more within the average
cyclist's means than formerly. The average charge for bed
and breakfast at the Irish hotels in my list is not more than 6s.

TRUST HOUSES, ETC.—As far as I know, there is not an
hotel in my list holding the appointment of the Royal Automobile Club, and very few of the Automobile Association.

I have included nearly all the houses run by the People's
Refreshment House Association (which are *not* "Trust
Houses"), and they are indicated in the list by the addition
of the sign P.R.H.A. These inns are in the hands of managers

who are paid a fixed salary, with a commission on the sale of all articles except alcoholic liquors, so that the managers have a pecuniary interest in the *bona-fide* traveller who wants meals or bed. Complaints or suggestions should be addressed to the Association at 193, Regent Street, London, W. 1.

OMITTED.—I have also omitted some houses, both licensed and unlicensed, which otherwise complied with our conditions, because they are " not open on Sundays "; and some whose prices would have come within our range but for the fatal and unjustifiable " Attendance 1s."

NO " SPECIAL TERMS."—No house in this list has paid, or will be allowed to pay, for inclusion. There is no arrangement, and there will not be, for discounts or special terms.

COMMERCIAL TEMPERANCE HOTELS.—I have included a great many temperance hotels of the " commercial " class, mainly found in the larger towns. They nearly always provide excellent accommodation, for no one knows better than the " commercial " where one eats well and sleeps well. It is true that at some of these houses, where accommodation is limited, and there is no " coffee-room " in addition to the " commercial " room, cyclists and other roadfarers are not anxiously sought. The custom of the commercial traveller is so much more regular and " all the year round " than that of the casual and seasonable wayfarer that the former is much more worth catering for. Just occasionally, too, it happens that the presence of " outsiders " in the Commercial Room is not welcomed by the old stagers, but a courteous word may always be relied on to put that right.

And it must be remembered that this class of resthouse is practically empty on Saturday and Sunday and on public holidays, and then becomes a most desirable place for the tourist. One proprietor told me last summer that he wanted his rooms full *every* day in the week, or it was difficult to make the place pay; and it was full of commercials from Monday to Friday.

BOARDING-HOUSES, Etc.—Of boarding-houses and farmhouses there are not many in the following list. Generally speaking, such places do not want one-night visitors. They lay themselves out for parties by the week or longer. (One-night travellers mean frequent changes of sheets—or should do.) The boarding-houses in this list either cater for the one-night traveller (or did so), or they are included because insufficient accommodation happens to be known to me otherwise in the place concerned. From the middle of July to the middle of September it is almost hopeless for the casual wayfarer to seek a night's lodging at farmhouses and seaside boarding-houses in the Lake District, North Wales, the South-West, the Derbyshire Peak country, the Yorkshire Dales, etc.

USING THE LIST.—The cyclist, with a journey in prospect, either point to point straightaway, or a roundabout tour, such

as one of the " potted tours " herein, should look up his route
on a good map, and compare the place-names on that route
with this list; thus he can plan it out in stages.

The addresses given are of widely different classes. When
two or more addresses are given for the same place, the wise
tourist will have a look at them all, and make his choice according to their appearance and the feel of his pocket. The order
in which they appear is not intended to suggest any other
precedence.

" 4½ N.W. BRIGHTON."—After most of the place-names
some details are given in brackets similar to the above heading.
Their purpose is to identify the places concerned on the map
and sometimes to distinguish them from others of the same
name. It should be carefully noted that " Eynsham 7 N.W.
Oxford " means that Eynsham is 7 miles north-west *from*
Oxford. It does *not* mean that Oxford is 7 miles to the north-
west of Eynsham. There are other uses for these notes in
brackets. Where I have no knowledge of a house suitable for
the list in a place where such is likely to be wanted, you are
sometimes told to " See so-and-so," upon reference to which
you will find a house or houses at other places within easy
cycling reach. I have made this provision in the case of a good
many seaside resorts, for it is often more convenient, comfortable, and economical to put up within a short ride of such places
than inside them.

SYMBOLS.—T. stands for a temperance hotel. R. stands
for all restaurants, cafés, bakeries, dairies, refreshment-rooms,
tea-gardens, etc., with bedrooms to let. There is often no difference, in fact, between T. and R. When no letter follows a
name (*e.g.*, Red Lion, Railway, Mannering Arms) a licensed
house is indicated; but the letter H. for hotel is sometimes
added where necessary for clearness. The letters P.H. are
used in the case of houses called Private Hotels, though I have
not discovered how they differ from other unlicensed resthouses. B.H. stands for a boarding house.

Places named after saints—St. Albans, St. Ives, etc.—will be
found altogether under St., not under Sa, nor under the various
Christian names.

England, Scotland, and Wales are together in the first list.
The second list consists of Ireland only.

MODEST MOTORISTS.—Such, I am certain, will find this
list useful. In the matter of shelter for motor-cycle or car, most
country inns will be found well enough provided. But T.'s and
R.'s are different. In these cases the motorist should choose
his house, deposit his passengers and bags, and inquire for the
nearest garage. If the cost of this is added to the bill at any
house on this list, it will still be a smaller total than he would
pay at the R.A.C. house, where the " garage " would also be an
extra as often as not.

GREAT BRITAIN.

ABBOTS BROMLEY (Staffs).—Bagot's Arms; Crown. See Hoar Cross.

ABERAYRON (15 S.W. Aberystwyth). — Monachdy Arms; Victoria.

ABERDARON (Carnarv.).—Ty Newydd.

ABERDEEN. — Urquhart's T., Regent's Quay; Aston H., 160, Union St.

ABERDOVEY.—Gwalia T.

ABERFELDY (Perth).—Crown T.; Breadalbane Arms.

ABERFORD (W. Yorks).—Swan.

ABERFOYLE (Perth).—McKellar's T.

ABERGAVENNY.—Victoria T., High St.; Swan.

ABERGELE.—Liverpool House; Jones' Metropole R.; Bee.

ABERYSTWYTH.—Gwalia T., North Parade; Alexandra T., opp. Station; Central T., Terrace Rd.; Skinners' Arms; Samuel's Brynceinion B.H., Waenfawr; and at Llanbadarn, 1m. E., Black Lion.

ABINGDON (6 S. Oxford).—T., 57, East St.; Plough; Midwinter's R.

ABINGTON, GREAT (Camb.).—Three Tuns.

ACCRINGTON. — Kendall's T., 163, Blackburn Rd.

ACTON BURNELL (8 S.E. Shrewsbury). — McDonell's B.H.

ADDERBURY (3½ S. Banbury).—Lane's Twyford R.

ADDLESTONE (2 S.E. Chertsey).—Rose T.

AINTHORPE (N. Yorks, 9 S.E. Guisboro').—Fox and Hounds.

AIRTON (W. Yorks, 5½ S.E. Settle).—Manor House.

ALCESTER (Warw.).—See Wixford.

ALDBOROUGH or ALDE-BURGH (Suff.).—Cross; R., 166, High St.

ALDBOURNE (6 N.E. Marlbro').—Crown; Mrs. Orchard, Church St.

ALDERMASTON (9 S.W. Reading).—Mrs. Arlott, Hull Cottage; Hind's Head, P.R.H.A. See Brimpton.

ALDERSHOT. — Oxford House T., Arthur St.; Carr's T., Station Rd.

ALDSWORTH (Glos, 6 S.W. Burford).—Sherbourne Arms.

ALEXTON (Leic., 3 W. Uppingham).—Wilton Arms.

ALFORD (Lincs).—Kew's T.; White Horse.

ALFORD (Aberdeen). — Coutts' T.

ALFRISTON (Sussex).—Market Cross H.

ALLENDALE (13 S.W. Hexham).—Forster's T.; Dale H.; King's Head.

ALLENHEADS (Northum.).—The H.

ALLENSMORE (5 S.W. Hereford, nr. Tram Inn Station).—Three Horseshoes P.R.H.A.

ALMONDSBURY (8 N. Bristol).—Swan.

ALNWICK.—Station T.; Tower T.; Nag's Head.

ALRESFORD (Hants). — See Four Marks and Ropley.

ALREWAS (5 N.E. Lichfield).—George and Dragon.

ALSOP (Derby, 6 N. Ashbourne).—New Inn, Tissington.

ALSTON (Cumb.). — King's Arms; Angel; Sun T.; Jackson's Albert House R.

ALTON (Hants).—Welcome T.; Crown. See Chawton and Holybourne.

ALVELEY (6 N.W. Kidderminster).—The Yews B.H., Turley Green.

AMBERLEY (Sussex).—Houghton Bridge H.

AMBLESIDE. — County T., Waterhead; Smallwood T.; Dixon's T.; Wansfell Tower P.H.; Robinson's T., Lake Rd.; Garside's T. and Myrtle Villa B.H., Compston Rd.

AMERSHAM COMMON (Bucks, Amersham 1½).—Tomlin's R., The Beeches.

AMESBURY (Wilts). — Phœnix T.; New Inn; Cockle's R.

AMLWCH (Anglesey). — Mona T., The Square.

AMMANFORD (Carmarth.).— Central T.

AMPTHILL (7 S.W. Bedford).— White Hart.

ANDOVER (Hants). — Blake's T.; Town Station T.; Aubrey's R.

ANNAN (Dumf.).—Maclean's T.

ANSDELL (1½ W. Lytham).— Dixon's R.

ANSTEY, EAST (Som., 4 S.W. Dulverton).—Froude Arms.

ANSTRUTHER EASTER (Fife). Commercial.

APETHORPE (N'hants, 5 S.W. Wansford). — King's Head, P.R.H.A.

APPLEBY. — Eden T.; Croft House B.H.

APPLECROSS (Ross and Cromarty). — McRae's T., Shore St.

APPLEDORE (3 N. Bideford).— Smallridge's B.H.

APPLETREEWICK (Wharfedale).—New Inn.

ARDLEIGH (4½ N.E. Colchester).—King's Head.

ARMATHWAITE (9 S.E. Carlisle).—Red Lion.

ARNCLIFFE (W. Yorks, Littondale). — Falcon; Beckwith's B.H.

ARRINGTON (Camb., 7 N. Royston).—Hardwick Arms.

ARROCHAR (Dumbart.).—Henderson's T.

ARUNDEL. — Wheatsheaf. See Walberton and Slindon.

ASCOT.—See Camberley.

ASCOT HEATH (6¼ S.W. Windsor). — Houlton's B.H., School Hill.

ASHBOURNE (Derby).— Barnes's R., Church St.; White Lion; Station H. See Mappleton.

ASHBURTON (Devon). — London H., West St.; Stancombe's T.

ASHBURY (Berks, 5 N.W. Lambourn). — Rose and Crown P.R.H.A.

ASHBY - DE - LA - ZOUCH.— Smith's R, 90, Market St.; Midland.

ASHCOTT (3 S.W. Glastonbury).—Piper's Inn T.; Albion Commercial.

ASHFORD (Derbys). — Oliver's B.H.

ASHFORD (Kent).—Fernley T.; and at Gt. Chart, 2 S.W., Swan.

ASHLEY HEATH (Staffs, 4 E.N.E. Mkt. Drayton).—Loggerheads.

ASHTON (Devon, 4 N. Chudleigh).—Manor Inn, P.R.H.A.

ASHURST (New Forest, 3 N.E. Lyndhurst).—Temp. H.

ASKRIGG (Wensleydale).—Commercial T.

ASPATRIA (Cumb.). — Waverley T., King St.

ASTON-BY-STONE (Staffs, 1½ S.E. Stone).—Crown.

ASTON CLINTON (3½ S.E. Aylesbury).—Swan T.

ASTON - ON - CLUN (Salop).— See Purslow.

ATHERSTONE (Warw.).—Central R., 94, Long St.; White Hart.

ATTLEBOROUGH (16 S.W. Norwich).—Angel.

AUCHENCAIRN (7½ S. Castle Douglas).—Auchencairn Arms.

AUDLEY (Staffs, 8 N.W. Newcastle).—Boughey Arms.

AVEBURY (Wilts).—Perry's R.

AVIEMORE (Inverness).— McLauchlan's T.

AVON (Hants, 4½ S. Ringwood).
—New Queen P.R.H.A.

AVONMOUTH (Glos). — Miles
Arms P.R.H.A.

AVONWICK (Devon, 2 S.
Brent).—Avon Inn P.R.H.A.

AXBRIDGE (Som.). — George.
See Cross.

AXMINSTER (Devon).—Samp-
son's T.; McLennan's Lynch
Villa B.H. See Hawkchurch.

AYLESBURY.—Vale T.; Grey-
hound; Horse and Jockey;
Goodridge's T.; Red Lion;
and at Hartwell, 2 S.W., Bugle
Horn.

AYLESFORD (3½ N.W. Maid-
stone).—Goddard's B.H., Rose-
cott.

AYLSHAM (Norf.).—Black Boy;
Dog. See Blickling.

AYNHO (6 S.E. Banbury).—
Cartwright Arms.

AYOT ST. PETER (Herts, 2
S.W. Welwyn).—Red Lion.

AYTON, EAST (4 S.W. Scar-
boro').—White Swan.

AYTON, GREAT (N. Yorks, 3
N.E. Stokesley). — Hodgson's
B.H., Stanley Grange.

BABRAHAM (6½ S.E. Cam-
bridge).—George.

BAGSHOT.—King's Arms.

BAINBRIDGE (Wensleydale).—
Preston's T.

BAKEWELL (Derby). — Castle
and Commercial. See Gt.
Longstone and Stoney Middleton and Youlgrave and Ashford.

BALA (N. Wales).—Bull Bach
T.; Blue Lion T.; Tegid T.;
Ship.

BALLACHULISH.—5 S. Duror
H.; 6 E. Glencoe H.

BALLANTRAE (Ayr).—Royal.

BALLASALLA (I.O.M.).—Cor-
rin's B.H., Newark Villa.

BALLATER (Aberdeen). — Far-
quharson's T.

BALLOCH (Loch Lomond).—
Tullichewan. See Gartocharn.

BAMPTON (Devon).—Gibbings'
T.

BANBURY (Oxon).—Blue Bird
T.; Spencer's T., Market Pl.

BANFF.—Crown T., Old Mar-
ket Pl.

BANGOR (Carnarv.). — Victoria
T., High St.; Rowlands T., nr.
Station; Railway.

BANGOR - ON - DEE (5 S.E.
Wrexham).—Red Lion.

BARDON MILL (Northum.).—
Fox and Hounds.

BARMOUTH (N. Wales).—Mid-
land T.; Richmond T.;
Morris's St. Anne's R.;
Roberts Ripon House B.H.

BARNARD CASTLE. — Robin-
son's T., nr. Station; Montalbo
T.; Three Horseshoes.

BARNET (11 N. London).—See
Gannick Corner, Potter's Bar,
Shenley, and South Mimms.

BARNSLEY (S. Yorks).—Tate's
T., Regent St. South; Commercial T., Market Pl.

BARNSTAPLE. — Central T.,
High St.; Massey T. and
Richmond T., Boutport St.;
Waverley T., Ivy St.; Junc-
tion T.; Broom's R., High St.

BARNTON (Ches., 2 N.W.
Northwich).—Red Lion.

BARNWELL (Northants, 2½ S.
Oundle).—Montague Arms.

BARROW - IN - FURNESS.—
Waverley T., nr. Station; Trevelyan.

BARTON - ON - HUMBER.—
George.

BARTON STACEY (Hants, 5
S.E. Andover).—Plough.

BASILDON (Berks, 2 S.E.
Streatley).—Crown P.R.H.A.

BASINGSTOKE. — Carlton T.,
Brook St.; Wheatsheaf; Sta-
tion; Andrew's Cosy R., Wote
St.

BATH.—Ralph's T., opp. Mid.
Station; Smith's T., opp. Pos-
tal Sorting Office; Victoria T.,
Southgate St.; Argyll T., opp.
G.W. Station; Full Moon,

Southgate St.; and at Batheaston, White Hart.

BATTLE (Suss.). — Chequers; Bailey's R. See Robertsbridge and Sedlescombe.

BAWTRY (9 S.E. Doncaster).— Barton's Manor House B.H. See Drakeholes.

BAYTON (Worc., 2½ S.E. Cleo Mortimer). — Wheatsheaf P.R.H.A.

BEACONSFIELD (Bucks).— White Horse.

BEAL (Northum. coast, opp. Holy Isle).—Plough P.R.H.A.

BEAMINSTER (6 N. Bridport). —White Hart. See Broadwinsor.

BEAUMARIS (Anglesey).— Westgate B.H., 52, Castle St.; Pier R., Castle St.

BECCLES (Suff.).—Gale's T.

BECKERMET (Cumb., 3 S. Egremont).—White Mare.

BECKINGTON (3 N.E. Frome). —Woolpack. See Standerwick.

BEDALE (N. Yorks).—Black Swan.

BEDDGELERT (N. Wales).— Plas Colwyn T.; Arthur's T.; Evans' R., Llewellyn Cottage; Mrs. Jones,, Erw Fair; Mrs. Powell, Glan Afon; Mrs. Jones, School House; Prince Llewellyn H.

BEDFORD.—Silver Grill R., 32, High St.; several T.'s by Midland Station.

BELBROUGHTON.— (Worc., 5 N.W. Bromsgrove).—Bell, P.R.H.A.

BELFORD (Northum).—Black Swan; Blue Bell.

BELLINGHAM (Northum).— Railway.

BELPER.— (Derby). — Jackson's R., Matlock Rd. See Holbrook.

BELVOIR (7 S.W. Grantham). —Peacock P.R.H.A.

BENEFIELD, UPPER (3 W. Oundle). — Wheatsheaf P.R.H.A.

BENSON (Oxon., 2 N.E. Wallingford).—T., Sheep St.

BENTHAM, LOW (W. Yorks). —Leeming's T.

BERE REGIS (Dorset).—Lane's B.H., North St.; Drax Arms.

BERKELEY (Bristol - Gloster Rd.).—Bennett's B.H., Old Vicarage; Prince of Wales, opp. Berkeley Rd. Station. See Woodford.

BERKHAMSTED, GREAT (W. Herts).—T., Castle St.; Swan.

BERKHAMSTED, LITTLE (4½ S.W. Hertford).—Five Horseshoes.

BERWICK - ON - TWEED.— Wood's T.; Avenue T.

BETHERSDEN (Kent, 5½ W. Ashford).—Bull.

BETHESDA (N. Wales).— Elias' Imperial T.

BETTWS - Y - COED.— Hughes's Tan-lan T.; Phillips' Fairhaven B.H.; Ancaster H.; Conway Falls T.

BEVERLEY (E. Yorks).— King's Head.

BEWDLEY (Worc.).—Royal.

BEXHILL (Suss.).—Star T., Western Rd.

BICESTER (Oxon.). — Berridge's R.; Mrs. Hadland, Ivy House, 32, North St.

BICTON (2½ N.W. Shrewsbury). —Four Crosses P.R.H.A.; Proctor's B.H.

BIDBOROUGH (2 S.W. Tonbridge).—Hare and Hounds.

BIDDULPH (4 S.E. Congleton). —Biddulph Arms, P.R.H.A.

BIDEFORD. — Kingsley T.; North Devon T.; Sanders' T., Buttgarden St.

BIDFORD-ON-AVON (Warw). —Cranhill Farm, Stratford Rd.

BIGGAR (Lanark). — Gunn's H.; Clydesdale.

BIGGLESWADE (Beds).— Royal Oak; Knott's R.

BIGRIGG (Cumb., 3 S.E. Whitehaven).—Brown Cow.

BILLESDON (8½ S.E. Leicester).—Queen's Head; White Hart.

BILLINGHAY (8½ N.E. Slea-ford).—Coach and Horses.

BILLINGSHURST (Suss.).—King's Arms.

BILSDALE (Valley, N.E. Yorks).—Buck at Chop Gate.

BIRMINGHAM. — Empire R., Smallbrook St.; Waverley T., corner High St. and Albert St.; Beaufort H., 21, Beaufort Rd., Fiveways; Carfax T., 499, Coventry Rd., Small Heath.

BISHOP AUCKLAND.—Shaw's T., Market Pl.

BISHOPS CAUNDLE (Dors., 5 S.E. Sherborne).—White Hart P.R.H.A.

BISHOPS STORTFORD.—Wilkins T., Moor St.; Albert T., South St.

BISHOPS WALTHAM (9½ S.E. Winchester).— Bungalow R., nr. Station.

BISPHAM (3 N. Blackpool).—Dawson's Ivy R.

BLABY (5 S. Leicester). — Dog and Gun.

BLACKBURN (Lancs). — Alma T., Bathurst St.; Mount T.

BLACKPOOL.—Best's T., Upper Queen St.; St. Alma T., 29, Central Parade; Victoria R., Waterloo Rd.; Myrtle, May Bell Avenue.

BLAENAU FESTINIOG.—Griffin T.; Gwalia T.

BLAIRGOWRIE (Perth).—Blairgowrie and Rattray T. See Bridge of Cally.

BLAKENEY (Forest of Dean).—King's Head; Mrs. Halford, Cherry Tree House, Viney Hill.

BLAKENEY (Norf., 5½ N.W. Holt).—White Horse.

BLANDFORD (Dorset).—King's Arms; Cullen's Cabin R.

BLEDLOW (Bucks, 1½ W. P's Risbro).—Red Lion.

BLETCHLEY.—Parker's Wilberforce T.; Swan.

BLICKLING (Norf., 1½ N.W. Aylsham). — Bucks Arms P.R.H.A.

BLOXHAM (3½ S.W. Banbury).—Red Lion.

BLYTH (Notts, 7 N.E. Worksop).—Angel; Ancliff's B.H.

BLYTHBURGH (Suff., 3½ W. Southwold). — Heath's Fair View B.H.

BOCKING (Essex, 1 N.E. Braintree).—King's Head.

BODMIN.—George's T.

BOGNOR.—Wall's R., Waterloo Sq.; Norfolk House B.H., Norfolk Sq.

BOLTON (Lancs). — Hamer's T.; Pack Horse.

BOLVENTOR (Corn., Bodmin Moor).—Jamaica Inn.

BONAR BRIDGE (Sutherland).—Mrs. Main, Bay View House.

BOOT (Cumb., 7 N.E. Raven-glass).—Sin's T.; Woolpack.

BORGUE (6 S.W. Kirkcud-bright).—Hutchinson's R.

BOROUGHBRIDGE (Som., 5 N.W. Langport).—King Alfred.

BOROUGHBRIDGE (W. Yorks).—T. H.; Black Bull; Anchor.

BOSCASTLE (Corn.).—Providence House; Petherick's B.H.; Atlantic T.

BOSHAM STATION (3 W. Chichester).—Holdom's B.H., Wildwood Corner.

BOSTON (Lincs). — Loveley's Albion T., West St.; Station.

BOSTON SPA (Yorks).—Crowden's Springfield B.H.

BOTLEY (Hants).—See Shedfield.

BOULMER (Northum., 5 E. Alnwick).—Fishing Boat.

BOURN (Lincs, 9 W. Spalding).—Angel; Six Bells; Marquis of Granby. See Edenham.

BOURNEMOUTH. — Tregonwell Arms T., Commercial

Rd.; Albany T., opp. Central Station; Nova R., Southbourne; Mayfair P.H., Upper Terrace Rd.

BOURTON-ON-THE-WATER (Glos.). — Mr. Hambidge, Gorse Dene, Rissington Rd.; Railway Inn.

BOVINGDON (Herts, 3 S.E. Berkhamsted).—Harrison's R., High St.

BOW (Devon, 8 W. Crediton).— White Hart.

BOWES (N. Yorks).—Unicorn.

BOXMOOR (Herts).—Day's R., Homeleigh, Green Lane.

BRACKLEY (7 N.W. Buckingham).—Tibbett's T.; Andrews' R.

BRACKNELL (Berks, 4 E. Wokingham). — Horse and Groom.

BRADFORD. — Metropole T., Forster Sq.; Mikado T., Godwin St.

BRADFORD - ON - AVON (Wilts).—Castle.

BRADWORTHY (12 S.W. Bideford).—Bradworthy H.

BRAEMAR (Aberdeen). — McHardy's B.H.

BRAILES (4 S.E. Shipston-onStour).—George.

BRAILSFORD (6 N.W. Derby). —Rose and Crown.

BRAINTREE (Essex). — Nag's Head. See Bocking.

BRAITHWAITE (2½ W. Keswick).—Royal Oak.

BRAMPTON (11 N.E. Carlisle). —Howard Arms T.; Shepherd's R.

BRANDIS CORNER (Devon, 5 E. Holsworthy). — Bickford Arms P.R.H.A.

BRANDON (5 E.S.E. Coventry).—Royal Oak, P.R.H.A.

BRANDON (Suff., 7 N.W. Thetford).—White Hart.

BRATTON (Wilts, 4 N.E. Westbury).—Belbin's R.

BRATTON FLEMING (7 N.E. Barnstaple).—White Hart.

BRAUNTON (5½ N.W. Barnstaple).—Gould's P.H.

BRAYWICK (1 S. Maidenhead). —Bartram's R.

BRECHIN (Forfar).—Crown.

BRECON.—Green Dragon T.; New Lion.

BRENDON (3½ E. Lynmouth). —Rockford.

BRENT KNOLL (Som., 2 N.E. Highbridge).—Fox and Goose.

BREWOOD (8½ S. Stafford).— Lion; Swan.

BRIDGE OF CALLY (4½ N.W. Blairgowrie).—Stalker's T.

BRIDGE OF ORCHY (12 N.E. Dalmally). — Inveroran T.; Kingshouse T.

BRIDGE OF URR (4 N. Castle Douglas).—T.H.

BRIDGE TRAFFORD (4½ N.E. Chester).—Nag's Head.

BRIDGNORTH (Salop).—Commercial H.: Collett's T.; Hearn's B.H.. Salop St.; Owen's R., Cann Hall.

BRIDGWATER (Som.). — Albany T.; Admiral Blake T.; White Hart, nr. station.

BRIDLINGTON. — Greening's T., 11, Quay Rd. See Reighton and Rudston.

BRIDPORT (Dors.).—Hodder's T.

BRIGG (Lincs).—Woolpack.

BRIGHTLINGSEA (10 S.E. Colchester). — Freemason's Arms; Fields B.H., 1, New St.

BRIGHTON.—Snelling's T., 40, Clifton St.; Gordon T. and Waverley T., both Queen's Rd.; Hurst's T., Richmond Place; Crown and Anchor. See Burgess Hill and Henfield and Poynings and Hurstpierpoint.

BRIGHTSTONE (Wight).— New Inn.

BRILL (Bucks, 7 N.W. Thame). Sun; Rose and Crown.

BRIMPTON (Berks, 2 W. Aldermaston).—Pine Apple.

BRISTOL.—Cathedral T., College Green; Smart's T., 220,

York Rd.; Don Cossack T., next G.P.O. Farther out, Swain's T., 350, Stapleton Rd., Eastville.

BRISTOL - GLOUCESTER ROAD.—See Stone and Berkeley.

BRIXHAM (S. Devon).— Doidge's T.; Waterman; Potter's, Parkham Villa B.H.

BRIXWORTH (7½ N. Northampton).—George.

BROADCLYST. (5 N.E. Exeter).—Red Lion P.R.H.A.

BROADHEMBURY (5¼ N.W. Honiton).—Red Lion P.R.H.A.

BROADWATER (1 N. Godalming on Guildford Rd.).— Broadwater T.

BROADWAY (Worc., 5 S.E. Evesham).—Swan; Mrs. King, St. Anthony, The Green.

BROADWINSOR (Dors., 3 N.W. Beaminster).—George.

BROCKENHURST (New Forest). — Cole's Watersgreen B.H.; Dear's R.

BROCKTON (Salop, 3 S.W. Shifnal).—Farmer's B.H.

BROMHAM (Wilts, 3½ N.W. Devizes).—Bell; Greyhound; both P.R.H.A.

BROMPTON (7 S.W. Scarbro). —Walker's B.H., Sunny Lodge.

BROMSGROVE (Worc.).—Central R., High St. See Belbroughton.

BROMYARD (Heref.).— Browne's T.; Falcon.

BROOK (New Forest, 1 W. Cadnam). — Bell, P.R.H.A.; Day's B.H.

BROUGH (Weston).—George; and at Stainmore, 3 S.E. Punch Bowl.

BROUGHTON-IN-FURNESS. —Old King's Head; Myer's R. and Mrs. Todd's B.H., both The Square. See Ulpha.

BROUGHTON (Peebles, 7 S. Broughton, 16 N. Moffat).— Crook Inn.

BUCKIE (Banff).—Reaper's T.

BUCKINGHAM.—Grand Junction; Swan and Castle; Railway Tavern; Mrs. Nobes, Masonic House, High St. See Finmere Station.

BUDE (Cornw.). — Banbury's Erdiston B.H.; Norfolk T.; Carrier's Arms; Ash, confectioner. See Stratton.

BUDLEIGH, EAST (Devon, 5 S.W. Sidmouth).—Feathers.

BUILTH (Upper Wye Valley).— Brynstone T.; Crown; Caeffynnon T.; Jones' T., High St.

BUNGAY (Suff.).—King's Head.

BURFORD (Oxon.).—Preston's B.H., High St.; also Mrs. Smith, next door; Lamb; Swan.

BURGESS HILL (9 N. Brighton).—Central T., Station Rd.

BURGHCLERE (Hants, 6½ N. Whitchurch). — Carnarvon Arms.

BURGHILL (3½ N.W. Hereford).—Lewis's Farm, The New House.

BURLESCOMBE (Devon, 4 N.E. Tiverton).—Lamb.

BURNHAM (Som., 7½ N. Bridgwater).—Lifeboat T.; Belmont T.

BURNHAM BEECHES (Bucks). —See Farnham Common.

BURNHAM-ON-CROUCH (Essex).—Railway.

BURNLEY (Lancs).—Manchester T.

BURNSALL (Wharfedale).— Bland's B.H., Manor House; Red Lion.

BURTON JOYCE (5 N.E. Nottingham).—Richardson's B.H. Rose Cott.

BURTON LEONARD (4 S.E. Ripon).—Royal Oak.

BURTON-ON-TRENT. — See Rolleston.

BURWARTON (9½ S.W. Bridgnorth). — Boyne Arms, P.R.H.A.

BURY (Lancs).—Howard T., Knowsley St.

BURY ST. EDMUNDS.—

Drake's Risbygate T.; Bell T.; Barlow's T.; Everard's H.

BUTLEIGH (Som., 4 S.E. Glastonbury).—Rose and Portcullis P.R.H.A.

BUTTINGTON (Montg., 2½ N.E. Welshpool).—Unicorn.

BUXTON. — Pendennis B.H., Devonshire Rd.; Waverley T.

BYLAND ABBEY (N. Yorks, 1½ N.E. Coxwold).—Abbey Inn; Mrs. Richardson, Mowbray House.

CADNAM (New Forest, 4 N. Lyndhurst). — C o a c h   a n d Horses. See Brook.

CAERPHILLY (7 N. Cardiff).— Clive Arms.

CAERSWS (Montg., 5½ N.W. Newton).—Buck's T.

CALDER BRIDGE (Cumb., 4 S.E. Egremont). — Stanley Arms.

CALLANDER (Perth).—Achray T.; Waverley T.

CALLINGTON (11 S. Launceston).—McColm's T.; Chubb's T.

CALNE (Wilts). — Bristow's P.H. See Sandy Lane and Derry Hill.

CALVERHALL, or Corra (Salop, 4½ S.E. Whitchurch).—Old Jack P.R.H.A.

CAMBERLEY (Surrey, 7 S.W. Ascot).—Wayside T., London Rd.

CAMBORNE (Corn.).—Perry's T., Commercial St.

CAMBRIDGE.—Livingstone T., nr. G.P.O.; Bird Bolt T., Hills Rd.; Central T., Market Hill; Tapling's B.H., 1, Park Parade.

CAMBRIDGE (Glos., 4 N.W. Dursley).—Baker's R., Nelson Cott.

CAMELFORD (C o r n w.).— Hooper's T.; Bridge T. See Hallworthy.

CANNOCK (Staffs).—Crown.

CANNOCK CHASE. — Lamb and Flag, Little Haywood; Clifford Arms, Gt. Haywood.

CANTERBURY.—Nash's Sunnyside T.; Westgate T.; Simkin's Cathedral R.; Fleece, The Parade; Falstaff, outside West Gate; Baker's T., St. George's St.

CAPEL (Surrey, 6 S. Dorking). —Wildsmith's B.H.; King's Head.

CAPEL CURIG (N. Wales).— Bryntyrch; Dolgam P.H.

CARDIFF.—Tresillian T. and Griffiths' T., both Caroline St.; Dumfries T.; Royal Clarence T., Tudor Rd.

CARDIGAN.—Grosvenor T.

CARISBROOKE (I.O.W.).— Smith's B.H., Mt. Olivet; Red Lion.

CARLISLE.—Chisham's T. and County T., both Botchergate.

CARLOPS (15 S.W. Edinburgh). —McGill's T.

CARLTON (Coverdale, 5 S.W. Middleham.—Foresters' Arms.

CARMARTHEN.—Jeremy's T., St. Peter St.

CARNARVON. — Station T.; Sportsman; King's Gate R., Castle Ditch; Castle T.; Mona, High St.; and at Cae-athraw, 1½ S.E., Bryngwana Inn.

CARNO (Montg., 11 N.W. Newtown).—Aleppo Merchant.

CARSTAIRS (4 E. Lanark).— Junction.

CARSTHORN (Galloway, 4½ S.E. New Abbey).—Steamboat.

CARTMEL (Furness, 6 E. Ulverston).—Ayers' R.

CASTLE ACRE (Norf., 4 N.W. Swaffham).—Ostrich.

CASTLE CARY (Som.).— George. See Ditcheat.

CASTLE COMBE (Wilts, 5½ N.W. Chippenham). — Jeffs' Bridge R.

CASTLE DONINGTON (Leic.). —Moira Arms.

CASTLE DOUGLAS (Kirkcud.). —Victoria T.

CASTLEMORTON (6 S.E. Malvern).—Feathers.

CASTLE RISING (4 N.E. King's Lynn).—Black Horse.

C A S T L E T O N (Derby).—Wright's R.; Mrs. Hall, Fern Cottage; Castle.

CATFIELD (Norf. Broads, 2½ S.E. Stalham).—Neal's B.H., Staith House; Clow, Lillington House.

CAUTLEY BECK (4 N.E., Sedbergh).—Cross Keys.

CAVENDISH (Suff., 7½ N.W. Sudbury).—Old Manor House B.H.

CEMAES BAY (Anglesey).—Vigour H.

CEMMES (Montg., 6 N.E. Machynlleth).—Penrhos Arms.

CEMMES ROAD (1½ S.W. preceding).—Dovey Valley H.

CERNE ABBAS (Dorset).—Elephant and Castle; Earwaker's R.

CHADDESLEY CORBETT (4½ S.E. Kidderminster).—Talbot; Central R.

CHAGFORD (Dartmoor).—Globe.

CHALE (I.O.W., 5¼ W. Ventnor).—Blackgang Chine H.

CHALFONT ST. GILES (Bucks).—Stacey's R.

CHALFONT ST. PETER (Bucks).—Greyhound.

CHAPEL-EN-LE-FRITH (Derby).—Royal Oak; Jolly Carter. See Cockyard.

CHARD (Som.).—Crown.

CHARING (Kent, 5½ N.W. Ashford).—Swan; King's Head; Holdstock's R.

CHARLWOOD (6 S. Reigate).—Bell's R.

CHATHAM.— Central T., Railway St.

CHAWTON (Hants, 1 S. Alton).—Grey Friar P.R.H.A.

CHEADLE (3 S.W. Stockport).—George and Dragon.

CHEDDAR (Som.). — Lewis's T.; West's Dairy; Valley, Union St.; Gilling's Riverside Farm; Stephens' Rose Cottage B.H. See Wedmore.

CHELMSFORD.—Barnard's T., High St.; Old Friars T., Friars Place; Red Cow T., Broomfield Rd.; Lion and Lamb.

CHELSFIELD (Kent, 1 N. Knockholt Stn.).—Rock and Fountain.

CHELTENHAM.—Imperial T., High St.; Carr's Central T., Clarence St.; Manchester T., Clarence St.; Pierpoint T.; Criterion T., Albion St.; Moultondale B.H. Pittville Circus Rd.; and at Staverton Bridge, 3 m. on Gloucester Rd., Pheasant.

CHENIES (Bucks).—Red Lion.

CHEPSTOW (Wye Valley).—White Hart T.; Dorothy R. and B.H.

CHERTSEY (Surrey). — Vine. See Addlestone.

CHESHAM (Bucks). — Chess Vale T. See Hawridge.

CHESHUNT (Herts, 14½ N. London).—T.H.

CHESTER.—Roslyn T. and Memphis T. and Windsor T., all City Rd.; Belgrave T., Foregate St.; Old Edgar R., Lower Bridge St.

CHEWTON MENDIP (Som., 5½ N.E. Wells). — Waldegrave Arms.

CHICHESTER. — Bedford T.; Four Chestnuts. See Nutbourne.

CHILHAM (5½ S.W. Canterbury).—Woolpack.

CHILLINGTON (S. Devon, 2 W. Torcross).—Union.

CHINNOCK, EAST (4 S.W. Yeovil).—Portman Arms.

CHINNOR (3½ W. Prince's Risbro).—See Oakley.

CHIPPENHAM (Wilts, Bath Rd.). — Ruskin T., Station Hill; Waverley T.; George. See Pewsham.

CHIPPENHAM (Cam., 4½ N.E. Newmarket).—Thorp Arms.

CHIPPING CAMPDEN (9½
S.E. Evesham). — Volunteer;
Lygon Arms.

CHIPPING NORTON (Oxon.).
—Blue Boar; Fox; Crown and
Cushion.

CHIRBURY (Salop, 3 N.E.
Montgomery).—Herbert Arms.

CHOP GATE (Bilsdale, N.
Yorks).—Buck.

CHORLEY (Lancs).—Red Lion.

CHUDLEIGH (10 S.W. Exeter).
—Clifford Arms.

CHUMLEIGH (N. Devon).—
King's Arms.

CHURCHILL (Som., 4 N. Ax-
bridge).—Churchill H.

CHURCH LAWFORD (4 N.W.
Rugby).—White Lion.

CHURCH LAWTON (5 S.W.
Congleton).—Lawton Arms.

CHURCH STRETTON (Salop).
—Sandford P.H., nr. Station;
Evans' B.H., 22, Sandford
Av.; Bucks Head.

CHURT (Surrey).—Pride of Valley.

CHWILOG (4 N.E. Pwllheli).—
Madryn Arms.

CINDERFORD (Forest of
Dean).—Old Engine; Swan.

CIRENCESTER (Glos.).—
Globe T.; Smith's Cotswold
T., West Market Place;
Viner's R., Market Place;
Swan.

CLACTON-ON-SEA. — Clifton,
Station Rd.; Castle T., nr.
pier; Victoria T., opp. Station;
Brunswick T.

CLARE (Suff., 6½ W. Long Melford).—Bear.

CLAYBROOK, GREAT (Leic.,
3½ N.W. Lutterworth).—Blue
Bell.

CLECKHEATON (W. Yorks).
—Bentley's T.

CLEETHORPES (Lincs).—Ar-
cadian T. and Dudley T., both
Alexandra Rd.; Turner's Pier
View B.H.

CLENT (Worc., 3½ S.E. Stour-
bridge). — Benwell's B.H.,
Walton Pool.

CLEOBURY MORTIMER (Sa-
lop).—King's Arms. See Bayton.

CLEVEDON (Som.). — Danes-
bury House T., nr. Station;
Bird's Atlantic R.

CLITHEROE (Lancs).—Cock-
bain's T.

CLOPHILL (Beds., 3½ E. Ampthill).—Flying Horse.

CLOTTON (Ches., 2½ N.W.
Tarporley).—Bull's Head.

CLOUGHTON (5 N.W. Scar-
bro). — Blacksmith's Arms
P.R.H.A.

CLOVELLY (N. Devon).—No.
33, No. 62, No. 74, No. 98, or
ask anywhere except at the
hotels.

CLOVELLY to Kilkhampton
Road.—West Country Inn.

CLUN (Salop).—Buffalo.

CLUNIE (Perth).—Inn.

CLYNNOGFAWR (9 S.W. Car-
narvon).—St. Benno H.

COBHAM (Surrey). — Oaktree
R.

COCKERMOUTH.—Grassmoor
T.; Fidler's T.; Apple Tree;
Waterloo.

COCKING (Suss., 2½ S. Midhurst).—Blue Bell.

COCKYARD (1 W. Chapel-en-le
Frith).—Hanging Gate.

CODICOTE (Herts, 8 S.E.
Hitchin).—Red Lion.

COGGESHALL (Essex).—
Chapel. See Feering.

COKER, EAST (2 S.W. Yeovil).
—New Inn.

COLCHESTER. — Shaftesbury
T., St. Nicholas Passage;
Peveril T. and Carlton T., both
North Hill.

COLEFORD (Forest of Dean).
—Waverley T.; King's Head;
Angel.

COLLINGHAM, SOUTH (5
N.E. Newark).—King's Head.

COLLUMPTON (Devon).—See
Cullompton.

COLNBROOK (7 W. Houns-
low).—Ostrich; Golden Cross.

COLWYN BAY.—Cartmell T.,
Station Rd.; Westminster T.

and Lewis's T., both Abergele Rd.; Metropole.

COLYFORD (E. Devon).—White Hart.

COMRIE (Perth). — Melville House; Barra House T., Drummond St.

CONGLETON (Ches.).—Bridge H.

CONINGSBY (Lincs, 7 S. Horncastle).—White Bull.

CONISTON (Lake Dist.).—Fairfield T.; Clifton Villa.

CONNEL FERRY (4½ N.E. Oban).—Burnbank T.

CONWAY (N. Wales).—Parry's Oak View T.; Manchester T.; Abram's T.

CORTON DENHAM (Som., 4 N. Sherborne).—Queen's Arms.

CORWEN (N. Wales).—Central Commercial; Eagle; Crown; Mrs. E. Peake, Woodbank.

COSHAM (4½ N. Portsmouth).—Over's T., Drayton.

COSTESSEY (4½ N.W. Norwich).—Falcon P.R.H.A.

COTEBROOK (2½ N.E. Tarporley).—Alvanley Arms.

COULSDON (5 S.W. Croydon).—Coppard's T., Smitham Bottom.

COUPAR ANGUS (Perth).—Royal.

COVENTRY.—London T., Jordan Well; Priory T., Bayley Lane; Victoria T. and Warwick T., both Warwick Row; Roslyn T., nr. Station.

COWBRIDGE (12 W. Cardiff).—Ancient Druid; Horse and Groom.

COWES (I.O.W.). — Garrett's Westbourne House T.

CRANAGE (Ches., 3½ N.E. Middlewich).—Dutton, Woodside Farm.

CRANBORNE (Dors.).—See St. Giles.

CRANBROOK (S. Kent).—Edwards' T.

CRANFIELD (8 S.W. Bedford).—Cross Keys.

CRANLEIGH, or Cranley (8 S.E. Guildford). — Onslow Arms.

CRAVEN ARMS (Salop).—Edge's T.; Thomas's T.

CRAWLEY (Suss.).—Albany T., High St.; Railway.

CREDITON (7½ N.W. Exeter).—Railway; Market House; Burden's R., 144, High St.

CREETOWN (Galloway).—Victoria T.; Barholm Arms.

CREWE (Ches.).—Greatbatch's T. and London T. and Ellis's T., all Nantwich Rd.

CREWKERNE (7 S.W. Yeovil).—Red Lion. See Haselbury.

CRICCIETH (N. Wales).—White Lion.

CRICKHOWELL (Breckn.).—Queen's T.; Cambrian Arms.

CRICKLADE (8 N.W. Swindon).—Vale, High St.

CRIEFF (Perth). — Young's Leven T., Comrie Rd.

CROMER. — Anderson's R., Hamilton Rd.; Haverhill House, Bond St.; Clarke's R.

CROOK (6 N.W. Bishop Auckland).—Wilson's R.

CROSS (Som., 1 W. Axbridge).—White Hart; Moorlands R.

CROSS-IN-HAND (Suss., 6 N.E. Uckfield).—Mrs. Jarvis, Fern Villa.

CROWLAND (8 N.E. Peterbro).—George.

CROXDALE (3 S. Durham).—Bridge P.R.H.A.

CROXTON (Camb., 4 E. St. Neots).—Spread Eagle.

CULLEN (Banff). — Seafield Arms.

CULLOMPTON (12½ N.E. Exeter).—White Hart; Rising Sun; Victoria T.

CULROSS (Fife). — Dundonald Arms.

CUMNOCK (Ayr).—Royal.

CUPAR (Fife).—Tontine.

CUXHAM (Oxon., 2 N.W. Watlington).—Pointer's Mill Farm.

DALBEATTIE (Kirkc.).—Donaldson's T.; Commercial; Maxwell Arms.

DALBY, GT. (Leic., 3 S.W. M. Mowbray).—Royal Oak.

DALMALLY (Argyll).—Cameron's B.H., Orchy Bank, Macdonald's B.H., Garten-aird.

DALMELLINGTON (Ayr).—Eglinton Arms.

DALRY (Kirkc.).—Gordon's T.

DANBURY (Essex).—Cricketers.

DARLINGTON.—Speedwell T., Victoria Rd.; Clarence T., Market Place.

DARTFORD (Kent).—Neale's Central T., Hythe St.

DARTMOUTH (S. Devon).—Moses' Commercial; Mrs. Bates' B.H., l'Esperance, Southtown.

DAVENTRY (Northants).—Bear; Leigh's T. See Norton.

DAWLISH (Devon).—Harris's T.; Partridge's B.H., Vaughan Ter.; Lansdowne R.

DEAL (Kent).—Central Commercial T., 143, High St.; New Inn, High St.; Swan.

DEDDINGTON (6 S. Banbury).—Unicorn.

DEDHAM (Ess., 3½ N.W. Manningtree).—Artis's B.H., High St.; Marlbro' Head.

DEIGHTON (5 S. York).—White Swan P.R.H.A.

DELAMERE (10½ N.E. Chester).—Fishpool Inn; Abbey Arms.

DENBIGH.—Royal Oak T.; Bull.

DENNINGTON (Suff., 2½ N. Framlingham). — Q u e e n ' s Head.

DENTDALE (N.W. Yorks).—Sportsman Inn, 4 m. up valley from Dent. At Dent, George and Dragon.

DENTON (Lincs, 4 S.W. Grantham).—Welby Arms P.R.H.A.

DERBY. — Berkeley T. and Carlton T., both London Rd.; Waverley T., Midland Rd.; Cameron's R., 10, Friargate.

DERRY HILL (Wilts, 2½ W. Calne).—Swan P.R.H.A.

DEVIZES.—Walker's T., High St.; Central T., Market Pl.

DIDCOT (Berks).—Royal Oak.

DIGSWELL HILL (Gt. North Rd., 1½ S. Welwyn).—Red Lion.

DISS (Norf., 2 W. Scole).—Waveney T.; King's Head. See Scole.

DITCHEAT (Som., 3 N.W. Castle Cary).—Manor House Inn.

DITCHLING (6 N. Brighton).—Bull.

DOCKRAY (Ullswater).—Donaldson's T.; Royal.

DODINGTON (Som., 8½ N.W. Bridgwater).—Castle of Comfort T.

DOLGELLEY.—Beechwood T.; Tyn-y-groes House; Ship.

DOLGOCH (4½ N.E. Towyn).—Williams' B.H., Waterfall House.

DOLYWERN (Glyn Valley, 5 W. Chirk).—Queen T. and B.H.

DONCASTER.— Fallas T., Hall Gate; Waverley T., St. George's Gate; Albany T., Baxtergate.

DONINGTON (Lincs, 8½ N.W. Spalding).—Red Cow.

DORCHESTER (Dors.).—Central T. and Dorchester T., both South St.; Coombe's R.

DORCHESTER (9 S.E. Oxford).—White Hart; Fleur de Lys.

DORKING (Surrey).—Dorking T., West St.; Goodson's R., High St.; Star and Garter.

DORRINGTON (6 S. Shrewsbury).—Horseshoes P.R.H.A.

DOUGLAS (I.O.M.).—Stanley T., Loch Promenade; Cunningham's Young Men's Camp.

DOULTING (Som., 2 E. Shepton Mallet).—Abbey Barn P.R.H.A.

DOVEDALE (Derby).—Small
T. at Milldale, 1 m. from Al-
stonfield. See also Mappleton.

DOVER.—Shaftesbury T., 153,
Snargate; Central T., next
King's Hall; Fowle's T., opp.
Harbour Station.

DOVERCOURT (with Har-
wich, Essex).—London T.,
High St.

DOWNHAM MARKET (11 S.
Kings Lynn).—Page's T.

DRAKEHOLES (Notts, 4 S.E.
Bawtry).—White Swan.

DREWSTEIGNTON (Devon, 4
N.W. Moretonhampstead).—
Drewe Arms; Piller's B.H.

DRIFFIELD (E. Yorks).—Fal-
cón; Buck.

DROITWICH (Worc.).—Bul-
lock's R., 44, High St.

DUFFTOWN (Banff). — Fife
Arms.

DUMBARTON. — 1 m. S.E.,
Dumbuck H.

DUMFRIES. — Nithsdale T.;
Fountain T.

DUNBAR.—Albert T.; Dunlop's
Hillside B.H.

DUNBEATH (Caithness).—
T.H.

DUNDEE.—Mather's T., Whitehall Pl.

DUNDONNELL (Ross and
Cromarty).—The H.

DUNFERMLINE (Fife).—Wil-
son's T., East Port St.

DUNMOW (Essex).—Chequers;
White Lion.

DUNOON (Argyll). — Douglas
T.

DUNS (Berwick).—Swan.

DUNSFORD (7½ S.W. Exeter).
—Royal Oak.

DUNSTABLE (Beds)—T., 17,
West St.; Hicks's T.; Red
Lion; "Avondale," Watling
St.

DUNSTER (Som., 3 S.E. Minehead).—Lock, baker; Foresters' Arms.

DUNTON GREEN (2 N.W.
Sevenoaks).—Miners' Arms.

DUNWICH (Suff., 4 S.W.
Southwold).—Barne Arms.

DURHAM.—Palmer's T., North
Rd.; Rose and Crown. See
Neville's Cross and Croxdale.

DURSLEY (Glos.).—Castle. See
North Nibley and Uley.

DURSTON (5 N.E. Taunton).
—Railway.

DWYGYFYLCHI (2½ W. Con-
way). — Roberts' R., Glen
Villa.

DYFFRYN (5 N.W. Barmouth).
—Glasfryn H.; Cromlech Commercial H.

DYFFRYN-CASTELL (11 W.
Llangurig).—D.C. Inn.

DYMOCK (Glos., 4 S. Led-
bury).—Beauchamp Arms.

EARLS COLNE (Essex, 3 S.E.
Halstead).—George.

EARLSTON (5 N.E. Melrose).
—Red Lion; and small T.

EASINGTON (E. Yorks, 6 N.
Spurn Point).—Neptune.

EAST ANSTEY (Som., 4 S.W.
Dulverton).—Froude Arms.

EAST AYTON (4 S.W. Scar-
bro).—White Swan.

EASTBOURNE.—Leaf Hall T.;
Clarence T., Terminus Rd.;
Hazleden T., Cavendish Pl.;
Westminster T., Hyde Gar-
dens; Waverley T., Junction
Rd.

EAST BUDLEIGH (Devon, 5
S.W. Sidmouth).—Rolle H.

EAST CHINNOCK (4 S.W.
Yeovil).—Portman Arms.

EASTCHURCH (Kent, Shep-
pey).—Castle.

EAST COKER (2 S.W. Yeovil).
—New Inn.

EAST DEREHAM (Norf.).—
Queen's T., Station Rd.

EAST HADDON (7 N.W.
Northampton).—Red Lion.

EAST ILSLEY (Berks, 9 N.E.
Newbury).—Crown and Horns.

EASTLEIGH (5½ N.E. South-
ampton).—Radnor T., High
St.

EASTNOR HILL (Heref., 2 E. Ledbury).—Somers Arms T.

ECCLEFECHAN (Dumfries).—Craig's R.

ECCLESHALL (7 N.W. Stafford).—King's Arms; Bell.

EDENBRIDGE (10 W. Tonbridge). — White Horse; Crown.

EDENHAM (Lincs, 2½ N.W. Bourne).—Five Bells P.R.H.A.

EDINBURGH.—Victoria T., 1, Erskine Pl.; Suttie's T., 20, South Bridge; Register T., 170, West Register St.; T., 24, Forth St.; West End T., 31, Lothian Rd.; Kenilworth T., 35, Leith St.; Donaldson's T., 25, Bath St., Portobello.

EDWINSTOWE (Dukeries, 2 S.W. Ollerton).—Royal Oak.

EGHAM (Surrey).—Pattle's Old House R.

EGLINGHAM (6 N.W. Alnwick).—Tankerville Arms.

EGREMONT (Cumb., 6 S.E. Whitehaven).—King's Arms.

EGTON BRIDGE (8 S.W. Whitby).—Station.

ELFORD (Staffs, 4 N.W. Tamworth).—Crown.

ELING (Hants, 1 S. Totton).—Anchor P.R.H.A.

ELLESMERE (Salop). — The Creamery, Watergate St.; Mrs. Griffiths, Market St.; Brownlow Arms.

ELLON (Aberdeen).—New Inn.

ELMSTEAD MARKET (4 E. Colchester).—King's Arms.

ELTON (Hunts, 4 N.E. Oundle).—Black Horse P.R.H.A.; Crown.

ELY (Camb.).—City T., Market Pl.; Greyhound; Minster T.

ENNERDALE (Cumb.).—Routen's T.

EPSOM (Surrey).—Ivydene R.

ESCOT (Devon, 2 N.W. Ottery St. Mary). — Fairmile Inn P.R.H.A.

ESCRICK (7 S.E. York).—Black Bull P.R.H.A.

ESKDALE (Cumb.).—Tyson's Gowrie B.H.

ESSENDON (Herts, 3 N.E. Hatfield).—Salisbury Crest.

EVESHAM.—Station T.; Granville T.; several T.s in High St.

EWHURST (Surrey, 8 S.W. Dorking).—Crown.

EXETER.—Richmond T., Richmond Rd.; Alcombe's T., Queen St.; St. David's T.; Northernhay T.

EXFORD (Som., Exmoor).—Wensley's T.

EXMOUTH (S. Devon).—Thorns Commercial T.; Williams' B.H., The Homestead.

EYAM (Derby, 5 N. Bakewell).—Bull's Head.

EYEMOUTH (Berwick).—Home Arms.

EYNSFORD (Kent, 5 N. Sevenoaks).—Dunmall's B.H., Hillcroft.

EYNSHAM (7 N.W. Oxford).—Swan; Red Lion.

FAIRFORD (Glos., 8 E. Cirencester).—White Hart.

FAKENHAM (Norf., 12 N.W. Dereham). — Lancaster T.: Crown; Lion.

FALKIRK (Stirling).—Munro's T.; Railway.

FALMOUTH.—Kneebone's T., 27, Arwenack St.; Bray's T., 9, Killigrew St.; West's Maenheere T.; Savage's T., Market St.

FAREHAM (Hants). — Pyle's R.; Foster's T., West St.

FARINGDON (Berks).—Crown; Orchard House.

FARNHAM (Surrey).—Carlton T. and Robin's T., both nr. Station; Railway H.

FARNHAM (Dors., 7 N.W. Cranborne).—Museum H.

FARNHAM COMMON (Bucks, 4 N. Slough).—Victoria.

FARNINGHAM (12 W. Rochester).—Bull.

FAVERSHAM (9½ N.W. Canterbury).—Tremain's T., Preston St.

FAWLEY (Hants Coast, 5 E. Beaulieu).—Falcon P.R.H.A.

FEERING (Essex, 2 S.E. Coggeshall, 1 N.E. Kelvedon).—Sun.

FELIXSTOWE.—Victoria T., Victoria St.; Central T., Hamilton Rd.

FELTON, WEST (4½ S.E. Oswestry, Holyhead Rd.).—Queen's Head P.R.H.A.

FELTON (Northum., 9 S. Alnwick).—Northumberland Arms.

FENNY STRATFORD (Bucks).—Timms' R., 31, High St. See Bletchley.

FERRYBRIDGE (Yorks, Gt. North Rd.).—Ramsey, motor and cycle depôt.

FERRYHILL (6 S. Durham).—Eldon Arms.

FESTINIOG (N. Wales).—Abbey Arms; Sun T.; Evans, Bryn Gwallen.

FILLONGLEY (Warw., 6 S.W. Nuneaton).—Anderton's R.

FILTON (4 N. Bristol).—Anchor.

FINCHAMPSTEAD (Berks, 3½ S.W. Wokingham).—Hilton's R.

FINDON (Suss., 4 N.W. Worthing).—Tugwell's B.H., North View.

FINGEST (Bucks, 7 N.W. Gt. Marlow).—Chequers.

FINMERE STATION (4½ W. Buckingham).—Shelswell Inn, P.R.H.A.

FLEETWOOD (Lancs) — Queen's T.

FLIMWELL (E. Sussex).—Lawrence's Postboy R.; Hare and Hounds.

FLINT.—Royal Oak.

FOLKESTONE.—Royal T., 194, Dover Rd.; Lawson's Junction T.; London R., 10, Harbour St.; "Chittenden," 18, Foord Rd. See Saltwood.

FONTHILL BISHOP (Wilts., 2 N.E. Hindon).—King's Arms P.R.H.A.

FORD (Stow-Tewkesbury Rd., 7 N.W. Stow).—Plough.

FORD (Northum., 6½ N.W. Wooler).—Wilson's T.

FORDINGBRIDGE (14 S. Salisbury).—Greyhound.

FORDWICH (2 N.E. Canterbury).—George and Dragon.

FORFAR.—New T., 34, Castle St.; Stag.

FORFAR - BRECHIN RD.—Finavon H., Esk Bridge, Tannadice.

FORMBY (7 S.W. Southport).—Café Royal.

FORRES (Elgin).—Munro's T.

FORT AUGUSTUS (Inverness).—Malvern R.; Chisholm's P.H.

FORT WILLIAM (Inverness).—Cochran's T.; Waverley T.; Central T.; Granite House T.

FOUR MARKS (Hants, 6 N.E. Alresford).—Windmill.

FOWEY (Cornw.). — Bourne's T.; King of Prussia; Globe, P.R.H.A.

FOWLMERE (Camb., 5½ N.E. Royston).—White Swan.

FRAMLINGHAM (Suff.).—See Dennington.

FRESHWATER (I.O.W.).—Saunders' T.; Medway B.H.

FRESSINGFIELD (Suff., 8 W. Halesworth).—Fox and Goose.

FROCESTER (Glos., 4 S.W. Stroud).—George.

FRODSHAM (10 N.E. Chester).—Bear's Paw.

FROME (Som.).—Sim's T.; Crown.

GADSHILL (3 S.E. Gravesend).—Sir John Falstaff.

GAERWEN (Anglesey).—Holland Arms.

GAILEY (Watling St.).—See Ivetsey Bank.

GAINSBOROUGH (Lincs).—King's Arms T.; Monsons Arms.

GAIRLOCH (by Achnasheen, Ross and Cromarty).—Duncan Ross's B.H., Strath; Macdonald's B.H., Kerrysdale.

GAIRLOCHY (Inverness).—Williamson's B.H.

GALASHIELS (Selkirk).—King's T.; Waverley T.; Maxwell's.

GALSTON (5½ E.S.E. Kilmarnock).—Portland Arms.

GANNICK CORNER (Gt. North Rd., 2 N.E. Barnet, 1 S.W. Potter's Bar).—Duke of York.

GARTHMYL (3 N.W. Montgomery).—Nag's Head.

GARTOCHARN (Loch Lomond, 3½ N.E. Balloch).—Gartocharn Inn.

GARVE (12 W. Dingwall).—Garve H.

GELDESTON (Norf., 2½ N.W. Beccles).—Wherry Inn.

GIFFORD (4 S.E. Haddington).—Tweeddale Arms.

GILLINGHAM (Dors., 4 N.W. Shaftesbury). — Weare's T., Newbury St.

GILSLAND (Cumb. Border, 7 N.E. Brampton). — Dacre House T.

GIRTFORD (Beds., Gt. North Rd., 4 N.W. Biggleswade).—Fuller's R., Bridge House.

GIRVAN (Ayr).—Gordon's T.

GLAISDALE (9½ S.W. Whitby).—Arncliffe Arms; Harrison's Applegarth Farm.

GLASGOW.—Penman's T., 939, Sauchiehall St.; Whyte's T., Candleriggs; Craiglea T., 59, Gibson St., Hillhead.

GLASTONBURY (Som.).—Rutland T.; Abbey T.; Brooks' Star T. See Meare and Street.

GLENCOE (Argyll).—Clachaig Inn.

GLENLUCE (Galloway, 8½ S.E. Stranraer).—Commercial.

GLENRIDDING (Ullswater).—Kilner's B.H., Rose Cottage. See Patterdale.

GLEN SHIEL (Ross and Cromarty).—Clunie Inn.

GLOUCESTER.—Newth's T., 10, Parliament St.; Pitt's T., 128, Barton St.; Empire T., Bleak House, Park End Rd.; Glevum T., Whitfield St.; Fleece, Westgate.

GLOUCESTER-BRISTOL RD.—See Stone and Berkeley.

GOBOWEN (Salop, 2½ N.E. Oswestry).—Hammond's T., nr. Station.

GODALMING (Surrey).—See Broadwater and Thursley.

GODMANCHESTER (just across Huntingdon Bridge).—Royal Oak; Railway.

GODSHILL (I.O.W., 5 N.W. Ventnor).—Griffin.

GODSTONE (6½ N.E. Reigate).—Bell; Corner House P.H.

GOGINAN (7½ E. Aberystwyth).—Evans's Druid R.

GOLSPIE (Sutherland).—Watson's T.

GOMSHALL (Surrey, 5 S.W. Dorking).—Compasses.

GORING HEATH (Oxon., 4 N.E. Goring).—King Charles Head, P.R.H.A.; Post Office R.

GOSFORTH (Cumb.).—Strands T.

GOTHAM (7 S.W. Nottingham).—Cuckoo Bush P.R.H.A.

GOUDHURST (Kent).—Church House T.; Station T.

GRANTHAM.—Barnett's T., 5, London Rd.; Cook's T., Westgate; Strathdon T., Watergate; Dysart T., nr. Post Office; Barley Mow; Blue Ram; Crossed Swords.

GRANTOWN AND KEITH RD. (Banff). — Dalnashaugh Inn.

GRASMERE (Lake Dis.).—Thornborough's T.; Baldry's Moss Grove P.H.; Usher's B.H., St. Oswald's; Dodgson's Kirk Allan R., next Church.

GRASSINGTON (Wharfedale).
—Commercial.

GRAVESEND (Kent).—Reeves'
T., 2, Harmer St.

GRAYS (Essex).—Victoria T.,
High St.

GRAYSHOTT (Hindhead, Sur-
rey-Hants).—Chubb's Queen's
R.

GT. ABINGTON (8 S.E. Cam-
bridge). — Three Tuns
P.R.H.A.

GT. AYTON (Yorks, 3 N.E.
Stokesley).—Buck.

GT. BEDWYN (Wilts, 4½ N.E.
Savernake).—Cross Keys.

GT. EASTON (Leic., 4 S.W.
Uppingham).—Castle.

GT. HAMPDEN (Bucks, 4 S.W.
Wendover).—Hampden Arms.

GT. HAYWOOD (5 S.E. Staf-
ford).—Clifford Arms.

GT. KIMBLE (Bucks, 3 S.W.
Wendover).—Bear and Cross.

GT. LONGSTONE (Derby, 3
N.W. Bakewell).—White Lion.

GT. MILTON (Oxon., 4 N.W.
Tetsworth).—Bell.

GT. MISSENDEN (Bucks, 4½
N.W. Amersham).—George's
T.

GT. NORTH ROAD (8 N.W.
Stamford, 13 S. Grantham).—
Ram Jam Inn.

GT. PARNDON (Essex, 5 N.W.
Epping).—Three Horseshoes.

GT. WITLEY (Worc., 5 S.W.
Stourport).—Hundred House.

GREENLAW (Berwick).—Black
Adder T.; Castle.

GREENODD (Furness).—Rob-
son's Woodview B.H., Penny-
bridge.

GRIMSBY.—Clarence T., Old
Market Pl.; Osborne Com-
mercial H.; Harrison's H.;
Grosvenor T., Flottergate.

GRINDLEFORD (Derby
Dales).—Mrs. F. Thompson,
Derwent R.

GRINSHILL (Salop, 4 S.
Wem).—Elephant and Castle.

GRONANT (Flint, 5 N.E.
Rhuddlan).—Gronant Inn.

GROOMBRIDGE (3½ S.W. Tun-
bridge Wells. — C r o w n
P.R.H.A.

GROSMONT (10 N.W. Mon-
mouth).—Angel.

GUERNSEY, St. Peter Port.—
Morris's B.H., 14, Saumarez
St.; Toms' B.H., Four Banks;
and at Belle Grêve Bay, Red
Lion.

GUILDFORD.—Connaught T.
and Weyside T., both nr.
bridge; Royal Arms T., North
St.; Imperial T., opp. G.P.O.;
Comber's Mount House T.;
Bull's Head.

GUILSBOROUGH (10 N.W.
Northampton).—Ward Arms.

GUISBOROUGH (N. Yorks).—
Pallister's R.

GULLANE (4 S.W. North Berwick).—Hope Field T.

GUNNERSIDE (Swaledale).—
Waggett's B.H., Lodge
Green. See Muker.

GURNARDS HEAD (Corn., 5½
S.W. St. Ives). — Gurnards
Head H.

HADDINGTON.—Black Bull;
George. See Gifford.

HADDON, EAST (7 N.W.
Northampton).—Red Lion.

HADLEIGH (Essex, 2 N.E.
Benfleet).—Castle.

HALESWORTH (Suffolk).—
King's Arms.

HALIFAX.—Maude's T., Broad
St.; others in Horton St.; Old
Cock.

HALLATON (Leic., 7½ N.E.
Mkt. Harbro).—Bewicke Arms.

HALLWORTHY (Corn., 5 N.E.
Camelford).—T.H.

HALSTEAD (Essex).—Ower's
Commercial T. See Earls
Colne.

HAMBLEDON (Hants, 6½ S.E.
Bish. Waltham).—New Inn.

HAMPTON LUCY (4 N.E.
Stratford-on-Avon). — Boat's
Head.

HANLEY (Staffs).—Central T., Stafford St.; Capesthorn T., Church St.

HARDRAW (Wensleydale, 1½ N. Hawes).—Green Dragon.

HARE HATCH (Berks, Bath Rd., 1½ N.E. Twyford).— Horse and Groom.

HARLECH (N. Wales).—Gorphwysfa T.

HARLESTON (Norf., 6½ S.W. Bungay).—Magpie.

HARMER HILL (6 N. Shrewsbury). — Bridgwater Arms P.R.H.A.

HARROGATE. — Beulah T., Beulah St.; Burns's B.H., 53, Valley Drive.

HARTLAND (N. Devon).— King's Arms; Anchor.

HARWICH.—See Dovercourt.

HASELBURY (Som., 2 N.E. Crewkerne). — White Horse P.R.H.A.

HASELOR (6 N.W. Stratford-on-Avon).—Crown.

HASLEMERE (Surrey).—Ewhurst Lodge B.H., Hill Rd.; Swan.

HASTINGS.—Connaught Hse., 19, Cambridge Rd.; Butelands, 3, Breeds Pl.; Washington T., Devonsire Rd.; Malvern House T. and Waverley T. and Gordon T., all Havelock Rd.

HATFIELD (Gt. North Rd., 20 N. London).—Salisbury T.

HATHERSAGE (Derby, 10 N. Bakewell).—Platt's B.H., Station Rd.

HAVANT (7 N.E. Portsmouth). —Clarke's T.

HAVERFORDWEST (Pembroke).—Railway T.; Mariners.

HAWES (Wensleydale). — Calvert's T.; Routh's T. See Hardraw.

HAWES JUNCTION (6 W.N.W. Hawes).—Moorcock.

HAWICK (Roxb.).—Victoria T., High St.; Gibson's T., Bridge St.

HAWKCHURCH (Devon, 3 N.E. Axminster).—Old Inn.

HAWKHURST (Kent, 4 S.W. Cranbrook).—Eight Bells.

HAWRIDGE (Bucks, 3 N. Chesham).—Full Moon.

HAY (20 N.W. Hereford).—Castle T.; Wye T.

HAYDON BRIDGE (7½ W. Hexham).—Haydon Bridge H.

HAYFIELD (Derby).—Pugh's Junction T.

HAYLE (Corn.).—Cornubia.

HEACHAM-ON-SEA (Norf.).— Limes T.

HEATHFIELD (Suss., 8 N. Hailsham).—Station T.

HELENSBURGH (Dumbart.).— Railway.

HELLIFIELD (Yorks, 5 S.E. Settle).—Craven T.

HELMSDALE (Sutherland).— Ross's T. See Port Gower.

HELSTON (Corn.). — Regent T.; Alpha P.H.; Lugg's T.

HEMPNALL (9 S. Norwich).— King's Head.

HEMYOCK (Devon, 7 E. Tiverton Junction).—Star.

HENFIELD (11 N.W. Brighton).—Rainbow T.

HENLEY - ON - THAMES (Oxon.).—Oxford T., Market Pl.; Bear; beware Regatta Week, 1st in July.

HENLEY-IN-ARDEN (10 W. Warwick).—Old Three Tuns; White Swan.

HENLOW (Beds., 5 N.W. Hitchin).—Five Bells.

HENSTRIDGE (Som., 6 S. Wincanton).—Virginia Ash H.

HEREFORD. — Farmer's T.; Doubleday's T.; Garrick H.; Hop Pole; Davies' H. See Stretton Sugwas and Burghill.

HEREFORD - HAY RD. (8 W.N.W. Hereford).—Portway Arms.

HERNE BAY (11 S.W. Margate).—Wiffen's T., Station Rd.; Waverley T. and Railway H., both High St.; Peacock's B.H., 12, Gosfield Rd.

HERTFORD. — White Hart; Farrow's R., Fore St.; Oliver's T., No. 9, Old Cross; and at 2 m. on Stevenage Rd., Sharpe, Old Windmill, Waterford. See also Stapleford.

HEVER (Kent, 7 S.E. Oxted).— Henry the Eighth.

HEXHAM (Northum.).—Hare's T.; Dodd's T.

HEYDON (Norf., 5 W. Aylsham).—Earle Arms P.R.H.A.

HEYTESBURY (Wilts, 4 S.E. Warminster).—Angel

HIGHBRIDGE (Som.).— George. See Brent Knoll.

HIGH FORCE (Teesdale).— High Force H.

HIGH HALSTOW (5½ N.E. Rochester). — Red Dog P.R.H.A.

HIGHWORTH (Wilts, 6 N.E. Swindon).—Saracen's Head.

HIGH WYCOMBE (Bucks).— Johns' T.; Railway T.; Candy's Farm, Lane End.

HINDHEAD.—See Grayshott.

HINDON (Wilts).—See Fonthill Bishop.

HITCHIN (Herts).—Leete's T., Station Rd. See Letchworth.

HOAR CROSS (Staffs, 4 S.E. Abbots Bromley).—Meynell Ingram Arms P.R.H.A.

HOCKLIFFE (Beds, 4 N.W. Dunstable).—White Hart.

HODDESDON (4 S.E. Hertford).—The Coffee Tavern.

HOLBEACH (Lincs, 7½ N.E. Spalding).—String of Horses.

HOLBROOK (Derby, 2½ S.E. Belper).—Greyhound.

HOLME (Norf., 3 N.E. Hunstanton).—White Horse.

HOLMROOK (Cumb., 2½ N. Ravenglass). — Lutwidge Arms.

HOLMWOOD (Surrey, 4 to 5 S. Dorking). — Adolphus' B.H.; White Hart, Beare Green.

HOLSWORTHY (Devon, 15 W. Hatherleigh).—Stanhope T.

HOLT (Norf.).—Gott's Morston B.H.

HOLT HEATH (4½ N.W. Worcester).—Red Lion.

HOLYBOURNE (Hants, 2 N.E. Alton).—White Hart.

HOLYWELL (Flint). — Cross Keys; King's Head.

HONITON (Devon). — Scott's T., High St.; Angel.

HOOK GREEN (Kent, 2 S.W. Lamberhurst). — Elephant's Head, P.R.H.A.

HOREHAM ROAD (Suss., 5½ N.W. Hailsham).—Baker's R.

HORNBY (8½ N.E. Lancaster). —Royal Oak.

HORNCASTLE (Lincs). — Imperial T.; Red Lion; Rodney.

HORNSEA (E. Yorks Coast).— Hodgkinson's Southsea B.H., Southgate; Alexandra.

HORSHAM (Suss.).—Waverley T., facing Town Hall; Carfax T.

HORSLEY (Northum., 3 N.W. Otterburn).—Redesdale Arms.

HORSMONDEN (Kent, 3 N.E. Lamberhurst).—King's Arms.

HUDDERSFIELD. — Waverley T., Market Pl.

HULL.—York T. and West Park T., both Anlaby Rd.

HUNGERFORD (Berks).— Crown; Plume; Buxcey's R., Bath Rd. See Newbury-Hungerford Rd.

HUNMANBY (E. Yorks, 2½ S. Filey).—Swan.

HUNSTANTON (Norf.).—Connaught P.H.; Brown Moth R., Agincourt Sq. See Holme.

HUNTINGDON.—Tuck's B.H., 97, High St. *See Godmanchester.*

HUNTLY (Aberdeen).—Huntly H.

HURSTBOURNE PRIORS (3½ N.E. Andover). — Portsmouth Arms P.R.H.A.

HURSTPIERPOINT (8 N. Brighton).—New Inn.

HUTTON - LE - HOLE (N.

Yorks, 3 N.W. Kirkby Moor-
side).—Crown.
HYTHE (Kent).—Wilberforce
T., 118, High St.; Sea View
H., Seabrook Rd. See Salt-
wood.

ILCHESTER (Som., 5 N.W.
Yeovil).—Dolphin.
ILFRACOMBE. — Montebello
T.; Claremont T., Fore St.;
Stentiford's B.H., 18, Brook-
dale Av.
ILKLEY (Wharfedale).—Carlton
T.; Waverley T.; Pawson's
Old Bridge R.
ILMINSTER (Som.).—George;
Hockaday's R.
ILSLEY, EAST (Berks, 9 N.E.
Newbury). — Crown and
Horses.
INELLAN (3½ S. Dunoon).—
Miss Stewart, Hazelcliff.
INGLETON (W. Yorks).—Slin-
ger's P.H.; Ingleborough H.;
Dodgson's B.H., Maythorn.
INVERARAY (Argyll).—T.H.
INVERKEILOR (Forfar, 6 N.
Arbroath).—Chance Inn.
INVERNESS. — Neish's T.,
Eastgate; McGilvray's T.
IPSWICH.—Nunn's T., Dial
Lane; Wolsey R., St. Nicholas
St.; Victoria T., Tavern St.;
Coach and Horses, Upp. Brook
St.; Waterloo T., Princes St.
IRVINE (Ayr).—Eglinton Arms.
ISLIP (Northants, 1 N.W.
Thrapston).—Woolpack.
ITCHEN ABBAS (Hants, 3½ W.
Alresford).—Stoneadge's River
View B.H.
IVETSEY BANK (Watling St.,
5 W. Gailey).—Bradford Arms
P.R.H.A.
IVYBRIDGE (S. Devon).—
King's Arms.

JERSEY, St. Helier's.—Mour-
ant's T., Broad St.; Halkett
H., Halkett Pl.; H. de l'Es-
planade; H. de l'Europe.
JEDBURGH (Roxb.).—Abbey
T.: Douglas T.

KEGWORTH (Leic., 5½ N.W.
Loughborough). — Flying
Horse.
KEIGHLEY (W. Yorks).—
Waverley T., Low St.
KELD (Swaledale). — Cathole
Inn.
KELSALL (7 E. Chester).—
Hardacre's B.H., the An-
chorage.
KELSO (Roxb.).—Border T.
KELVEDON (12 S.W. Colches-
ter).—Star and Fleece. See
Feering.
KEMSING (Kent, 2 N.E. Seven-
oaks).—Chequers.
KEN BRIDGE (1 N.E. New
Galloway).—T.
KENDAL. — Waverley T.;
Webb's T.; Sand Area T., nr.
Station; Rainbow; Union
Tavern.
KENILWORTH (4 N. War-
wick).—Waite's Castle R.;
Maisey's B.H., North Chase.
KENNETT (Camb., 6 N.E.
Newmarket).—Bell.
KESSINGLAND (4½ S.W. Low-
estoft). — Thacker's B.H.,
Swiss Cott.
KESWICK.—Storey's Derwent-
water T.; Waverley T., Main
St.; Ramsay's B.H., 78, Main
St.; Bank Tavern.
KETTERING.—Palmer's Albion
T., Market Pl.; Waverley T.,
Station Rd.; Victoria R.
KETTLEWELL (Wharfedale).
—Blue Bell; King's Head;
Carradice's B.H.
KIBWORTH (Leic., 6 N.W.
Mkt. Harbro).—Coach and
Horses.
KIDDERMINSTER. — Anchor,
Worcester St.; Grosvenor T.,
nr. Station.
KIDLINGTON (5 N. Oxford).—
Black Horse.
KILKHAMPTON (N. Corn., 4
N.E. Stratton).—London Inn
P.R.H.A.
KILKHAMPTON - CLOVELLY
RD.—West Country Inn.

KILLIN (Perth).—McGregor's Tay View B.H.

KILMARNOCK.—Station T.

KILNSEA (E. Yorks Coast).— Blue Bell.

KILNSEY (Wharfedale).—Anglers' Arms.

KILSBY STATION (Northants, 4 S.E. Rugby).—Railway.

KILWORTH, SOUTH (Leic.). —White Hart.

KIMBOLTON (10 S.W. Huntingdon).—George.

KINETON (Warw.). — Swan; Glenroy B.H., Warwick Rd.

KINGSBRIDGE (S. Devon).— South Hams T.; Albion; Anchor.

KINGS BROMLEY (Staffs, 5 N. Lichfield).—Royal Oak.

KINGSCLERE (Hants, 9 N.W. Basingstoke).—Crown.

KINGS LANGLEY (Herts).— Rose and Crown.

KINGS LYNN.—Balding's T., Portland St.; Patt's T.; Lowe's T., Norfolk St.

KINGSTON LISLE (Berks, 4½ W. Wantage). — Plough P.R.H.A.

KINGSTON - ON - THAMES.— Sanders' R., 32, High St.

KINGTON (Heref., 7 S.W. Presteigne). — Cambrian T., Bridge St.; Rogers' T., Duke St.; Burton House H.

KINGUSSIE (Inverness).—Waverley T.; Silverford B.H.

KIRKBY LONSDALE (Westm.). — Garlick's T.; Waverley T.; Vale of Lune T.

KIRKBY MOORSIDE (N. Yorks).—George and Dragon.

KIRKBY STEPHEN (Westm.). —Smith's T.

KIRKCALDY (Fife). — Anthony's T.

KIRKCUDBRIGHT.—Commercial.

KIRK IRETON (Derby, 3 S.W. Wirksworth).—Barley Mow.

KIRK LANGLEY (4½ N.W. Derby).—Meynell Arms.

KIRKMICHAEL (I.O.M.).— Quayle's B.H.; Church View.

KIRKWHELPINGTON (Northum., 12 W. Morpeth).—Moffatt's Cliffside B.H.

KIRRIEMUIR (Forfar).— Thrums T.; Airlie Arms.

KIRTON LINDSEY (Lincs, 6 S.W. Brigg).—Queen's Head.

KNARESBOROUGH (W. Yorks). — Holiday Camp (tents), York Pl., May to Sept.; Commercial T.; Crown.

KNEESALL (Notts, 3½ S.E. Ollerton).—Old Angel.

KNIGHTON (Radnor).—Chandos T.; Swan.

KNOCKIN (Salop, 5 S.E. Oswestry).—Bradford Arms.

KNOLLS GREEN (Ches., 3½ E. Knutsford).—Pollitt's R.

KNOWLE (Warw., 9½ S.E. Birmingham).—Clark's B.H., Hampton Lane.

KNOWL HILL (3 N.E. Twyford, 4½ S.W. Maidenhead).— New Inn.

KNOWSLEY (Lancs, 3 N.W. Prescot).—Derby Arms.

KNUTSFORD.—Smith's Argyll B.H., Market Pl. See Ollerton.

KYLE OF LOCHALSH (10 S.W. Strome Ferry).—T.H.

KYLE SKU (7 S. Scourie).— Inn.

LACEBY (4 S.W. Grimsby).— Waterloo.

LALEHAM (Midd., 2 S.E. Staines).—Post Office.

LAMBERHURST (6½ S.E. Tunbridge Wells). — Newell's Springbank Farm. See Hook Green.

LAMBOURN (Berks, 8 N.W. Hungerford).—Red Lion.

LAMPETER (Card.).—Walter's T.

LANARK. — Bonnington T.; Victoria and Station.

LANCASTER.—Trevelyan T., Church St.; Castle T.; Elm House T., Meeting - house

Lane; Farmer's Arms; Railton's T., nr. Station.

LAND'S END.—Thomas's T., Penwith House; and at 3 m. S.E., Logan Rock Inn, Trereen.

LANGDALE, LITTLE (Lake Dis.). — Wear's Blea Tarn Farm; Pepper's B.H., Dale View.

LANGDON BECK (7 N.W. Middleton-in-Teesdale). — The Inn.

LANGDON HILL (Essex, 5 S. Billericay).—Crown.

LANGFORD (Som., 6 N.E. Axbridge).—Langford H.

LANGHOLM (Dumfries).—Eskdale T.

LANGWATHBY (11 N.E. Appleby).—Yeo's T.

LAUDER (Berwick).—Lauderdale T.

LAUNCESTON. — Castle T.; Dolphin T.; Harris's T.

LAVENHAM (Suff., 5 N.E. Long Melford).—Swan.

LAVINGTON, WEST (Wilts, 5 S. Devizes). — Churchill Arms.

LEAMINGTON.—York T., 5, Spencer St.; Avon T., 9, High St.; Westminster T., 33, Bath St.; Guernsey T., Church St.

LEATHERHEAD (Surrey).— Duke's Head.

LECHLADE (Glos., 3 S.E. Fairford).—Giles's T.; Crown.

LEDBURY (13 S.E. Hereford). —Old Talbot; New Inn; Biddulph Arms P.R.H.A. See Eastnor Hill.

LEEBOTWOOD (Salop, 4 N.E. Ch. Stretton). — P o u n d P.R.H.A.

LEEDS. — Parker's T., opp. Grand Theatre; Wilson's T., 35, New Briggate; Plant's T., 8, Eldon Ter., Woodhouse Lane; Victoria, Gt. George St.; Alma House, 20, Vernon Rd.

LEEK (Staffs).—Neville's T.

LEICESTER. — Grosvenor T.

and Edinburgh T. and Cobden T., all New Walk.

LEIGH-ON-SEA.— Crowhurst's Cyclists' House, London Rd.

LEIGHTON BUZZARD (Beds). —Plume of Feathers; Swan.

LEIGHTON-ON-SEVERN (3½ N.W. Much Wenlock).—Big Tree.

LENHAM (Kent, 8½ S.E. Maidstone).—Dog and Bear.

LEOMINSTER (12 N. Hereford).—Waverley T., Etnam St.; Owen's R., Etnam St.; Hill's R., Draper's Lane.

LETCHWORTH, Garden City (3 N.E. Hitchin).—Garden City T., Station Rd.; Guest House, Leys Av.; Fox, at Willian, P.R.H.A.

LEVEN (Fife).—Star.

LEWES.—Best's T., 29, High St.; Black Horse, Western Rd.

LEYBURN (Wensleydale).— Black Swan; Smithson's T.

LICHFIELD.—Shaw's T., Bird St.; Castle.

LIFTON (Devon, 4½ N.E. Launceston).—Arundel Arms.

LINCOLN.—Alexandra T., Norman Pl.; Tuxford's Waverley T. and Trevelyan T. and Knight's T. and Doncaster T., all High St.

LINLITHGOW.—St. Michaels.

LIPHOOK (Hants, 8½ N.E. Petersfield).—Dale's R., Station Rd.

LISS (Hants, 4 N.E. Petersfield). —Station.

LISKEARD (Corn.).—Stag.

LITTLEHAMPTON (S u s s. Coast).—Cyprus T., 58, High St.

LITTLE HEREFORD (2½ W. Tenbury). — Barton's Woodbine B.H.

LITTON (W. Yorks, Littondale).—Queen's Arms.

LIVERPOOL.—Shamrock T., St. George's Cres.; Inglewood T., Norton St., off London Rd.; City Caterers T., 48A, Lime St.; Morley's T. 85,

Mount Pleasant and Antrim T., 73, ditto.

LLANARMON (Ceiriog Valley, 7½ S.W. Llangollen).—West Arms.

LLANBADARN FYNYDD (10 N.E. Rhayader).—New Inn.

LLANBEDR (3 S. Harlech).— Plas Newydd T.

LLANBERIS.—Idan T.; Railway T.; Prince of Wales; Rowlands P.H., Glan Eilian; Min-y-don, 10, High St.

LLANBRYNMAIR (10 E. Machynlleth).—Wynnstay Arms.

LLANDEGLA (Denb., 7 S.E. Ruthin).—Crown.

LLANDILO (15 N.E. Carmarthen).—Imperial T.; Castle.

LLANDRILLO (5 S.W. Corwen).—Dudley Arms.

LLANDRINDOD WELLS.— Central T., High St.; Geisha R., Temple St.

LLANDUDNO.—West End T., Gloddaeth St.; Moon's T.; others in Vaughan St.; Penrhyn Holiday Camp, Little Orme.

LLANEGRYN (4 N. Towyn).— Cefn Coch H.

LLANELLY.—Grand T.; Cleveland T., nr. Station.

LLANFAIR (Mont., 8 W. Welshpool).—Bon Marché T.

LLANFAIRFECHAN (7 S.W. Conway). — Fenton's Bryn Celyn B.H.; Sunfield P.H., Valley Rd.

LLANFAIRPWLL, etc. (Anglesey).—Penrhos Arms.

LLANFROTHEN (6½ N.E. Harlech).—Brondanw Arms.

LLANFYLLIN (Montg.).— Eagle.

LLANGADOCK (7 N.E. Llandilo).—Railway.

LLANGEFNI (Anglesey).— Rowland's Mona R.

LLANGOLLEN. — Grapes; Bridge End H.; Homeland T., Bridge St.; Waverley T.; Dee T.; Mrs. Roberts, Green Bank; Jenny Jones R.

LLANGURIG (4½ S.W. Llanidloes).—Blue. Bell; Black Lion.

LLANIDLOES (Montg.).— Humphries T.; Gwalia R.; Lewis, Eithinog Farm.

LLANRHAIADR (14 S.W. Oswestry).—Powis T.

LLANRWST (Denbigh).— King's Head; Boot.

LLANSILIN (6 W.S.W. Oswestry).—Wynnstay Arms.

LLANTWIT MAJOR (4½ S.W. Cowbridge).—Cross Keys.

LLANWRDA (4 S.W. Llandovery).—Royal Oak.

LLANBYTHER (5 S.W. Lampeter).—Black Lion.

LLANYMYNECH (6 S.W. Oswestry).—Lion; Swannick's Hillside B.H.

LOCHALSH (8 S.W. Strome Ferry).—Airdferry H.

LOCHMABEN (Dumf.).— King's Arms.

LOCKERBIE (Dumf.).—Blue Bell.

LOCKTON (N. Yorks, 5 N.E. Pickering).—Durham Ox.

LONDON.—See Section 15, page 69.

LONG COMPTON (5 S.E. Shipston-on-Stour).—Taylor's R.; Red Lion.

LONG MELFORD (Suff.).— Black Lion. See Lavenham.

LONGNOR (6 S.E. Buxton).— Cheshire Cheese.

LONGSTOCK (Hants, 1 N. Stockbridge). — Peat Spade P.R.H.A.

LONG SUTTON (Lincs, 4 S.E. Holbeach).—Bull.

LONG SUTTON (Som., 3 E. Langport).—Devonshire Arms.

LONGTOWN (9 N.W. Carlisle). —Bush; Graham Arms.

LOOE (Corn.). — Martin's Dairy.

LOPPINGTON (Salop, 3 N.W. Wem).—Bradford Arms.

LOSTWITHIEL (Corn.).— King's Arms; Talbot.

LOUDWATER (Bucks, 7 N. Maidenhead).—Crown.

LOUGHBOROUGH. — Station H., Derby Rd.; Beacon R., Baxtergate.

LOUTH.—Briggs' T.

LOWESTOFT.—Bridge T., 8, Commercial Rd.; Garfield T., Bevan St.; Clyffe T., on front. See Kessingland.

LUDLOW.—Blythwood House T.; Dobson's Royal Oak T., Tower St.

LULLINGTON (6¼ S. Burton-on-Trent).—Colville Arms.

LULWORTH, EAST (Dors., 5½ S.W. Wareham).—Weld Arms.

LULWORTH, WEST (Dors. Coast, 8¼ S.W. Wareham).— Castle; Hazard R.

LUTON.—Franklin T., George St.; Cowley's T., Church St.

LUTTERWORTH (Leic.).— Hind; Denbigh H.; T.H., Church St. See Monks Kirby.

LUXULYAN (Corn., 3 N.W. St. Blazey).—Mrs. Tinney.

LYBSTER (Caithness Coast).—Portland Arms.

LYDBURY NORTH (Salop, 2 S.E. Bishop's Castle).—Powis Arms P.R.H.A.

LYDNEY (Forest of Dean).— Swan; Feathers.

LYDD (Kent).—George.

LYME REGIS (Dors. Coast).— Baker's Cosy T., Broad St.; Walker's R., 52, Broad St.

LYMINGTON (Hants Coast).— Anglesey T.

LYNDHURST (New Forest).— Jessamine B.H., Romsey Rd. See Ashurst.

LYNMOUTH (Devon).— Moore's T., Nelson Cottage.

LYNTON.—Pow's Stourton B.H., by Post Office; Crown.

LYTHAM.—Arley T., Central Beach. See Ansdell.

MABLETHORPE (Lincs Coast).—West's T.; Berry's R.

MACCLESFIELD.—Hayes' T., Jordangate; Bull's Head.

MACHYNLLETH. — Eagle's Commercial.

MAENTWROG (2 W.S.W. Festiniog).—Mrs. Lloyd Hughes, Llys Twrog.

MAIDENHEAD. — Rose and Callingham's R., 14, Bridge Rd. See Knowl Hill and Bray Wick.

MAIDEN NEWTON (Dors., 7½ N.W. Dorchester). — White Horse.

MAIDSTONE. — Central T., Week St.; Stockwell's T., Gabriel's Hill; Victoria, Week St.

MALDON (Essex).—Simon's T., Market Hill; Walton's T., Cromwell Hill; Chequers; Rose and Crown.

MALHAM (W. Yorks).—Clark's T.; Buck; Lister's Arms; and at Bell Busk, Aire View B.H.

MALMESBURY (Wilts).—Rapley's T.

MALTON (21 N.E. York).—Oldfield's T., Castlegate.

MALVERN.—Tooley's Central T., St. Anne's Rd.

MANCHESTER. — Sydney T., All Saints, Oxford Rd.; Griffin's T., 142, Corporation St.; Veever's T., 22, Piccadilly; Foley's T., 504, Moss Lane East.

MANNINGTREE (Essex).— White Hart.

MANSFIELD (Notts).—Clifton T., Terrace Rd.; Gresham T., Church St.

MAPPLETON (Dovedale, 1½ N.W. Ashbourne).—Okeover Arms T.

MARCH (14 E. Peterbro).— Fisher's Railway T.

MARESFIELD (2 N. Uckfield). —Bedford's B.H., Mill House.

MARFORD (3 N.E. Wrexham). —Trevor Arms.

MARGATE.—Knapp's Parade R.; Murna House T., Royal Cres.; Buttifant's T., Hawley Sq.; O'Sullivan's B.H., 8, Garfield Rd.

MARKET DEEPING (Lincs).—Hare's B.H., Church St.; New Inn.

MARKET DRAYTON (Salop). —See Ashley Heath.

MARKET HARBOROUGH (Leic.).—Victoria T., nr. Station; Murkitt's Central R.

MARKET RASEN (13½ N.E. Lincoln).—Gordon Arms.

MARKET WEIGHTON (E. Yorks).—Half Moon; T., High St.

MARKYATE (Herts, 4½ S.E. Dunstable).—Red Lion.

MARLBOROUGH (Wilts).—Holland's Angel T.; Royal Oak.

MARYPORT (Cumb.).—Waverley T.

MASHAM (8 N.W. Ripon).—Commercial P.H.; College Villa B.H., College Lane.

MATFIELD (4 S.E. Tonbridge). —Star P.R.H.A.

MATLOCK.—Oriental T., nr. P.O.; Derwent T., Dale Rd. At Matlock Bath, Peveril T.

MAYBOLE (9 S.W. Ayr).—King's Arms.

MAYFIELD (7½ S. Tunbridge Wells).—Royal Oak.

MEARE (Som., 3 N.W. Glastonbury). — Ring of Bells P.R.H.A.

MEARS ASHBY (3 S.W. Wellingboro). — Griffin's Head P.R.H.A.

MEDBOURNE (6 N.E. Mkt. Harbro).—Horse and Trumpet.

MELKSHAM (Wilts).—King's Arms. See Lacock.

MELMERBY (8½ N.E. Penrith). —Toppin's T.

MELROSE (Roxb.).—Waverley T. See Earlston.

MELTON MOWBRAY.—George. See Dalby.

MELVERLEY (Salop, 4 N.W. Westbury Station).—Royal Hill Inn.

MENAI BRIDGE.—Marquis T., Mona Rd.; Penrhos Arms.

MERE (Wilts, 4 N.E. Gilling-ham). — Reynolds' T. See Stourton.

MERROW (2 N.E. Guildford).—T.H.

MERSTHAM (Surrey).—Joliffe Arms.

MERTHYR TYDVIL.—Central T.

METHWOLD (Norf., 3¼ S.E. Stoke Ferry).—George.

MIDDLESBROUGH (N. Yorks).—Shaftesbury T., Albert Rd.; Clifton T., by Station.

MIDDLESMOOR (Nidderdale). —Crown.

MIDDLETON-IN-TEESDALE (Durham). — Commercial T., Market Pl.; Cleveland Arms.

MIDDLEWICH (Ches.).—Red Lion.

MIDHURST (12 N. Chichester).—Crown; New Inn.

MILDENHALL (Suff.).—Bell.

MILFORD (5½ S.W. Guildford). —Red Lion.

MILFORD HAVEN (Pemb.).—Lord Nelson.

MILLOM (Cumb.). — Central T.

MILNATHORT (Kinross).—Thistle.

MILTON ABBAS (Dors.).—Hambrough Arms.

MINCHINHAMPTON (3½ S.E. Stroud).—The Institute.

MINEHEAD (Som.).—Holloway T.; Elgin Tower H.; Glen Rock T., 13, The Avenue; Rendell's Blenheim R.

MINSTERLEY (9 S.W. Shrewsbury).—Bath Arms.

MITCHELDEAN (Forest of Dean).—White Horse.

MOFFAT (Dumf.).—Fleming's T.; Black Bull.

MOLD (Flint).—Star.

MONK'S KIRBY (6 N.W. Rugby, 6 W. Lutterworth).—Denbigh Arms P.R.H.A.

MONMOUTH. — Dorothy R.; Monnow R.; Butchers' Arms; Angel; May Hill; Webb's B.H., 7, Church St.

MONTGOMERY (6 S. Welsh-
pool).—Old Bell T.

MORCHARD RD. STATION
(Devon, 6 N.W. Crediton).—
Sturt Arms.

MOREBATTLE (7 S.E. Kelso).
—Temple Hall.

MORECAMBE (3½ N.W. Lan-
caster).—De Lacy's T., Central
Promenade; Pearson's B.H.,
9, Claremont Rd., West End;
Birtle's T. and Stoddard's T.,
both Euston Rd.

MORETONHAMPSTEAD (12
S.W. Exeter).—Stanleick's T.;
Bell.

MORETON - IN-THE-MARSH
(Glos.).—White Hart; Smith's
R., High St.

MORPETH (15 N.N.W. New-
castle). — Queen's Head;
George and Dragon.

MORVILLE (Salop, 3 N.W.
Bridgnorth).—Acton Arms.

MORWENSTOW (Corn., 6 N.
Bude). — Bush; Cholwill's
B.H., Kathleen Cottage.

MOTCOMBE (Dors., 1½ N.W.
Shaftesbury). — Royal Oak
P.R.H.A.

MOTTRAM ST. ANDREW
(Ches., 2½ N.W. Prestbury).—
Wright's B.H.

MOUNTSORREL (4 S.E.
Loughboro).—Barker's B.H.,
149, Loughbro' Rd.

MUCH BIRCH (6½ S. Here-
ford).—Warmelow Tump.

MUCH MARCLE (5½ S.W. Led-
bury). — Walwyn Arms
P.R.H.A.

MUCH WENLOCK (14 S.E.
Shrewsbury).—Stork; Swan
and Falcon; Cooper's R., Barrow St.

MUKER (Swaledale). — Mrs.
Harker's B.H.; Queen's
Head; Farmers' Arms. See
Gunnerside.

MULLION (Corn., 6½ S. Helston).—Old Inn.

MUNDESLEY (Norf.).—Trim-
mer's B.H., 5, Manor Rd.

MUNDFORD (Norf., 4½ N.E.
Brandon).—Crown.

NAFFERTON (9½ S.W. Brid-
lington).—Cross Keys.

NAILSWORTH (Glos., 4 S.
Stroud).—Railway.

NAIRN (15 E.N.E. Inverness).
—Waverley T.

NANTGWYNANT (13 N.E.
Beddgelert). — Jones, Llyndy
Ucha Farm.

NANTWICH.—Queen's T., Pil-
lory St.

NAZEING (4 N.W. Epping).—
King Harold's Head.

NEATH (8 N.E. Swansea).—
Waverley T.

NESSCLIFF (8 N.W. Shrews-
bury).—Old Three Pigeons,
P.R.H.A.; Nesscliff H.

NETHER STOWEY (Som., 7½
N.W. Bridgwater).—George;
Rose and Crown; Mrs. Bind-
ing, 63, Keenthorne.

NETTLEBED (Oxon., 5 N.W.
Henley).—Bull.

NEVILLES CROSS (1 S.W.
Durham).—Nevilles Cross H.

NEWARK.—Castle T., 38, Castlegate; Thompson's T., 21,
Cartergate; Robin Hood, Lom-
bard St.

NEWBALD, NORTH. — See
North Newbald.

NEWBRIDGE (Denb., 2 S.W.
Ruabon).—Royal Oak.

NEWBRIDGE-ON-WYE (Rad-
nor, 7 S.E. Rhayader).—
Crown T.

NEW BRIGHTON (Ches.).—
Davies' R., 10, Atherton St.

NEWBURY (Berks).—Guildhall
T., Mansion House St.;
Cripps' Broadway Dairy;
George and Dragon; Ireland's
R., London Rd.; Litten P.H.
See next.

NEWBURY - HUNGERFORD
RD.—Halfway House.

NEWCASTLE EMLYN (9
E.S.E. Cardigan). — Emlyn
Arms.

NEWCASTLE - ON - TYNE.
—Clyde T.; Queen's T., 37,

Westmorland Rd.; Waverley
T., Newgate St.; Hume's T.,
Wentworth Pl.

NEWCASTLETON (Liddes-
dale).—Grapes.

NEWDIGATE (6 S.E. Dork-
ing). — Aitchison's Camp,
tents, Easter-Sept.

NEWENT (8 N.W. Gloucester).
—Devonia R.; George.

NEW GALLOWAY (Kirkc.).—
Kenmure Arms. See Ken
Bridge.

NEWLANDS VALE (S.W. of
Keswick).—Newlands Inn.

NEWMARKET (13 E. Cam-
bridge). — Newmarket T.,
Market St. See Chippenham.

NEWNHAM BRIDGE (Worc.,
3½ E. Tenbury).—Talbot.

NEWNHAM (11 S.W. Glouces-
ter).—Cosy R.

NEWPORT (Mon., 12 N.E. Cardiff).—Morrish's T.; Central
Y.M.C.A.

NEWPORT (I.O.W.). — Wel-
come T., High St.

NEWPORT (Essex, 3½ S.W.
Saffron Walden).—Star and
Garter.

NEWPORT (Salop, 11 W.S.W.
Stafford).—Raven and Bell.

NEWPORT (Pemb., 6 N.E.
Fishguard).—Farmers' Arms.

NEWPORT PAGNELL
(Bucks).—Swan.

NEWQUAY (N. Corn. Coast).—
Cliff P.H., 24, Cliff Rd.;
Prospect House, East St.

NEW QUAY (Card., 5 S.W.
Aberayron).—Black Lion.

NEW RADNOR (6 N.W. King-
ton).—Eagle.

NEW ROMNEY (Kent, 8 S.W.
Hythe).—Ship.

NEWTON (Lincs, 3 N.W.
Falkingham). — Red Lion
P.R.H.A.

NEWTON (N. Yorks, 3 S.W.
Guisbro).—King's Head.

NEWTON ABBOT (S. Devon).
—Welsh's T., New St.;
Churchill's T.; Queen's.

NEWTON POPPLEFORD (3
N.W. Sidmouth).—Exeter Inn
P.R.H.A.

NEWTON STEWART (23 E.
Stranraer).—Kay's Creebridge
P.H.; Patterson's T.; Gallo-
way Arms; Grapes.

NEWTOWN (7½ S.W. Mont-
gomery).—Lion.

NEWTON LINFORD (6 N.W.
Leicester). — Harrison, Yew
Tree Farm.

NIBLEY, NORTH.—See North
Nibley.

NITON (I.O.W.).—Royal Sand-
rock.

NORTHALLERTON (N.
Yorks).—Railway.

NORTHAMPTON.—Dodd's T.,
Bridge St.; Carlton T., 25,
Gold St.; Foxon's T. and Ben-
son's Castle T., both Black
Lion Hill; Propert's T. and
Spencer's T., both Marefair;
Waverley T., Guildhall Rd.

NORTH BERWICK.—See Gul-
lane.

NORTH CADBURY (Som., 5
S.W. Wincanton).—Catash Inn
P.R.H.A.

NORTHINGTON (Hants, 7
N.E. Winchester).—Woolpack
P.R.H.A.

NORTH NEWBALD (E.
Yorks, 4 S.E. Mkt. Weighton).
—New Inn.

NORTH NIBLEY (Glos., 2
S.W. Dursley).—White Hart.

NORTHOP (3½ S. Flint).—Red
Lion.

NORTH PETHERTON (Som.,
2 S. Bridgwater).—George.

NORTH TAWTON (Devon, 6½
N.E. Okehampton).—Ring of
Bells.

NORTHWICH (Ches.).—Dodd's
R., 103, Manchester Rd.;
Richardson's B.H., 16, Vic-
toria Rd.

NORTON (Salop, Bridgnorth-
Shifnal Rd.).—Hundred House.

NORTON (2 N.E. Daventry).—
White Horse P.R.H.A.

NORWICH.—Central T., Tomb-

land; Carlton T., Prince of
Wales Rd.; Goffin's T., 18,
Exchange St.

NOTTINGHAM. — Little John
Café; Bowden T., Queen's
Walk; Avondale T., 43, Castle
Gate; Cade's T., 18, Hamp-
den St.; Shakespeare T., nr.
Victoria Station.

NUNEATON (9 N. Coventry).—
Needwood T., Coton Rd.;
Windsor T.

NURSLING (5 W.N.W. South-
ampton). — H o r n s I n n
P.R.H.A.

NUTBOURNE (Suss., 6 W.
Chichester).—Holiday Camp,
huts, tents, etc.

NUTLEY (Suss., 5 S.W. Uckfield).—Nutley H.

OAKHAM (Rutl.).—Railway;
White Lion.

OAKLEY (Oxon., ½ W. Chin-
nor).—Wheatsheaf.

OARE (Wilts, 4 S.W. Marlbro).
—White Hart P.R.H.A.

OBAN.—County T.; Windsor
T.; Waverley T.; McDonald's
B.H., 3, Victoria Pl.

ODIHAM (6½ S.E. Basing-
stoke).—New Inn; Tuns.

OKEHAMPTON (D e v o n).—
Webb's T.; Red Lion T.; Cen-
tral T., Fore St.; Plume of
Feathers; London.

OKEHAMPTON - CREDITON
ROAD.—See Bow.

OLDHAM (Lancs).—Hassall's
T., Yorkshire St.

OLLERTON (Ches., 2 S.E.
Knutsford).—Dun Cow. See
Kneesall.

OLNEY (11 S.E. Northampton).
—Bull; Queen.

OMBERSLEY (3½ W. Droit-
wich).—Mrs. Bedford, Wellington House.

ORMSKIRK (12 N.E. Liver-
pool).—King's Arms.

ORTON LONGVILLE (2 S.W.
Peterbro). — Gordon Arms
P.R.H.A.

OSMOTHERLEY (6 N.E.
Northallerton).—King's Head.

OSWESTRY. — Criterion T.,
Beatrice St.; Bartlett's T.,
Albion Hill; Matthews T.;
Oriel T., Bailey St.

OTTERBURN (Northum.).—
See Horsley.

OTTERY ST. MARY (12 N.E.
Exeter).—King's Arms. See
Escot.

OTTRINGHAM (E. Yorks, 3
N.W. Patrington). — White
Horse.

OULTON BROAD (Norf.).—
Waveney H.

OUNDLE (Northants). — T.,
West St.; Cross Keys; Talbot.
See Warmington and Barnwell
and Benefield.

OVERTON (7½ S.W. Basing-
stoke).—Red Lion.

O X F O R D. — Exchange T.,
George St.; Becket T. and
Flory's T., both Becket St., nr.
Station; Dodson's T., 1, Bot-
ley Rd.

OXTED.—Old Bell.

PADSTOW (Corn.).—At Tre-
vone, 2 W., " St. Helens,"
B.H.

PAIGNTON (S. Devon).—Tor-
bay T. and Clark's T., both
Torbay Rd.

PAINSWICK (7 S.E. Gloucester).—T., by church gates;
Bell.

PAINSWICK HILL (2 N.
Painswick). — Gardner's Castle Bungalow B.H.

PARRACOMBE (Devon, 4½
S.W. Lynton). — Fox and
Goose.

PATELEY BRIDGE (Nidder-
dale).—Pudsey's T.

PATRICK B R O M P T O N
(Yorks, 4 N.W. Bedale).—
Wilson's Ashlar House B.H.

PATRINGTON (E. Yorks).—
Hildyard Arms.

PATTERDALE (Lake Dis.).—
White Lion. See Glenridding.
Patterdale and Glenridding are

1 m. apart at S. end of Ullswater.

PEEBLES.—Forester's T.

PEEL (I.O.M.).—Mrs. Lewin, 16, Derby Rd.; Cashin's B.H., Castlemere.

PEMBRIDGE (Heref., 7 W. Leominster).—Greyhound.

PEMBROKE.—Lion.

PEMBROKE DOCK.—Bush.

PENDEEN (Corn., 2½ N. St. Just).—Roberts, Higher Bojewyan Farm.

PENKRIDGE (6 N. Stafford).—Littleton Arms.

PENN (Bucks, 4 S.W. Amersham).—Crown.

PENNAL (3 W. Machynlleth).—Mrs. Evans, Brynian Bychain; Miss Williams, Griandy St.

PENRHYNDEUDRAETH (3½ E. Portmadoc).—Morris's Osmond R., High St.

PENRITH. — Waverley T., Crown Sq.; Albion T.; Central T.

PENSHURST (4 S.W. Tonbridge).—Station T.

PENTRE VOELAS (Denb.).—Thomas's Mill House B.H.; P.V. Arms.

PENYBONT (5 N.E. Llandrindod Wells).—Bufton's R.

PENZANCE.—Robins's Cornwall R., Causewayhead; Opie's T., Princes St.; Central T.

PERSHORE (8 S.E. Worcester).—Swan; Salmon's R.

PERTH.—Gowrie Douglas R.; Fraser's T.

PETERBOROUGH. — Bedford T., Queen St.; City T., Broad Bridge St.; Royal T., Westgate; Albion T., North St.

PETERHEAD (Aberdeen).—Palace.

PETERSFIELD (19 N.E. Portsmouth).—Bell; T., the Square; Blue Anchor; Terry's T.; Southcote B.H., Nyewood.

PETWORTH (Suss., 14 N.E. Chichester). — Wheatsheaf; Angel.

PEWSEY (Wilts).—See Wootton Rivers.

PEWSHAM (Wilts, 1½ S.E. Chippenham).—Swan.

PICKERING (N. Yorks).—Hugill's T.; Horseshoe; Castle.

PILLING (Lancs, 5 N.W. Garstang).—Simpson's New Hall B.H.

PILNING (9 N. Bristol).—King's Arms at Redwick.

PITLOCHRY (Perth).—Reid's T.

PLYMOUTH.—Pearse's T., 145, Union St.; Arthur's T., Buckland Ter.; St. Michael's T., North Rd. Station; Hacker's T., Athenæum Ter.; London T., Millbay Station.

PLYMSTOCK (3 S.E. Plymouth). — Plymstock Inn P.R.H.A.

POCKLINGTON (E. Yorks, 7 N.W. Mkt. Weighton).—New Red Lion.

POLRUAN (Corn., ferry from Fowey).—Mrs. Stephens and Mrs. Tyro, both West St.

PONTERWYD (Card.).—At 2 m. N.E., Dyffryn Castell Inn.

PONTYPOOL (Mon., 10½ N. Newport). — Waverley T., Crane St.

POOLE (5 W. Bournemouth).—Wynglade T.; Commercial T., Market St.; Longfleet T.

PORT GOWER (Suth., 2 S.W. Helmsdale).—T.H.

PORTHCAWL (G l a m.).—Brace's Central R., John St.

PORTHLEVEN (Corn., 2½ S.W. Helston).—Commercial.

PORT ISAAC (N. Coast Corn.).—Donnithorne's B.H.; Mrs. Panter, "Holmleigh," Port Gaverne.

PORTMADOC (11 E. Pwllheli).—Williams' Llys Eifion T., 41, High St.

PORTOBELLO (3 E. Edinburgh).—Donaldson's T., Bath St.

PORTREATH (Corn., 4 N.W. Redruth).—Portreath H.

PORTSMOUTH. — Washington
T., Pearl Buildings; North's
T., Cambridge Junc.; Royal
T., Commercial Rd.; Boyd's
T., 20, Landport Ter.; Mad-
din's T., Station St.; and at
Southsea, Victoria and Albert
T., 76, Albert Rd., and York
T., Hambrook St.

PORTSOY (8¼ W. Banff).—
Matthews' T.

PORTWAY (9 W.N.W. Here-
ford, 12 E. Hay).—Portway
Arms.

PORT WILLIAM (Wigtown).
—Monreath Arms.

POTTERS BAR (3 N. Barnet).
Old Robin Hood. See Gan-
nick Corner.

POTTON (Beds, 4 N.E. Biggleswade).—Rose and Crown.

POYNINGS (6 N.W. Brighton).
—Royal Oak.

PRESTATYN (4 E. Rhyl).—
Raven T. and B.H.

PRESTEIGNE (6¼ N.E. New
Radnor).—Frost's R., 3, Here-
ford St.; Duke's Arms. See
Whitton.

PRESTON (Lancs).—Worth's
T., 3, Latham St.; West End
T., 22, Fishergate Hill.

PRINCES RISBOROUGH
(Bucks).—At Cadsden, 2 N.E.,
Plough. See Bledlow.

PRUDHOE-ON-TYNE (11 W.
Newcastle).—Adam and Eve.

PULFORD (5 S. Chester).—
Huskisson's R.

PURSLOW (Salop, 2 W. Aston-
on-Clun).—Purslow Hundred
House, P.R.H.A. · ·

PWLLHELI.—London T., High
St.; Lewis's Bodorwel B.H.,
Abererch Rd.; Crown.

QUORN (Leic.).—White Horse.

RADSTOCK (Som.).—Fir Tree.
See Writhlington.

RAGLAN (7 S.W. Monmouth).—
Crown.

RAINHAM (4 E.S.E. Chatham).
—White Horse.

RAMSEY (Hunts).—Lion.

RAMSEY (I.O.M.).—Waterloo.

RAMSGATE. — Wellington T.
and Central T., both High St.;
Dawson's T., Chatham St.;
York House T., York Ter.; Ar-
tillery Arms.

RAVENGLASS (Cumb. Coast).
—Pennington Arms. See Holmrook.

RAWTENSTALL (Lancs).—
Queen's.

READING.—Café Royal, 60,
King's Rd.; Lodge T., King's
Rd.; Albany T., Greyfriars
Rd.; Thomas's R., 60, King's
Rd.; Rumming's T., 16, Lon-
don St.; Jackman's T., West
St.; Welcome R., Cross St.;
Britannia Tavern, Caversham
Rd.

REDBOURN (Herts, 4½ N.W.
St. Albans).—Bull.

REDCAR (Yorks Coast).—
Weatherill's Pier T.; Swan.

REDDITCH. — Royal; White's
R., Unicorn Hill.

REDHILL (Surrey).—Foster's
T.; Warwick H., Station Rd.

REDMIRE (Wensleydale).—
King's Arms.

REDRUTH (Corn.).—Oates' T.,
nr. Station; Alma T., Alma
Pl.; Lamb and Flag T.; Harris's R., 59, Fore St.

REETH (Swaledale).—Wallis,
Victoria House; King's Arms.

REIGHTON (5½ N.W. Bridlington).—Dotterel Inn.

RETFORD (Notts, Gt. North
Rd.). — Albany T., Bridge
Gate; Aldridge's T., nr. Sta-
tion; Howard's T., Grove St.;
Butchers' Arms.

RHAYADER (Wye Valley).—
Glan-nant T.; Butchers' Arms;
Bear's Head; Clark's B.H.,
Glandwr House.

RHUDDLAN (N. Wales).—
Mariners' Arms; New Inn.

RHYL.—Grosvenor T., facing
Station; Mostyn T., High St.;
Penmaen T., 77, Wellington
Rd. See Gronant.

RICCALL (4 N. Selby).—Grey-hound.

RICHMOND (Swaledale).—Fleece.

RICKMANSWORTH (Herts).—Turner's Old Tannery B.H., Mill End.

RIDGMONT (Beds, 4 S.W. Ampthill).—Red Lion.

RINGWOOD (New Forest).—Briggs' Montagu House T., by Station; Albany R., West St. See Avon.

RIPLEY (3½ N.W. Harrogate).—Hornsley's R.

RIPON. — Parker's Kirkgate House T., opp. Cathedral; Yoredale T., nr. Station.

RIVERHEAD (Kent, 1½ N.W. Sevenoaks).—Townsend's R.

ROBERTSBRIDGE (Suss., 5 N. Battle).—Langham T.

ROCHDALE.—Willett's Crescent T., Drake St.

ROCHE (Corn., 5 N.W. St. Austell).—Victoria.

ROCHESTER.—Speedwell T., opp. Central Station; Alexandra T.; City T., 3, High St.; Gordon T., 91, High St.

ROCKBEARE (6¼ E. Exeter).—Crown and Sceptre P.R.H.A.

ROCKINGHAM (Northants).—Sondes Arms.

ROLLESTON (3 N.W. Burton-on-Trent). — Spread Eagle P.R.H.A.

ROMALDKIRK (5 N.W. Barnard Castle).—R o s e and Crown.

ROMSEY (Hants).—Newman's B.H., Oak Cottage; Sawyers' Arms; Bridge T a v e r n; Brown's R.; Mrs. Cole, 90, Palmerston Rd.

ROPLEY (Hants, 4 E. Alresford).—Chequers.

ROSS (Wye Valley). — P.H., Eddy St.; Gwalia T., Broad St.; Watkins R.; George; Carlton R.; Nag's Head; Pheasant.

ROSTHWAITE (6 S. Keswick).—Royal Oak.

ROTHBURY (11 S.W. Alnwick).—Station.

ROTHERHAM (Yorks).—Glencoe T., Station Rd.

ROTHES (Elgin). — Seafield Arms.

ROTHWELL (Northants).—Red Lion.

ROWSLEY (Derby).—Buckley's B.H., 28, Chatsworth Rd.

ROYDON (W. Essex).—New Inn.

RUABON (Denb.).—Wynnstay Arms. See Newbridge.

RUDSTON (5 W. Bridlington).—Bosville Arms.

RUFFORD (5½ N.E. Ormskirk).—Fearn's Avondale R.

RUGBY. — Campbell T., by Parish Church; Coronation T., Station Rd.; Eagle T., Market Pl.

RUSHDEN (Northants).—Waggon and Horses; T., 5, Newton Rd.

RUTHIN (Denb.).—Cross Keys T.; Wynnstay Arms.

RYDE (I.O.W.).—Victoria T., 33, High St,; Prince of Wales; Rajah Brooke, Monkton St.; Britannia R.

RYE (Suss.).—Cinque Port Café.

SAFFRON WALDEN. — Abbey T., High St.

SALISBURY.—Three Swans T., Market Sq.; Bridge House T., 18, Dews Rd.; Nelson T., by Stations; Coach and Horses; Williams' T., 21, New Canal. See Wilton.

SALTBURN (Yorks. Coast).—Darley's T., Milton St.

SALTWOOD (betw. Folkestone and Hythe).—Castle.

SAMPFORD ARUNDEL (2 S.W. Wellington, Som.).—Red Ball.

SANDBACH (4½ N.E. Crewe).—Hungerford T.; Bear's Head.

SANDOWN (I.O.W.). — Mrs. Futcher, 4, Albert Rd.

SANDWICH.—Fleur de Lys; Nutley's B.H., Strand St.

SANDY LANE (Wilts, 4 S.W. Calne).—George P.R.H.A.

SANQUHAR (Dumf.).—T.H.

SARN (9 W. Pwllheli).—Penrhyn Arms.

SAWSTON (7 S.E. Cambridge). —White Lion.

SAXMUNDHAM (S u ff.).— White Hart.

SCARBOROUGH. — Waverley T. and Stafford T., both opp. Station; Bielby's B.H., 54, Cambridge St.; Holiday Camp, King St.; Talbot, Queen St. See Brompton and Cloughton and East Ayton.

SCOLE (Norf.).—Scole Inn (Old White Hart).

SEAL (1½ N.E. Sevenoaks).— Crown Point Inn P.R.H.A.; Kentish Yeoman.

SEATHWAITE (Borrowdale).— Pepper's B.H., Raingauge Farm.

SEATOLLER (Borrowdale).— Pepper's B.H., White House.

SEATON (S. Devon).—Gould's.

SEDBERGH (N.W. Yorks).— Nelson's T.; Red Lion. See Cautley Beck.

SEDGEFIELD (Durham).— Hardwick Arms.

SEDLESCOMBE (Suss., 3 N.E. Battle).—Queen's Head.

SELSEY (7 S. Chichester).— Terry's B.H., 4, South View.

SENNEN (Land's End).—Nicholas' B.H., Maryon Cottage; First and Last H.

SETTLE (W. Yorks).—Castleberg T.; Hoyle's T.

SEVENOAKS. — Rose and Crown; White Hart; Lime Tree T., London Rd. See Riverhead, Seal, Dunton Green, and Kemsing.

SHAFTESBURY (N. Dorset).— Ship. See Motcombe.

SHANKLIN (I.O.W.).—Jones's T., Regent St.

SHAP (Westmr.).—King's Arms.

SHARNFORD (Leic., 4½ S.E. Hinckley).—Old Star.

SHAWBURY (7 N.E. Shrews-bury).—Elephant and Castle; Post Office B.H.

SHEDFIELD (Hants, 3 E. Botley).—Black Horse.

SHEFFIELD.—City T., 160, The Moor; Unwin's Surrey T., Victoria St.; Hamilton T., 17, Eyre St.

SHENLEY (Herts, 5 N.W. Barnet).—White Horse; Hull's Wheatsheaf Farm.

SHENSTONE (Staffs, 3 S. Lichfield).—Plough and Harrow.

SHEPPERTON (2 E. Chertsey). —Old King's Head.

SHEPTON MALLET (Som.).— Bell; Red Lion; T., Market Pl. See Doulting.

SHERBORNE (D o r s.).— Plume of Feathers P.R.H.A.; Central T.; Crown P.R.H.A.; Cross Keys; Mrs. Andrews, 9, Ludbourne Rd.

SHERINGHAM (Norf. Coast). —Cedars P.H., South St.

SHIELDAIG (Ross and Crom.). —McLean's T.

SHIFNAL (Salop).—Jones' R., 13, Victoria Rd. See Brocton.

SHIPSTON - ON - STOUR.— White Horse; Stour B.H.

SHIPTON - UNDER - WYCH-WOOD (Oxon.).—Crown.

SHOREHAM (Suss.). — Royal George; at Lancing, Sussex Pad.

SHORWELL (I. of W.).—Crown.

SHOTLEY BRIDGE (Durham). —Crown and Swords.

SHREWSBURY.—Barley Mow, Abbey Foregate; Carlton T., College Hill; Bates B.H., 58, Wyle Cop; Marshall's H., Castle Gates; Old Post Office H.; Central T., Butcher's Row. See Bicton.

SIDBURY (Devon, 3 N. Sidmouth).—Red Lion.

SIDMOUTH (16 S.E. Exeter).— Hucker's T., Fore St. See Sidbury.

SILLOTH (Cumb.). — Silloth Hydro.

SITTINGBOURNE (Kent).—
Waverley T., Station St.

SKEGNESS.—Osborne T., High
St.; Pelham B.H., Wainfleet
Rd.

SKIPTON (W. Yorks). — Old
George; Garner's R., Belmont
Bridge.

SLEAFORD (Lincs).—Waverley
T., Ingram Ter.; Beesley's
R.s, Westgate and Southgate;
Still H.

SLINDON (4 W. Arundel).—Sir
Geo. Thomas Arms.

SLOUGH (2 N.E. Windsor).—
Bennett's B.H., 15, King's
Rd. See Farnham Common.

SOMERTON (Som., 5 N.E.
Langport).—White Hart; Red
Lion.

SOUTHAM (Warw.).—Black
Horse.

SOUTHAMPTON.—Central T.,
Western Shore; City T., Ble-
chynden Ter.; Heathfield T.,
West Park Rd.; Mascot R.,
High St.; Bunday's B.H., 58,
Portland Ter. See Eastleigh
and Nursling.

SOUTHEND (Essex).—Carlton
T., Warrior Sq.; Imperial R.,
Victoria Av.

SOUTH MIMMS (3 N.W. Bar-
net).—Plough.

SOUTHMINSTER (Essex, 8
S.E. Maldon). — Rose and
Crown.

SOUTH MOLTON (Devon).—
Gatting's Laurel Cottage B.H.

SOUTH TAWTON (Devon, 2
E. Sticklepath).—Seven Stars.

SOUTHWELL (Notts).—
Crown; Cromwell House,
Westgate.

SOUTHWOLD (Suff. Coast).—
Station H. See Wangford.

SPALDING (Lincs).—Waver-
ley T.; Cross Keys.

SPARKFORD (Som., 5 S.W.
Castle Cary).—Sparkford Inn
P.R.H.A.

SPELDHURST (2½ N.W. Tun-
bridge Wells).—George and
Dragon P.R.H.A.

SPILSBY (Lincs). — White
Hart.

SPURSTOW (Ches., 7 W.
Nantwich).—Crewe Arms.

ST. ALBANS.—St. Hilda's T.,
opp. Mid. Station; Clarendon
T., Market Pl.; Pendragon T.,
London Rd.

ST. ANDREWS (Fife Coast).—
Cross Keys; Linksgate B.H.,
10, Golf Pl.

ST. ASAPH (N. Wales).—Barlow's B.H., Elwy View; Railway H.

ST. AUSTELL (Corn.).—Davies'
T., North St.; Mennear's T.;
Queen's Head.

ST. BLAZEY (Corn.).—See
Luxulyan.

ST. BRIAVELS (7 N. Chep-
stow).—Taylor's Moat House
R.

ST. COLUMB (Corn.).—Rail-
way and Commercial.

ST. DAVIDS (Pemb.).—City H.

ST. GILES (Dors., 2 S.W. Cranborne).— Bull P.R.H.A.

ST. IVES (Corn.).—Curnow's
T., opp. P.O.; Bunney's T.

ST. IVES (Hunts).—Central T.;
Parrot H.

ST. JOHN'S CHAPEL (Wear-
dale).—King's *Head*.

ST. JUST (Corn.).—Commercial
H.; Gill's T. See Pendeen.

ST. KEVERNE (Corn.).—
White Hart.

ST. NEOTS (Hunts).—New
Inn; King's Head; Royal Oak.

ST. OSYTH (10 S.E. Col-
chester).—Red Lion.

STAFFORD.—Waverley T., nr.
G.P.O.

STAINDROP (Durham).—
Royal Oak.

STAINES (Midd.).—Mikado R.,
10, High St.

STALBRIDGE (Dors., 7 E.
Sherborne).—Red Lion.

STALHAM (Norf., 6 S.E. North
Walsham).—Railway.

STAMFORD (Lincs, Gt. North
Rd.).—Hosken's T., 14, Barn
Hill; Red Lion T.; Crown.

STANDERWICK (Som., 1½ S.E. Beckington).—Bell.

STANDON (8 N.E. Hertford).—Windmill.

STANHOPE (Durham, Weardale).—Phœnix.

STANSTED (Kent, 2½ N. Wrotham). — Milton's B.H., Brattle Pl.

STANSTEAD ABBOTS (4 E. Hertford).—Pied Bull.

STAPLEFORD (2½ N. Hertford). — Woodhall Arms P.R.H.A.

STAPLEHURST (8 S. Maidstone).—Bell.

STARBECK (2 E. Harrogate).—Mrs. Johnson, 8, Beech Grove Ter.

STEVENAGE (Herts, 4 S.E. Hitchin).—Central T.; Marquis of Lorne.

STICKLEPATH (Devon, 4 N.E. Okehampton).—Taw River H. See South Tawton.

STILTON (Hunts, Gt. North Rd.).—Coleman's B.H.

STIRLING.—McKillop's County T.; Arcade T., King St.

STOCKBRIDGE (6½ S. Andover).—Ship T. See Longstock.

STOCKPORT.—Albany T., 80, Wellington R. South.

STOCKTON - ON - TEES.—Washington T., Wellington St.

STOKE FERRY (Norf., 6 S.E. Downham Mkt.).—Crown.

STOKE GABRIEL (Devon 4 S.E. Totnes).—Church House Inn P.R.H.A.

STOKE MANDEVILLE (3 S.E. Aylesbury).—Bell.

STOKENCHURCH (Bucks).—King's Arms.

STOKESLEY (N. Yorks).—See Bilsdale.

STOKE-ON-TRENT. — Trew's Waverley T., Glebe St.; Rhodes' T., Winton Ter., Leek Rd.; Cauldron T., Stoke Rd.

STOKE-UNDER-HAM (6 W. Yeovil).—Fleur de Lys.

STONE (Glos., 4 S.W. Berkeley).—At Falfield, 1 m. S., New Inn; and at Woodford ¼ m. N., Fox.

STONE (7 N. Stafford).—Unicorn. See Aston-by-Stone.

STONEHAVEN (15 S.W. Aberdeen).—County T., Railway Rd.

STONEY MIDDLETON (Derby, 4½ N. Bakewell).—Moon.

STONEHOUSE (Lanark).—Black Bull.

STONOR (Oxon., 4 N.W. Henley).—Stonor Arms.

STONY STRATFORD (8 N.E. Buckingham).—Victoria T.; Bull.

STOURPORT (Worc.).—Swan.

STOURTON (Wilts, 3 N.W. Mere). — Spread Eagle P.R.H.A.

STOW (7 N.W. Galashiels).—Russell's.

STOW-ON-THE-WOLD (Glos.).—Rimell's T.; Unicorn; White Hart; Talbot.

STRANRAER (Wigtown).—McQuistin's T., George St.; Ely Pl. T.

STRATFORD - ON - AVON.—Royal R., Bridge St.; Emm's R., Sheep St.; Lansdown T. and Victoria T., both Wood St.; New Bull's Head R., Ball St.

STRATHAVEN (Lanark).—Central T., Kirk St.

STRATTON (Corn., 1½ E. Bude).—Bay Tree T.; Bank House R.; and at Marhamchurch, 2 m. S., Kennacott Farm.

STREATLEY (Berks). — See Basildon.

STREET (1½ S.W. Glastonbury).—Bear T., High St.

STRELLEY (Notts, 2 E. Ilkeston).—Broad Oak P.R.H.A.

STRETTON (Rutl.).—See Gt. North Rd.

STRETTON SUGWAS (3 N.W. Hereford).—Kite's Nest H.

STRINES (Derby, 2 S.E. Marple).—Dicker's Highfield Bungalow.

STROUD (9 S. Gloucester).— Grosvenor T., Russell St.

SUDBURY (Suff.).—Black Boy; Orbell T., Station Rd.; White Horse.

SUTTERTON (Lincs, 6 S.W. Boston).—Angel.

SUTTON-ON-TRENT (Notts). —Dolphin.

SWAFFHAM (Norf.). — Chapman's T., Market Pl.

SWANAGE.—Albany T.; Tyrrell's Queen's R.

SWANSEA.—Monico T., High St.; Gt. Western T., by Station.

SWINDON. — Albion T., 1 Bridge St.; Central T., Regent St.; Midland T., Newport St.; King's Arms.

SYSTON (5 N. Leicester).— Hanging Gate.

TADCASTER.—Londesborough.

TALGARTH (Brecon, 7 S.W. Hay).—Castle; Evans' Imperial R.

TALLINGTON (Lincs, 4 E. Stamford). — Kesteven Arms P.R.H.A.

TALSARNAU (3 N.N.E. Harlech).—Ship Aground; Mrs. Jones, Glan Morfa.

TALYCAFN (3 S. Conway).— Tyn-y-groes H.

TAL-Y-LLYN (Merion., 2 N. Upper Corris).—Minfford T.

TAMWORTH (Staffs).—Swan.

TARPORLEY.—See Clotton.

TATTENHALL (7 S.E. Chester).—Bear P.R.H.A.

TAUNTON.—Drayton T., nr. Station.

TAVISTOCK.—South Western T.; Cornish Arms; New Market H., P.R.H.A.

TAWTON, NORTH.—Ring of Bells.

TAYNUILT (13 E. Oban).— McNiven's B.H., Aros Villa.

TEBAY (Westm.).—Cross Keys.

TEIGNMOUTH. — Partridge's T., Station Rd.

TENBURY (Worc.). — Ship; Mattey's B.H., 33, Cross St. See Little Hereford and Newnham Bridge.

TENBY (S. Wales). — South Wales T., St. George St.

TETBURY (Glos.).—Gethin's R., Long St.; White Hart.

TETSWORTH (Oxon., 3 S.W. Thame).—Swan.

TEVERSALL (Notts, 3½ W. Mansfield).—Carnarvon Arms.

TEWIN (Herts, 3½ S.E. Welwyn).—Rose and Crown.

THAME (15 E. Oxford).— Swan. See Tetsworth.

THATCHAM (Berks, 3 E. Newbury).—White Hart; New Inn.

THAXTED (Essex, 6 N. Dunmow).—Enterprise T.

THEALE (5 S.W. Reading).— Railway; Red Lion.

THETFORD (Norf.).—Central T., Market Pl.; Crispe's T., Wells St.

THIRSK.—T., Market Pl. See Topcliffe.

THORNBURY (12 N. Bristol). —Moody's R., High St.

THORNE (9 N.E. Doncaster).— White Hart.

THORNEY (7 N.E. Peterbro).— Rose and Crown P.R.H.A.

THORNFORD (Dors., 3 S.W. Sherborne). — King's Arms P.R.H.A.

THORNHILL (9 N.W. Stirling).—Crown.

THORNHILL (14 N.W. Dumfries).—Hastings T.

THORNTON - LE - DALE (N. Yorks).—Buck.

THORPE-LE-SOKEN (12 S.E. Colchester).—Maid's Head.

THRAPSTON (Northants).— Swan; White Hart. See Islip.

THRELKELD (3½ N.E. Keswick).—Horse and Farrier.

THURSO (Caithness). — Harper's, Traill St.; Station H.

THWAITE (Swaledale, 1 N.W. Muker).—Joiners' Arms.

TINGEWICK (3 S.W. Buckingham).—White Hart.

TINGRITH (Beds, 4 E. Woburn).—Swan P.R.H.A.

TINTAGEL (N. Corn.).—Fry's P.H.; Clifton P.H.

TINTERN (Wye Valley).—Rose and Crown; Smith's B.H., The Manor.

TITCHFIELD (Hants, 2 W. Fareham).—Bugle.

TIVERTON (12 N. Exeter).— Gay's T., St. Peter St.

TONBRIDGE.—Burr's R., 156, High St. See Bidborough and Penshurst.

TOPCLIFFE (4½ S.W. Thirsk). —Swan; Black Bull.

TORCROSS (S. Devon).—See Chillington.

TORQUAY.—Woolley's T., 83, Union St.; Browne's T., Fleet St.

TORRINGTON (N. Devon).— Globe; Victory R., High St.

TOTLAND BAY (I.O.W.).— Godsell's R.

TOTNES (S. Devon).—Roberts' Commercial H.; Elizabethan R.; Day's B.H., 74, High St.; Higham's R., 83, High St.

TOTTON (Hants).—See Eling.

TOWCESTER.—Lewis's Central R.; Dainty R., High St.; Talbot.

TOWYN.—St. Cadvan's T., College Green; Mrs. Pugh, 29, Idris Villas. See Llanegryn.

TRAWSFYNYDD (12 N. Dolgelley).—Highgate T.

TRECASTLE (Brecon).—Bear House.

TREGONY (Corn., 6 E. Truro). —Town Arms.

TRING (Herts, 5 N.W. Berkhamsted).—George.

TROWBRIDGE (Wilts).—Cotswold T.; George.

TRURO.—Fletcher's T.; Gulley's R.

TUNBRIDGE WELLS.—Hunter's T., 18, High St.; Alexandra T., opp. G.P.O.; Maslen's

T., 70, High St.; Crescent T., Crescent Rd.

TUNSTALL (Suff., 2 S.E. Wickham Mkt.). — Green Man P.R.H.A.

TURRIFF (Aberdeen). — Fife Arms.

TUXFORD (Notts, 6½ S. Retford).—T., Eldon St.

TWYFORD (Berks).—Bull. See Hare Hatch and Waltham St. Lawrence and Knowl Hill.

TYDWEILIOG (9 W. Pwllheli). —Ship.

TYNEMOUTH.—Waverley T.; Sainsbury's T.

UCKFIELD (Suss.).—Bellingham's T., High St.; Bell; Mrs. Reed, 4, The Croft.

UGLEY OR OAKLEY (Essex). —White Hart.

UGTHORPE (7 W. Whitby).— Black Bull.

ULEY (Glos., 2 E. Dursley).— King's Head.

ULLAPOOL (Ross and Crom.). —Royal.

ULLSWATER. — See Glenridding and Patterdale.

ULPHA (4½ N. Broughton-in-Furness).—Traveller's Rest.

ULVERSTON (Furness).—Martin's T., Queen St.; Simpson's B.H., 3, Benson St.

UMBERLEIGH (6½ S.E. Barnstaple).—Rising Sun.

UPPINGHAM (Rutl.). — The Hostel, High St. See Alexton and Gt. Easton.

UPSTREET (5½ N.E. Canterbury).—Ship; Florence.

UPTON SNODBURY (6 E. Worcester).—Royal Oak.

USK (Mon.).—Three Salmon.

UTTOXETER (13 N.E. Stafford).—Elkes's New T., High St.; Waverley T., Bridge St.; Cross Keys; Titterton's R.

UXBRIDGE (Midd.).—Middleton's T., St. Andrews; Railway T., Vine St.; Brookfield T.

VENTNOR (I.O.W.).—Rayner's T.; Crab and Lobster; Prince of Wales. See Chale.

VYRNWY (Montg.).—Jones's B.H., Bryn Vyrnwy, foot of lake.

WADDESDON (5 N.W. Aylesbury).—Bell.

WADEBRIDGE (Corn.).—Cornish Arms; Commercial.

WADESMILL (Herts, 2 N. Ware).—Feathers.

WADHURST (6 S.E. Tunbridge Wells).—Queen's Head; Old Vine.

WAINFLEET (Lincs, 9 S.E. Spilsby).—Angel.

WAINHOUSE CORNER (Corn., 9 N.E. Camelford).—The Inn.

WAKEFIELD.—Cornhill T. and Waverley T., both Westgate.

WALBERTON (3 W. Arundel). —Royal Oak, Avisford Hill.

WALL (Northum., 3 N.W. Hexham).—Smith's Arms.

WALLINGFORD (Berks).— Tombs' T.

WALSINGHAM, LITTLE (Norf., 4½ S. Wells).—Black Lion.

WALTHAM (4 N. Chelmsford). —White Hart.

WALTHAM ST. LAWRENCE (2½ N.E. Twyford). — Bell P.R.H.A.

WANGFORD (Suff., 3½ N.W. Southwold).—White Lion.

WANSFORD (Gt. North Rd., 8 W. Peterbro').—Paper Mills Inn. See Apethorpe.

WANTAGE (Berks).—King Alfred's Head; Cosy Café.

WARE (Herts).—See Wadesmill and Hertford.

WAREHAM (Dors.).—Old Castle; Red Lion.

WARESLEY (Hunts, 4 N.E. Potton). — Duncombe Arms P.R.H.A.

WARKWORTH (Northum.).— Mason's Arms.

WARMINGTON (Northants; 2½

N.E. Oundle).—Hautboy and Fiddle.

WARMINSTER (9 S. Trowbridge).—Old Bell; Box's Magnet T.

WARNFORD (Hants, 6 N.E. Bish. Waltham).—George.

WARNHAM (Suss., 2 N.W. Horsham).—Greets Inn.

WARRINGTON.—Ward's T., nr. Bank Quay Station; Maddock's T., Sankey St.

WARSOP (Notts, 5 N.E. Mansfield).—Mrs. Hovell, Cleveland Villas.

WARWICK. — Aylesford T., High St.; Dale T., Old Sq.; Castle R., Smith St.

WASDALE HEAD (Cumb.).— Wilson's T.; also Wilson's at Burnthwaite.

WASS (N. Yorks, 2 N.E. Coxwold).—Wombwell Arms.

WATCHET (Som. Coast).— West Somerset H.

WATERLOOVILLE (Hants, 6 N. Portsmouth). — Queen's P.H.

WATFORD (Herts). — Lime Tree T., 33, High St.; Woolger's R., St. Albans Rd.

WATLINGTON (Oxon.).—Soldiers' Memorial Club.

WAVERTON (4 S.E. Chester). —Black Dog.

WEDMORE (Som., 4 S. Cheddar).—George.

WELLINGBOROUGH (10 N.E. Northampton). — Granville T.

WELLINGTON (Salop):— Swan, Watling St. Cross Roads; Cock.

WELLINGTON (Som., 8 S.W. Taunton). — Shaplands, Fore St.; Hutching's R., North St.; King's Arms. See Sampford Arundel.

WELLS (Norf.).—Railway. See Walsingham.

WELLS (Som.).—Jefford's T.; City T.; Red Lion T., Moggs' R., High St.; Mitre P.H.; Clarence.

WELSHPOOL (Montg.).—
White Lion. See Buttington.

WELWYN (Herts, 4 N. Hat-
field).—See Digswell Hill and
Ayot St. Peter and Tewin.

WELWYN GARDEN CITY (3
N. Hatfield).—Cherry Tree.

WEM (10½ N. Shrewsbury).—See
Grinshill and Loppington.

WENDOVER (5 S.E. Ayles-
bury).—See Gt. Kimble and Gt.
Hampden.

WENTBRIDGE (10 N.W. Don-
caster).—Saxby's R.

WEOBLEY (Heref., 7 S.W. Leominster).—Lion.

WEST BURTON (Wensleydale,
2 S. Aysgarth).—Fox and
Hounds.

WESTBURY (Wilts, 4½ S.
Trowbridge). — Lopes Arms.
See Bratton.

WEST FELTON (4½ S.E. Os-
westry).—Punch Bowl.

WEST MEON (Hants).—Red
Lion.

WESTON - BY - WELLAND (4
N.E. Mkt. Harbro).—Wheel
and Compass.

WESTON-SUB-EDGE (Glos., 2
N.W. Campden). — Seagrave
Arms.

WESTON - SUPER - MARE.—
Oxford T., Beach Rd.; La
Marguerite T., Oxford St.;
Star R., Meadow St.

WESTON ZOYLAND (Som., 3
S.E. Bridgwater). — Three
Greyhounds.

WEST PENNARD (3 E. Glas-
tonbury).—Red Lion P.R.H.A.

WEST WOODBURN
(Northum., 4 N.E. Bellingham).—Fox and Hounds.

WEST WYCOMBE (2½ N.W.
High Wycombe).—Black Boy.

WEYMOUTH. — Tett's T.,
King St.; Bishop's T. and
Royal's T., both St. Thomas
St.; Southwell's Isis B.H.;
Stoneleigh T., 5, Royal Ter.

WHEATLEY (5 E. Oxford).—
Merry Bells T., High St.

WHICHFORD (Warw-Oxon, 2
N.E. Long Compton).—Cook's
Mill Farm.

WHITCHURCH (Devon, 2 S.E.
Tavistock).—Whitchurch Inn
P.R.H.A.

WHITCHURCH (Hants, 7 N.E.
Andover).—Kingsley T.

WHITCHURCH (Salop, 20 N.
Shrewsbury).—Alexandra T.,
High St.; Dawson's T., Sta-
tion Rd.

WHITEGATE (Ches., 3½ S.W.
Northwich).—Plough.

WHITEHAVEN (Cumb.).—
Waverley T., Tangier St. See
Bigrigg.

WHITLAND (14 W. Carmar-
then).—Railway P.R.H.A.

WHITLEY BAY (Northum.
Coast).—Lewis's Haven House
T., Promenade; Cusworth's
Esplanade T.

WHITTINGTON (Salop, 2 N.E.
Oswestry). — White Lion
P.R.H.A.

WHITTLESEY (5 E. Peterbro).
—Falcon.

WHITTON (Radnor, 3½ N.W.
Presteigne). — Whitton Arms
P.R.H.A.

WICK (Caithness).—Caledonian.

WICKHAM (Hants, 4 N. Fareham).—King's Head.

WICKHAM MARKET.—White
Hart. See Tunstall.

WICKWAR (Glos.).—New Inn.

WIDDECOMBE (8 S.W. More-
ton Hampstead).—Old Inn.

WIGTON (11½ S.W. Carlisle).—
Royal Oak T.

WIGTOWN (Galloway).—Galloway Arms.

WILDBOARCLOUGH (6 S.E.
Macclesfield).—Sigley's Dane
Cottage B.H.

WILLENHALL (Staffs).—
Kent's R., Market Pl.

WILLERSEY (Glos., 7 S.E.
Evesham).—Bell; New Inn.

WILTON (3 N.W. Salisbury).—
Bell P.R.H.A.

WIMBORNE (Dors.).—Three
Lions; Griffin; King's Head.

WINCANTON (Som.). — See North Cadbury.

WINCHCOMBE (6¼ N.E. Cheltenham). — G e o r g e; Mrs. Major.

WINCHESTER.—Oriel T., City Rd.; Sharp's Carfax T., Station Hill; North Dene P.H., Sussex St.; Castle H.; Bond's B.H., 3, Gladstone St.

WINDERMERE. — Cristopherson's T.; Waverley T.; Tyson's B.H., 7, Alexandra Rd.

WINDSOR. — Harley House P.H., 14, Park St.; Tower House P.H., Thames St.; Nell Gwynne R., 5, Church St.; Chantler's Cosy R., Peascod St.

WINSFORD (Ches., 5 S. Northwich).—Golden Lion.

WINSTER (3 S. Bowness-on-Windermere).—Brown Horse.

WINSTER (Derb., 4 N.W. Matlock).—Winfield's B.H., East Bank View.

WINTERINGHAM (N. Lincs). —Bay Horse.

WISBECH (Camb.). — Royal; Crawford's T.

WITHAM (8 N.E. Chelmsford). Spread Eagle.

WITHAM FRIARY (Som., 5 S.W. Frome).—Seymour Arms P.R.H.A.

WITHERNSEA (Yorks Coast). —Barton's Victory R.

WIVELISCOMBE (S o m.).— White Hart.

WIXFORD (Warw., 2 S. Alcester).—Fish.

WOKINGHAM (7 S.E. Reading).—Red Lion; Osmond's R., Peach St.

WOLVERHAMPTON. — Clarence T., Queen St.; Imperial T., Princes Sq.; Royal T., Railway St.

WOLVERTON (2 N.E. Stony Stratford). — Crauford Arms P.R.H.A.

WOODBRIDGE (Suff.).—Bull.

WOODBURY (7 S.E. Exeter).— Hall's Bakery, Church St.

WOODCHURCH (Kent, 4 E. Tenterden). — Pearson, Redbrook Farm.

WOODFORD (Gloster-Bristol Road, 3 S. Berkeley).—Fox.

WOODHALL SPA (Lincs).— Hallatt's Ingledew B.H.

WOODLANDS (4 N.W. Doncaster). — W o o d l a n d s Inn, P.R.H.A.

WOODSTOCK (8 N.W. Oxford).—White's Blenheim Park B.H.

WOOLHAMPTON (Berks, Bath Rd.).—Rising Sun.

WOOLSTON (Warw.). — See Brandon and Church Lawford.

WOOLSTONE (Berks, 6 S. Faringdon). — White Horse P.R.H.A.

WOORE (Salop).—Swan.

WOOTTON RIVERS (Wilts, 5 N.E. Pewsey).—Royal Oak.

WORCESTER. — Lyttelton T., Broad St.; Central T., the Cross; Lea's Pierpoint T., Pierpoint St.; Diglis H., nr. Cathedral.

WORKINGTON (C u m b.).— Green Dragon.

WORKSOP (Notts).—Waverley T.

WORTHEN (Salop, 3½ W. Minsterley).—White Horse.

WORTHING (Suss.).—Victoria T., by Station; Waverley T., Chapel Rd.; Bedford T., Montagu St.; Clark's R., Bath Pl.

WOTTON - UNDER - EDGE (Glos., 4 S. Dursley).—Falcon; Matthews' R., Church St.

WRAGBY (11 N.E. Lincoln).— Turner Arms.

WRAXALL (6 W. Bristol).— Battleaxes, P.R.H.A.; and at 1 m. N.E., Failand Inn P.R.H.A.

WRAY (10 N.E. Lancaster).— George and Dragon.

WREXHAM (Denb.). — Westminster T., Grosvenor Rd.; Thomas' T., 16, Chester St.; Trevor's T.; Jones's Commercial T Queen St. See Marford.

WRITHLINGTON (Som., 1 E. Radstock).—Fir Tree P.R.H.A.

WROTHAM (Kent).—Horse and Groom. See Stansted.

WROXHAM (7 N.E. Norwich). —Castle; Nokes' R.

WYMESWOLD (Leic., 4½ N.E. Loughbro).—Windmill.

WYMONDHAM (10 S.W. Norwich).—King's Head; Mallow's P.H.

YALDING (6½ S.W. Maidstone). —Anchor.

YARMOUTH, GREAT.—Clarence T., 7-9, Regent Rd.; White Horse.

YATTENDEN (Berks, 12 N.W. Reading).—Royal Oak.

YATTON (Som., 7 N. Axbridge). —Prince of Orange.

YEOVIL (Som.).—Fernleigh T., nr. Station; Albany T., Middle St. See E. Chinnock and E. Coker.

YORK.—Minster T., St. Martin's Cres.; Burns's T., Rougier St.; Ebor T., Low Ousegate; Haddakin's T., 106, Micklegate; Cromwell T.; Commercial T., 45, Micklegate; Grapes, Tanner Row.

YOULGRAVE (Derby, 3½ S.W. Bakewell).—Thornhill Arms.

YOXFORD (Suff., 4 N. Saxmundham).—Three Tuns.

ZENNOR (Corn.). — Tinners' Arms.

IRELAND.

ABBEYFEALE (Lim.). — Central.

ACHILL ISLAND. — Johnstone's H. and Sweeney's H., Achill Sound; Mountain View H., Doogort; Amethyst House, Keel.

ANTRIM.—Masserene Arms.

ARDARA (18 N.W. Donegal).— Ardara T.; Brennan's.

ARDEE (14 N.W. Drogheda).— Ruxton Arms.

ARKLOW.—Railway and Commercial.

ARMAGH. — Westbrook T.; Beresford Arms.

ATHLONE.—Ramsay's

AUGHNACLOY (Tyrone).—Imperial.

AUGHRIM (Wicklow). — Lawless's.

BAGNALSTOWN (Carlow).— Ward's.

BALLAGHADERIN (Roscommon).—Commercial.

BALLINA (Mayo).—Moy.

BALLINASLOE (12 S.W. Athlone).—Flanagan's.

BALLINTOY (Antrim Coast).— Carrick-a-Rede H.

BALLYBAY (11 S.E. Monaghan).—Leslie Arms.

BALLYCASTLE (Antrim Coast). —Clermont T.

BALLYGAWLEY (Tyrone). —Stewart Arms T., and one opposite.

BALLYLIFFIN (Don., 12 N. Buncrana).—Ballyliffin H.

BALLYMENA (Antrim).—Albert T.

BALLYNAHINCH (Down).— The B'hinch H., High St.

BALLYSADARE (4 S.W. Sligo). —Hotel.

BALLYSHANNON (14 S.W. Donegal).—Royal T.

BANGOR (Mayo, 20 W. Crossmolina).—Miss Hickson's.

BANNOW (Wexford).—Atlantic.

BANTRY.—McCarthy's.

BELFAST. — Robinson's T., Donegal St.; Menteith's T., York St.; Crown; Byron T., Gt. Victoria St.

BELMULLET (Mayo).—Erris; Royal; Sea View.

BERAGH (7 S.E. Omagh).— Cassidy's.

E

BLESSINGTON (19 S.W. Dublin).—Downshire Arms.

BORRIS (Carlow). — Commercial.

BOYLE (Roscom.). — Rockingham Arms.

BUNCRANA (12 N.W. Londonderry).—Atlantic.

BUNDORAN (Donegal Bay).—O'Gorman's.

BURTONPORT (Don., 5 N.W. Dungloe).—O'Donnell's.

BUSHMILLS (5 E. Portrush).—Halliday's T.

CAHIRCIVEEN (Kerry).—Railway.

CAHIRDANIEL (Kerry, 7 S.E. Waterville).—See Darrynane.

CALLAN (Kilkenny).—Central; Callanan's.

CAPPOQUIN (10 W. Dungarvan).—Walsh's.

CARLOW.—Club House T.

CARNDONAGH (Donegal).—O'Doherty's.

CARNLOUGH (Antrim Coast). —Londonderry Arms.

CARRICK (Donegal).—Hotel.

CARRICKFERGUS (Antrim).—Imperial.

CARRICKMACROSS (14 W. Dundalk).—Shirley Arms.

CARRICK - ON - SHANNON. —Bush.

CARRICK-ON-SUIR. — Kirwan's.

CARRIGART (Don., 16 N. Letterkenny).—Patton's.

CASHEL (Tipper).—Ryan's Central; Stewart's Rock; Corcoran's.

CASHEL BAY (Galway).—Zetland.

CASTLECOMER (14 W.S.W. Carlow).—Wandesforde Arms.

CASTLEISLAND (Kerry).—Imperial.

CASTLEROCK (6 N.W. Coleraine).—Mullan's.

CASTLETOWN - B E R E - HAVEN (Cork).—Berehaven.

CASTLEWELLAN (Down).—Commercial.

CAVAN.—Imperial T.: Bridge; Farnham.

CHARLESTOWN (Mayo, 6 E.N.E. Swineford).—Imperial.

CHARLEVILLE (Cork).—Madden's.

CHURCHILL (N. Donegal).—Wilkins.

CLAREMORRIS (Mayo, 15 S.E. Castlebar).—St. Colman's.

CLIFDEN (Connemara). — Lyden's.

CLONAKILTY (Cork, 13 S.W. Bandon).—O'Donovan's.

CLONES (Monaghan).—Erne; Lennard Arms; Dunne's.

CLONMEL. — Magner's; Hearn's.

CLOYNE (Cork, 5 S. Middleton).—Dunne's.

CLOYNES (Monaghan).—Lennard Arms.

COLERAINE (Londonderry).—Westbrook T.

CONG (Mayo, 27 N.W. Galway). —Tourists and Anglers.

CORK.—Windsor, King St.; Munster, Coburg St.

CREESLOUGH (Donegal Coast).—Sharkey's.

CROLLY BRIDGE (Don., 2 S.W. Gweedore).—Inn.

CULLENSTOWN (15 S.W. Wexford, on Bannow Bay).—Atlantic.

CUSHENDALL (Antrim Coast). —Delargy's.

DARRYNANE (Kerry, 7 S.E. Waterville).—Keating's.

DERRYBEG (Donegal Coast).—McBride's.

DINGLE.—Benner's.

DONEGAL.—Smullen's Crown; Imperial.

DROGHEDA.—Central.

DROMAHAIR (Leitrim).—Abbey.

DUBLIN.—Westbrook T., Rutland Sq.; St. Andrews T., Exchequer St.; Ivanhoe T., 8, Harcourt St.; Edinburgh T., 56, Upper Sackville St.

DUNDALK. — Lorne; Queen's Arms.

DUNGANNON (Tyrone).—Myrdith T.; Ranfurley Arms.

DUNGARVAN (W a t e r f.).— Lawlor's T.; Devonshire Arms.

DUNGLOE (D o n e g a l).— Sweeney's; Dougherty's.

DUNLAVIN (Wickl.). — Imperial.

DUNMANWAY (Cork).—Railway; West End H.

EDGWORTHSTOWN (Longf.). —Imperial.

ELPHIN (9 S.W. Carrick-on-Shannon).—Elphin H.

ENNISCORTHY (W e x f.).— Railway.

ENNISKERRY (Wicklow).— Leicester Arms.

ENNISKILLEN (Ferman.).— Reynolds' T., Forthill St.; Railway.

ENNISTYMON (Clare).—Commercial.

FALCARRAGH (Donegal).— McGinley's; and at Gortahook, 3 S.W., McFadden's.

FERMOY (Cork).—Imperial.

FERNS (Wexford). — Bolger's Commercial.

GALWAY.—Mahon's, Forster St.

GARVAGH (12 S. Coleraine).— Imperial.

GIANT'S CAUSEWAY (Derry). —Kane's Royal.

GLENARIFF (Antrim Coast).— McCormack's. T.

GLENBEIGH (Kerry). — Glenbeigh H.

GLENCAR (Kerry, 10 S.W. Killorglin).—Breen's Glencar H.

GLENCOLUMBKILL (Donegal).—McNele's.

GLENGARRIFF (Cork).—Post Office.

GLEN OF THE DOWNS (Wicklow).—Glen View.

GLENTIES (Donegal).—O'Donnell's.

GLIN (Limerick).—Conway's.

GORESBRIDGE (11 E. Kilkenny).—Commercial.

GOREY (Wexf.). — Railway; Rams Arms.

GORT (Galway).—Commercial.

GREYSTONES (Wicklow).— Railway.

GOUGANEBARRA LAKE (Cork, 16 W. Macroom).— Cronin's.

GWEEDORE. — See C r o l l y Bridge and Middletown.

INCHIGEELA (Cork, 9 S.W. Macroom).—Lake.

KANTURK (Cork).—Lucey's.

KENMARE (Kerry). — O'Sullivan's, Henry St. See next.

KENMARE-SNEEM ROAD.— Doran's Templenoe B.H., $3\frac{1}{2}$ W. Kenmare.

KILCULLEN (Kildare).—Bardon's.

KILDARE.—Commercial.

KILDYSART (Clare). — Commercial.

KILLARNEY.—Sheheree House, off Muckross Rd.; Castle H., New St.; and at Muckross, 2 m., O'Sullivan's.

KILLORGLIN (13 N.W. Killarney).—Railway.

KILLYBEGS (Donegal Coast). —Coane's; Gannon's; Roger's.

KILMACRENAN (Donegal).— Taylor's.

KILLMALLOCK (Limerick).— Central.

KILRUSH (Clare, 9 S.E. Kilkee).—Williams's.

KNOCKLONG (10 S.W. Limerick).—Railway.

LARNE.—King's Arms.

LEENANE (Galway).—King's.

LETTERFRACK (Galway).— The H.

LETTERKENNY (Donegal).— McCarry's; Hegarty's.

LIMERICK.—McMahon's T., O'Connell St.; Globe T.; Glentworth.

LISDOONVARNA (Clare).—Atlantic View.
LISMORE (Waterf.).—Blackwater Vale.
LISTOWEL (Kerry).—Listowel Arms.
LONDONDERRY. — Diamond T.; Melville, Foyle St.
LURGAN (20 S.W. Belfast).—Star T.; Brownlow Arms.

MACROOM (24 W. Cork).—Williams's.
MAGHERA ('Derry).—Walsh's; Commercial.
MALLOW (Cork). — Moran's Central.
MARYBOROUGH (Queens.).—Aird's Central; Horan's.
MIDDLETON (Cork).—Middleton Arms.
MIDDLETOWN (Donegal, 5 N.W. Gweedore).—McBride's.
MILFORD (Donegal, 10 N. Letterkenny).—Stewart's R.
MILLTOWN-MALBAY (Clare Coast).—Central.
MITCHELSTOWN (Cork).—Royal.
MOHILL (Leitrim). — Knott's Commercial.
MOUNT CHARLES (4 S.W. Donegal).—Commercial T.
MOUNTRATH (Queens.).—Railway.
MOVILLE (Donegal Coast).—Prospect.
MULLINGAR (Westmeath).—Walsh's.

NAAS (20 S.W. Dublin).—Royal.
NAVAN.—Central.
NENAGH (Tipp.).—O'Meara's.
NEWCASTLE (Down Coast).—Central T., Main St.
NEWPORT (Mayo, 7 N. Westport).—Chambers'.
NEW ROSS (13 N.E. Waterford).—Globe.
NEWRY.—Newry H.; Victoria.
NEWTOWN BARRY (Wexf.).—King's Arms.
NEWTOWN BUTLER (Ferman.).—Maguire's T.

NEWTOWN STEWART (Tyrone).—Black Bull.

OLDCASTLE (Meath).—Napier Arms.
OMAGH (Tyrone).—Milligan's T.
OUGHTERARD (17 N.W. Galway).—Murphy's.

PETTIGOE (16 N.E. Ballyshannon).—Aiken's.
PORTADOWN (A r m a g h).—Queen's; Imperial.
PORTGLENONE (9 W. Ballymena).—Victoria.
PORTRUSH (Antrim Coast). Eglinton.
PORTSTEWART (3 W. Portrush).—Carrig-na-cule T.

RANDALSTOWN (5 N.W. Antrim).—McAuley's.
RAPHOE (15 S.W. Londonderry).—Holmes's.
RATHDRUM (9 S.W. Wicklow).—Walsh's.
RATHKEALE (9 S.W. Limerick).—Pigott Arms.
RECESS (Galway, 12 E. Clifden).—Joyce's B.H., Cloonacarton.
ROSCOMMON.—Crealy's.
ROSCREA (Tipp.).—Central.
ROSTREVOR (Down Coast).—Craig-a-vad.
ROUNDSTONE (G a l w a y Coast).—Kinton's T.
SAINTFIELD (11 S.E. Belfast). —McRobert's.

SKIBBEREEN (Cork).—West Cork; Eldon.
SLIGO.—Central Commercial, Ratcliffe St.
SNEEM (15 S.W. Kenmare).—Sheehan's.
STEWARTSTOWN (Tyrone).—Imperial.
STRABANE (Tyrone). — Commercial.
SWANLINBAR (C a v a n).—Veitch's T.

THURLES (Tipp.).—Hayes'.
TIPPERARY.—Carroll's.
TRALEE.—Central, Denny St.
TRAMORE (7 S. Waterford).—
Avondale.
TRIM (Meath).—Central.
TULLAMORE (Kings.).—Char-
leville Arms.
TULLEW (Carlow).—Slaney's;
Bridge.

VALENCIA.—Royal.

VIRGINIA (Cavan, 6 N.E. Oldcastle).—Headfort Arms.

WATERFORD. — Metropole;
Adelphi.
WATERVILLE (Kerry Coast).
—Foley's T. See Darrynane.
WESTPORT (Mayo Coast).—
Railway; Joyce's P.H.; and at
Rossmoney, Kilcovne's H.
WICKLOW.—Bridge.

NORTHERN FRANCE.
(Normandy, Brittany, etc.)

ABBEVILLE (Somme).—H. de
France.
ALENCON (Orne).—H. du
Grand-Cerf.
ANDELYS, LES (Eure).—H. des
Fleurs at Petit Andely.
ANTRAIN (Ille-et-V.). — H.
Grandmaison.
ARGENTAN (Orne).—H. du
Cheval Blanc.
ARQUES - LA - BATAILLE
(Seine-Inf.).—H. du Chemin
de Fer.
ARROMANCHES (C a l v.).—
Grand H.
AUDERVILLE (M a n c h e).—
H. du Soleil Levant.
AUMALE (Seine-Inf.).—H. du
Dauphin.
AURAY (Morbihan).—H. du
Lion d'Or.
AVRANCHES (Manche). — H.
Bonneau; H. d'Angleterre.

BALLEROY (Calvados).—H. de
la Place.
BAPAUME (Pas-de-Calais).—
H. du Pas de Calais.
BARENTIN (Seine-Inf.).—H.
du Chemin de Fer.
BARENTON (Manche).—H. de
France.
BARFLEUR (Manche).—H. du
Port.
BAYEUX (Calvados).—H. du
Lion d'Or.
BEAUMONT - LE - ROGER
(Eure).—H. du Lion d'Or.

BEAUVAIS (Oise).—H. de la
Poste.
BECHEREL (Ille-et-V.).—H.
du Centre.
BELLEME (Orne).—H. Saint-
Louis.
BELLE-ILE (Morbihan).—At-
lantic-Hôtel; H. du Com-
merce.
BERNAY (Eure).—H. du Lion
d'Or, rue d'Alençon; H. du
Cheval-Blanc.
BERNEVAL-SUR-MER (nr.
Dieppe).—H. le Val Fleuri.
BINIC (C. du N.).—H. de l'Uni-
vers.
BLANGY-SUR-BRESLE (Seine-
Inf.).—H. de la Poste.
BREHAT, ILE DE (C. du N.).
—H. du Port.
BRETEUIL (Oise).—H. du
Globe.
BRIGNOGAN (Finis.).—H. des
Bains de Mer.
BRIOUZE (Orne).—H. de la
Poste.
BULLY-GRENAY (P. de C.).—
H. Moderne.

CAEN (Calv.).—H. de France;
if it is race week here, clear
out.
CALAIS.—H. du Commerce et
Excelsior.
CALLAC (C. du N.).—H. du
Centre.
CANY-BARVILLE (Seine-Inf.).
—H. du Commerce.

CARENTAN (Manche).—H. du Commerce.

CARHAIX (Finist.).—H. de France.

CARNAC (Morb.). — H. des Voyageurs.

CARROUGES (Orne). — H. Saint-Pierre.

CARTERET (Manche).—H. de la Mer.

CARVIN (P. de C.).—H. Laloux.

CAUDEBEC (Seine-Inf.).—H. du Havre.

CAULNES (C. du N.).—H. de la Poste.

CAYEUX-SUR-MER (Somme). —H. du Commerce; H. Central.

CHATEAULIN (Finist.).—H. de la Grand'maison.

CHATEAUNEUF (nr. St. Malo). —H. de la Croix d'Or.

CHATEAUNEUF DU FAOU (Finist.).—H. Belle-Vue.

CHERBOURG (Manche).—H. Moderne.

CONCARNEAU (Finist.).—H. de France.

CONDE (Calv.).—H. de Normandie; H. du Lion d'Or.

CORLAY (C. du N.).—H. des Voyageurs.

COUTANCES (Manche).—H. de la Gare.

COYE (Oise).—H. des Etangs.

CROZON (Finis.).—H. Moderne.

CREIL (Oise).—H. du Chemin de fer.

CROISILLES (P. de C.).—H. des Voyageurs.

CROTOY, LE (Somme).—H. du Commerce.

DAMVILLE (Eure).—H. de la Poste.

DINAN.—H. Marguerite; H. de Paris.

DIVES-SUR-MER (Calv.).—H. des Voyageurs.

DOMFRONT (Orne).—H. du Commerce; H. de la Poste.

DOUARNENEZ (Finis.). — H. du Commerce.

DOUDEVILLE (Seine-Inf.).— H. de France.

DOULLENS (Somme).—H. des Quatre-Fils-Aymon.

DUCEY (Manche).—H. du Lion d'Or.

DUCLAIR (Seine-Inf.).—H. du Chariot d'Or.

ELVEN (Morb.).—H. du Lion d'Or.

EPERNAY (Marne).—H. Moderne.

ERQUY (C. du N.).—H. des Bains.

ETABLES (C. du N.).—H. Continental.

ETEL (Morb.).—H. de la Gare et de la Plage.

EU (Seine-Inf.).—H. du Commerce.

FALAISE (Calv.).—H. de Normandie.

FAOU, LE (Finis.).—Restaurant du Marché.

FAOUET, LE (Morb.).—H. du Lion d'Or; H. de la Croix d'Or.

FAUQUEMBERGUE (P. de C.).—H. de l'Univers.

FERTE-MACE, LA (Orne).—H. du Cheval-Noir; H. du Grand-Turc.

FLEURY - SUR - ANDELLE (Eure).—H. du Vexin.

FOUESNANT (Finis.).—H. des Pommiers.

FOUGERES (Ille-et-V.).—H. de l'Ouest.

FRUGES (P. de C.).—H. du Cheval-Noir.

GAILLON (Eure).—H. du Soleil d'Or.

GENETS (Manche, nr. Avranches).—H. des Voyageurs.

GER (Manche).—H. des Voyageurs.

GISORS (Eure).—H. Moderne.

GOURIN (Morb.).—H. du Cheval-Blanc.

GRAND-CAMP-LES-BAINS (Calv.).—Grandcamp H.

GRANVILLE (Manche). — H. des Bains.

GUER (Morb.).—H. de France.

GUINGAMP (C. du N.).—H. du Commerce; Grand H. de France.

HAM (Somme).—H. de France.

HARFLEUR (Seine-Inf.).—H. du Commerce.

HAVRE, LE.—Hotel-Restaurant Belle-Vue, 14, Place Gambetta; H. des Négociants, rue Corneille; H. Victoria, 37, quai de Southampton.

HESDIN (P. de C.).—H. de France; H. du Commerce.

HONFLEUR (Calv.).—H. du Cheval-Blanc; H. d'Angleterre.

HUELGOAT (Finis.).—H. de France.

ISLE-AUX-MOINES (Bay of Morbihan).—H. Belle-Vue.

IVRY-LA-BATAILLE (Eure).— H. Saint-Martin.

JOSSELIN (Morb.). — H. de France.

JUGON (C. du N.).—H. de l'Ecu.

JUVIGNY - SOUS - ANDAINE (Orne).—H. des Voyageurs.

LAMBALLE (C. du N.).—H. des Voyageurs, nr. Station.

LANDIVISIAU (Finis.).—H. du Commerce; H. du Léon.

LANNION (C. du N.).—H. de France.

LAVAL (Mayenne).—Gd. H. de Paris; H. de l'Ouest.

LESNEVEN (Finis.). — H. Grande-Maison.

LISIEUX (Calvados).—H. de France et d'Espagne.

LOC-TUDY (Finis.).—H. des Bains.

MALESTROIT (Morb.).—H. de l'Aigle d'Or.

MAREUIL - SUR - OURCQ (Oise).—H. du Soleil d'Or.

MAUBEUGE (Nord).—H.-Restaurant Rouneau.

MAURON (Morb.).—H. Grand-Maison.

MAYENNE.—Moderne-Hotel.

MENTONE (Riviera).—H. Gay.

MERU (Oise).—H. du Centre.

MESLE - SUR - SARTHE, LE (Orne).—H. du Cheval-Blanc.

MONT - SAINT - MICHEL (Manche).—H. Duval, also called Cheval-Blanc; H. de la Croix-Blanche.

MONTAUBAN (Ille-et-V.).—H. de l'Ouest.

MONTEBOURG (Manche).— H. Alexandre Bienaimé.

MONTFORT (14 W. Rennes).— H. Joly.

MONTFORT - SUR - RISLE (Eure).—H. du Soleil d'Or.

MORLAIX (Finis.).—H. Branellec; H. Bozellec (up Station Hill).

MORTAGNE (Orne).—H. du Grand-Cerf.

MORTAIN (Manche).—H. de la Poste.

MOULINS ⊦ LA - MARCHE (Orne).—H. du Dauphin.

NACQUEVILLE (Manche).—H. du Village Normand.

NANTES.—H. des Trois-Marchands, 26, rue d'Erdre.

NEUBOURG, LE (Eure).—H. de la Poste; H. Breuvron.

NEUFCHATEL (Seine-Inf., 20 S.E. Dieppe).—Lion d'Or; Grand-Cerf.

NICE (Riviera).—H. Colbert, 34, rue Lamartine; H. Français, 3, avenue Malausséna.

NOYELLES - SUR - MER (Somme).—H. des Voyageurs.

OMONVILLE - LA - ROGUE (Manche).—H. de la Mer.

ONIVAL (Somme).—H. de la Plage.

ORANGE (Vaucluse).—H. du Louvre, avenue de la Gare.

ORBEC (Calv.).—H. de Lisieux.

ORLEANS.—H. Sainte-Catherine; Terminus-Hôtel.

OUISTREHAM (Calv.).—H. de l'Univers.

PACY-SUR-EURE (Eure).—H. St. Lazare.

PAIMPOL (C. du N.).—Grand H.; H. Gicquel.

PAIMPONT (15 N.E. Ploermel). —H. Nicolas.

PARAME (opp. St. Malo).—H. Continental, summer only.

PARIS.—Pension de famille Grégoire, 34, rue d'Alésia.

PIERREFONDS (Oise). — H. des Ruines; H. de l'Enfer.

PERROS-GUIREC (C. du N.). —Gd. H. des Bains; and at Trestraou, a mile away, H. des Bains.

PLANCOET (C. du N.).—H. des Voyageurs.

PLESTIN-LES GREVES (C. du N.).—H. des Voyageurs.

PLEYBEN (Finis.).—H. de la Croix-Blanche.

PLOERMEL (Morb.).—H. de France.

PLOUAY (Morb.).—H. du Commerce; H. des Voyageurs.

PONT - AUDEMER (Eure).— Don't stay here.

PONT-CROIX (Finis.).—H. des Voyageurs.

PONT-DE-L'ARCHE (Eure).— H. de Normandie.

PONT-L'ABBE (Finis.).—H. des Voyageurs.

PONT-SCORFF (Morb.).—H. des Voyageurs.

PONTIVY (Morb.).—H. de la Gare; H. des Voyageurs.

PONTORSON (Manche). — H. de Bretagne; Ancienne Maison Guichard; H. de l'Ouest; H. du Chalet.

PONT-REMY (Somme).—H. de la Station.

PONT-STE.-MAXENCE (Oise). —H. du Lion d'Or.

PORTBAIL (Manche).—H. des Voyageurs

PRECY-SUR-OISE (Oise).—H. du Centre.

QUIMPER (Finis.).—H. Templet; H. de la Paix.

QUIMPERLE (Finis.).—H. du Commerce, high town.

REGNEVILLE (Manche).—H. de la Gare et de la Mer.

RENNES (Ille-et-V.).—H. Duguesclin.

RHEIMS.—H. du Nord, about 30 f. a day.

RIVA-BELLA (Calv.).—H. du Châlet.

R O C H E - BERNARD, LA (Morb.).—H. de l'Espérance.

ROSCOFF (Finis.).—H. des Bains de Mer.

ROSTRENEN (C. du N.).—H. du Commerce.

ROUEN.—H. de Normandie, 9-13, rue du Bac; H. de Dieppe, rue Verte; H. de Rouen et du Commerce, rue du Bac; H. Lisseau, nr. river.

STE. ANNE - D'AURAY (Morb.).—H. de France.

ST. AUBIN - DU - CORMIER (Ille-et-V.).—H. des Voyageurs.

ST. AUBIN - SUR - MER (Calv.).—H. Bellevue.

ST. BRIAC (Ille-et-V.).—H. du Centre.

ST. CAST (C. du N.).—H. du Centre.

ST. BRIEUC (C. du N.).—H. du Commerce; H. de la Croix Rouge.

ST. HILAIRE - DU - HARCOUET (Manche).—H. de la Poste.

ST. JEAN-DU-DOIGT (Finis.). —H. Saint-Jean.

ST. LUNAIRE (nr. Dinard).— H. d'Angleterre et des Bains.

ST. MALO. — H. Central-Benoît; H. de Provence; H. du Louvre.

STE. MARGUERITE - SUR - MER (Seine-Inf.).—Pension de famille du Clos de Capriment.

ST. MEEN (Ille-et-V.).—H. Deshayes.

ST. OMER (P. de C.).—H. des Voyageurs.

ST. PIERRE - DU - VAUVRAY (Eure).—H. du Chemin de Fer.

ST. PIERRE - QUIBERON (Morb.).—H. des Pins, plage de Penthièvre.

ST. POL-DE-LEON (Finis.).—H. de France.

ST. SAUVEUR-LE-VICOMTE (Manche).—H. des Voyageurs.

ST. SERVAN (opp. St. Malo).—H. de la Poste.

SARZEAU (Morb.).—H. Jouen.

SEES (Orne).—H. du Cheval-Blanc.

SOTTEVILLE - SUR - MER (Seine-Inf.).—H. de Sotteville chez Zabel.

SOURDEVAL (Manche).—H. du Commerce.

THIBERVILLE (Eure).—H. du Lion d'Or.

TILLY-SUR-SEULLES (Calv.). —H. du Nord.

TREBEURDEN (C. du N.).—H. de la Plage ; H. d'Angleterre.

TREGASTEL (6 N.W. Lanmeur).—Gd. H. Primel.

TREGUIER (C. du N.).—H. Lalauze, on quay.

TREVOU-TREGUIGNEC (5 m. from Perros-Guirec).—H. des Flots.

VAL-ANDRE, LE (C. du N.).— H. du Verdelet, 1½ m. from Pléneuf.

VERNEUIL (Eure).—H. du Saumon.

VERNON (Eure). — H. des Fleurs.

VERSAILLES. — H. de la Chasse, rue de la Chancellerie.

VIEUX-MOULIN (Oise).—H. Bailly-Reulier.

VILLEDIEU - LES - POELES (Manche).—H. du Louvre.

VIMOUTIERS (Orne).—H. du Soleil d'Or.

VITRE (Ille-et-V.).—H. des Voyageurs.

INDEX.

	PAGE
Ankle Action	15
Antrim	68
Battlefields, French ...	82
Bearings	17
Belgium, Note on... ...	84
Border Tour	61
Brakes, Use and Care ...	37
Bristol, Avoiding 54, 55
Bristol Channel	53
Brittany 79, 80
Broads, Norfolk	61
"B.S.A. Pattern" ...	14
Camping Club of G.B. & I.	36
Camping Kit, addresses ...	36
Capes, Waterproof ...27-30
Capes, Carrying	29
Caps and Hats	30
Cardiff-Weston Steamers	53
Care of Bicycle	17
Centre, Touring from ...	30
Chains, Care of 17, 18
Chain-line	37
Change-speed Gears ...	11
Chateaux of Loire ...	80
Children on Carriers ...	16
Chiltern Hills	57
Choosing a Bicycle ...	5
Clyde Steamers	63
Connemara...	67
Cornwall	51
Cotswolds	49
Couplings, Cycle	16
Crank-length	8
C.T.C. Address	36
Dartmoor	50
Derbyshire Dales... ...	43
Devon and Somerset ...49, 50
Drinks	32
Enamelling and Renovation	24
Exmoor 49, 50
Fenland ... ... 58 ; 61
Fog, Lamps in	23
Footpaths	36

	PAGE
Frame-height ...	7 ; 36
France, Resthouse List ...	131
France, Touring in ...	76
French Battlefields ...	82
Galloway	62
Gearcases	5
Glasgow, avoiding ...	64
Gloves	35
Guide-books	35
Heavy Riders	6
Hemorrhoids	35
Highlands, Scottish ...63, 64
Holland, Note on ...	84
Hundred in a Day ...	31
Ireland 65-68
Kent	56
Kerry	66
Killarney	66
Ladies' Bicycles 8, 9
Ladies on Tour	27
Lake District 37-40
Lamps, Oil...	21
Lamps, Acetylene ...	22
Lamps, Electric	23
Lamp-spring, Broken ...	22
Laws and Customs of Road	32
Learning to Ride	14
Leggings	28
Light Riders 6, 9
Loire Chateaux	80
London, Approaching ...	69
London, Avoiding ...	72
London, Resthouses ...74, 75
London, Tours from ...56-60
London, Routes through	71
Long Cranks	8
Luggage, Carrying ...	25
Medical Matters 34, 35
Norfolk Broads	61
Normandy 80-82
North Wales	45

INDEX—*continued*.

	PAGE
Oiling Up	17
Paris, Roads to	82
Peak District	43
Position on Bicycles ...	7
Potted Tours 37-85
Punctures, Finding ...	19
Railway Rates	37
"Rational" Dress ...	9,10
Resthouse Directory—	
Britain	88
,, ,, Ireland	127
,, ,, France	131
Rheumatism	34
Road-racers	7
Roman Rims	37
Rules of the Road ..	32
Saddle, Care of	17
Saddle, Position	7
Saddles, Anatomical ..	35
Scottish Border	61
Scottish Highlands ...63, 64
"Second-hand Bargains"	12
Shoes and Stockings ...	35
Side-car, Bicycle	16
Sleeping-bags	36
Storing Bicycles 17, 21
Surrey, Sussex, Tours in...58-60

	PAGE
Tandems	11
T. C. F. Address	36
Thames Tour	57
Three-speed Hubs ...	11
Toe-clips	15
Traffic Riding	8
Tramcars, Overtaking ...	32
Traps for Unwary	12
Tricycles	12
Trossachs	64
Tweed Valley	61
Two-speed Gears	11
Tyres, Handling and Repair	19
Unsound, Cycling for ...	34
Variable Gears	11
Varicose Veins	34
Wales, North	45
Wales, South	48
Waterproof Clothing ...	27
Western Rivers	47
Wet Weather Riding ...	27
Wicklow	65
Wight, Isle of	58
Women's Bicycles ...	8, 9
Wye Valley	47
Yorkshire Dales	40

Tea.

Explore
your
England.

A cup of tea, how refreshing.

It is so jolly to arrange a run through sequestered lanes to a favourite spot for tea.

It adds enormously to the delight of the ride on a

Rudge-Whitworth
Britain's Best Bicycle
the bicycle that is so easy to ride.

Standards - - - £7.0.0

Aero Specials - - £9.7.6

Rudge - Whitworth
de Luxe ($\substack{\text{Three Speed} \\ \text{Gear}}$) £14.14.0

1924 Catalogue with beautifully Coloured Front Cover, post free from

Rudge-Whitworth Ltd. Coventry

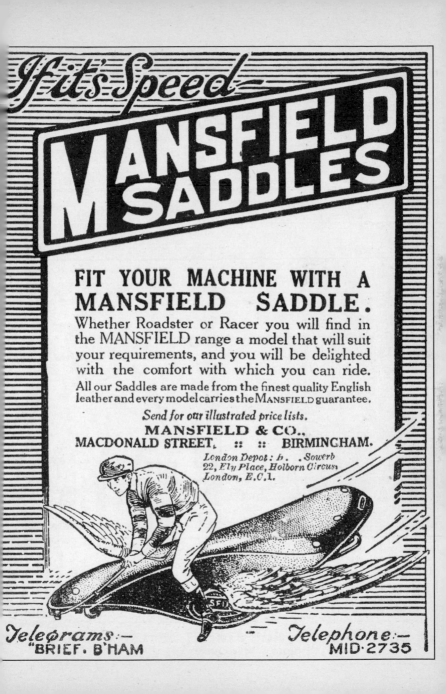

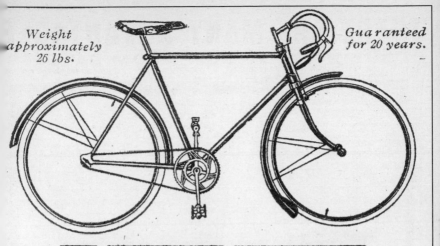

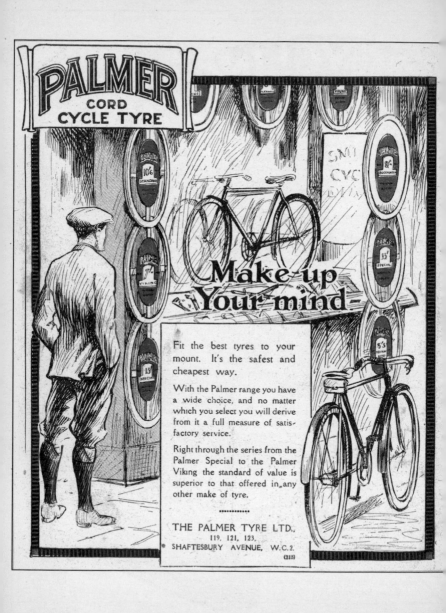

BICYCLING TIME!

The smooth, easy running of a Rudge-Whitworth bicycle is like a perpetual wind behind you. Its utter silence is welcome alike in green lanes and busy streets. So are the new coupled brakes that give you complete command of the machine down one-in-four goat tracks or streets alive with traffic.

The strength of a Rudge-Whitworth bicycle is a thing to marvel at. Always there seems a reserve of strength—at times of stress and strain you can depend upon it entirely.

You see, the Rudge-Whitworth people have been building bicycles for so long that they know exactly what you want in a bicycle, and what a bicycle must do for you. So they have made a machine so perfect in all its parts that they are able confidently to guarantee it not for one, two, five or ten years, but for ever and ever.

Twenty shillings down allows you to ride a Rudge-Whitworth bicycle within a day or two.

Published in Great Britain in 2013 by Old House books & maps
Midland House, West Way, Botley, Oxford OX2 0PH, United Kingdom.
4301 21st Street, Suite 220B, Long Island City, NY 11101, USA.
Website: www.oldhousebooks.co.uk

A CIP catalogue record for this book is available from the British Library.
ISBN-13: 978 1 90840 262 2
Originally published *c.* 1923 as *The Kuklos Annual* by The Daily News Ltd, London.
Illustrations from *Cycling* magazine, 1924–9.
Printed in China through Asia Pacific Offset Limited

13 14 15 16 17   10 9 8 7 6 5 4 3 2 1

PUBLISHERS' NOTE: The page numbers to be found in this reproduction are exactly as per
the original book. They have been retained in order to indicate, at a glance, where illustrations
from other sources have been inserted – an un-numbered page which interrupts the original
pagination indicates inserted material.